Google Rules

# Google Rules

*The History and Future of Copyright*
*Under the Influence of Google*

**JOANNE ELIZABETH GRAY**

Oxford University Press is a department of the University of Oxford. It furthers the University's objective of excellence in research, scholarship, and education by publishing worldwide. Oxford is a registered trademark of Oxford University Press in the UK and certain other countries.

Published in the United States of America by Oxford University Press
198 Madison Avenue, New York, NY 10016, United States of America.

Library of Congress Cataloging-in-Publication Data
Names: Gray, Joanne Elizabeth, author.
Title: Google rules : the history and future of copyright under the influence of Google /
    Joanne Elizabeth Gray.
Description: New York : Oxford University Press, 2020. | Based on author's thesis (doctoral—
    Australian Catholic University, 2018) issued under title: Google rules : an analysis of Google's
    influence on copyright law and practice. | Includes bibliographical references and index.
Identifiers: LCCN 2019034239 (print) | LCCN 2019034240 (ebook) | ISBN 9780190072070 (hardback) |
    ISBN 9780190072094 (epub) | ISBN 9780190072100 (online)| ISBN 9780190072087 (updf)
Subjects: LCSH: Copyright. | Copyright and electronic data processing. | Google. | Google (Firm)—
    Influence. | Authors and publishers—Effect of technological innovations on.
Classification: LCC K1420.5 .G73 2020 (print) | LCC K1420.5 (ebook) | DDC 346.04/82—dc23
LC record available at https://lccn.loc.gov/2019034239
LC ebook record available at https://lccn.loc.gov/2019034240

9 8 7 6 5 4 3 2 1

Printed by Integrated Books International, United States of America

**Note to Readers**
This publication is designed to provide accurate and authoritative information in regard to the subject matter covered. It is based upon sources believed to be accurate and reliable and is intended to be current as of the time it was written. It is sold with the understanding that the publisher is not engaged in rendering legal, accounting, or other professional services. If legal advice or other expert assistance is required, the services of a competent professional person should be sought. Also, to confirm that the information has not been affected or changed by recent developments, traditional legal research techniques should be used, including checking primary sources where appropriate.

*(Based on the Declaration of Principles jointly adopted by a Committee of the American Bar Association and a Committee of Publishers and Associations.)*

You may order this or any other Oxford University Press publication
by visiting the Oxford University Press website at www.oup.com.

*For Victor—this book began when you did.*

# CONTENTS

Preface  xiii
Acknowledgments  xvii

1. A Brief History of Digital Copyright and Google: Politics, Ideologies, and Agendas  1
   Copyright's Foundational Tension: In Service of Both Public and Private Interests  3
   Copyright's Foundational Objectives in the Digital Age  5
   Digital Copyright Politics: The Search for a New Model of Control  6
   An Ideological Setting: The Laissez-Faire Evolution of the Digital Environment  10
   The Advent of Google  13

2. The Value and Function of Copyright: Why the Copyright Debate Matters to Us All  19
   The Conventional Wisdom of Copyright as a Private Property Right  20
   Politically Constructed Concepts of Authorship and Creativity  21
   Social, Cumulative, and Appropriated Creativity  22
   Authors' Rights: The Labor and Personality Theories of Copyright  25
      Labor Theory: The Liberating Nature of Private Property  26
      Personality Theory: Private Property for Self-Actualization  28
   An Economic Theory of Copyright: Private Property for Market Transactions  29
      The Economic Model—Copyright as an Economic Incentive  30
   A Cultural Theory of Copyright  33
      Human Flourishing, the Social Human, and a Cultural Democracy  34
      Cultural Theory, Creativity, and Copyright  37

Why the Cultural Theory Approach to Understanding Copyright
    Is the Right Approach for the Digital Age  38
Conclusion  40

3. "Innovate First, Permission Later": Google's Copyright Policy
    Agenda  41
    Google's Innovation Idealism  42
    In a Digital Economy, Copyright Is Economic Policy  45
    Copyright and Creativity—Valuing Innovation over Tradition  47
    What, Then, Should Policymakers Do? "Balanced" Copyright for the
        Digital Age  49
    A Flexible Fair Use Exception—The Gold Standard for Balanced
        Copyright  50
    Safe Harbors for Online Intermediaries—The Second Pillar of
        Balanced Copyright  54
    Google's Plan for Addressing "Piracy"—Leave It to Innovation!  60
    Conclusion  62

4. Google vs. The Copyright Tradition: Litigating "Innovate First,
    Permission Later"  65
    Copying the Entire Internet  66
    Testing the Legality of Automated Copying of Websites—*Field
        v. Google*  67
    A Second Test—*Parker v. Google*  69
    Copying Other People's Photos—*Perfect 10 v. Google*  70
        In-Line Linking—What Does It Mean to Serve Content over the
            Internet?  71
        But What About Those Thumbnail Copies?!  72
    A Public Interest Deal  74
    If We Can Copy Websites and Images, Then Why Not Books?  74
        Perhaps Making Full Copies of Books Is Pushing Things Too Far?
            A Proposed Settlement (2008)  76
        Google Books Is a Fair Use of Authors' Works—The District Court
            Decision (2013)  77

Copying for a Searchable Database Is a Quintessentially Fair Use—
The HathiTrust Decision (2014)  79
Displaying Snippets Is Fair Too—The Second Circuit Decision
(2015)  79
The Significance of the Google Books Decision  81
Google's Obligation to Monitor for Copyright Infringement—*Viacom
v. YouTube*  83
Was YouTube Entitled to Intermediary Safe Harbor?  83
Viacom: YouTube Knew All About Its Users' Infringement!  84
Google: YouTube Has No Obligation to Monitor for or Investigate
Infringement!  85
No Duty to Monitor—The District Court Decision (2010)  86
But Did YouTube Have Actual Knowledge of Infringement? The
Second Circuit Decision (2012)  87
The Path to a Settlement  87
Copying Oracle's API—*Oracle v. Google*  88
The Java Platform and Google's Android  88
So, What Exactly Did Google Copy?  89
No Copyright Protection for the Java API—The District Court
Decision (2012)  90
Oracle's API Is Protected by Copyright—The Federal Circuit
Decision (2014)  91
Google's Copying Was a Fair Use—A Jury Decision (2016)  93
The Jury Was Wrong—The Federal Circuit Decision (2018)  94
Conclusion  95

5. The Problems of Google News in Europe  97
Aggregating News Articles  98
The Problems of News Media in the Digital Age  100
Agency France Presse—United States  102
Copiepresse—Belgium  103

Federazione Italiana Editori Giornali—Italy  105
Leistungsschutzrecht für Presseverleger—Germany  106
Digital Publishing Innovation Fund—France  107
Article 32 of the Ley de Propiedad Intelectual—Spain  108
Digital News Initiative—European Union  109
European Commission Copyright Directive—European Union  110
Conclusion  113

6. Google's Private Copyright Rule-Making and Algorithmic
Enforcement  117
Large-Scale Algorithmic Notice and Take-Down  118
Beyond Notice and Take-Down: Sanitizing Search  119
Further Beyond: Content ID on YouTube  121
Governed by Google: Private Copyright Rule-Making, Algorithmic
    Enforcement, and the Public Interest  127
Conclusion  133

7. From Access to Monopoly: The Results and Complexities of Google's
Copyright Logic  135
Google's Access Paradox  135
Economic Consequences of Google's Monopoly Power: The Capacity
    for Anticompetitive Practices  140
The Cultural Consequences of Monopoly Power in an Information
    Market  144
Political Consequences of Google's Monopoly Power—Private
    Regulatory Power  145
Democracy and Concentrated Private Power in the Digital
    Environment  147
Conclusion  150

8. Conclusion: Achieving Public Interest Outcomes in a Digital
Environment Dominated by Monopolistic Technology Firms  151
Directly Addressing Google's Monopoly Power  152

Imposing Public Interest Responsibilities upon Google 156
Public Interest Copyright Law Reforms 157
Self-Regulating in the Public Interest 159
Conclusion 164

Notes 165
Index 217

I believe strongly in the value of a vibrant and diverse creative world. For most of my career, I have worked closely with artists, people who create music and art. I see up close the contribution they make to our society—enriching and enlightening. Copyright has also played a central role in my professional life. Copyright protects art, music, and other creative expression and is important for building a career from a creative practice. But for most of my career, I've felt that there's something amiss with how copyright functions and with how the policy debate typically plays out. Too much attention is given to established industry players, and the concepts central to the copyright orthodoxy appear divorced from actual creative practice and the interests of actual artists.

Several years ago, it occurred to me that Google might represent a turning point in the history of copyright. Here was a technology giant arguing for changes to copyright laws to support more public access to works and creative freedoms. Could Google be a corporate white knight? Or were Hollywood and Rupert Murdoch correct in thinking Google is a parasite set to destroy all possibility for commercial success in the creative industries? Of course, once I looked into it, I quickly realized both estimations of Google were inaccurate. I discovered that the story of Google and copyright is thorny and complex, with consequences that reach far beyond artists, art, and the media and entertainment industries. The story of Google and copyright is also about the impact of technological change, the distribution of power in society, and the shape of contemporary democracy.

In this book, I explore and evaluate Google's relationship to copyright law. I examine Google's copyright agenda, its legal, commercial, and political conflicts over copyright, and Google's approach to copyright in practice. The first part of the book shows how the public interest suffers in a digital copyright policy debate dominated by powerful industry stakeholders. The second part explores Google's contributions to digital copyright politics and the copyright policies that Google enforces across its own platforms. In the concluding chapters of the book, I identify the implications of Google's current position in digital copyright governance for the public interest and propose pathways for confronting Google's accumulation of economic, political, and social power.

Copyright is central to much of what Google does, and, because Google is a powerful and motivated multinational corporation that is likely to seek to influence copyright law for the foreseeable future, I hope lawmakers and other copyright stakeholders, including the public, will benefit from my analysis and evaluation of Google's activities in this space. Copyright laws impact us all—copyright is one of the key levers for regulating the social and cultural conditions of our time. Accordingly, I have tried to make this book accessible and engaging to the widest possible audience. As creators, lawyers, policymakers, educators, entrepreneurs, engineers, internet users, parents, and children, we are all stakeholders in the digital copyright policy debate.

A quick note on terminology. In 2015, Google Inc. restructured, and now Google operates as a wholly owned subsidiary of parent company Alphabet. Google is Alphabet's largest subsidiary. Google's key internet-related businesses, including Search, YouTube, and Android, remain within Google. The businesses unrelated to Google's internet activities—for example, in the areas of health sciences, drones, and self-driving cars—operate as separate subsidiaries of Alphabet. Given Google's continued dominance within the broader corporate entity, as well as its continued focus upon activities that relate most directly to copyright law, in this book, rather than adopting "Alphabet" to describe the political and economic activities of the restructured entity, I continue to use "Google."

In this book, while I talk about the activities and motivations of Google, I of course understand that a corporation does not think or seek anything for itself. A corporation is directed by owners and management—by real people working collectively and as individuals. Yet when the decisions and activities of the people working for an organization are viewed in the aggregate, and in the context of an economic purpose, we can attribute to a corporation an overarching strategy, principles, and agenda.[1] In Google's case, key individuals lead a company with a clear economic purpose, and it is possible to identify an overarching strategy and a copyright policy agenda underpinned by political and economic principles.

I was able to establish Google's vision for copyright, including Google's preferred policies, legislation, and reforms, through an examination of almost forty submissions made by Google to government agencies in jurisdictions throughout the world as part of law-reform public consultations undertaken between 2005 and 2016. To locate these submissions, I researched every one of the 189 countries in the World Intellectual Property Organization (WIPO) member state database to determine which countries had conducted public consultations on copyright law amendments or reforms between 2005 and 2016. To obtain a copy of Google's submission to a public consultation, I made contact with copyright agencies (or other relevant agencies) in each jurisdiction. In many cases, Google had made its submission publicly available. Collecting and analyzing these submissions allowed me to get around the well-known difficulties in obtaining candid on-the-record interviews with technology companies. Policy submissions are a reliable source of formal proposals (and analysis) made directly by Google, and they complemented my collection of other primary sources including case law, policy documents, and company information regarding Google's business structure and practices.

Finally, I think it is important to state that while the parameters of this book may be narrowly set—upon one company and one area of intellectual property law—I see it as a contribution to a broader and multifaceted conversation about a new generation of monopolistic companies, born from the technological developments of the digital age, the social, political, and economic influence they have acquired in contemporary society, and what exactly we might be able to do about it.

## ACKNOWLEDGMENTS

In completing this book, I owe sincere appreciation to the following people. Professor Brian Fitzgerald and Dr. John Gilchrist for their intellectual, professional, and personal support over the past several years. To Alex Flach at Oxford University Press for his assistance in the development of my work. To Professor Pamela Samuelson for facilitating my time as a visiting researcher at UC Berkeley, during which I gained valuable perspective that informs this book. To Chris Rodley for answering my countless questions. To Professor Nic Suzor for his thoughtful feedback. To Catherine McCormack for her diligent research assistance. To Caroline Gasteen for her help in the final stages of my work. To the ever-patient Ben Hassell. And to my mother, Suzanne McCormack, for all the time and effort she devotes to me—always—but especially as a grandmother to my son. Because of her efforts, I have time to research and write.

# A Brief History of Digital Copyright and Google

## Politics, Ideologies, and Agendas

It is easy to assume that a swift rise to power is an uncomplicated rise to power. In a few short years after its inception, Google rose to dominate the digital environment, becoming the primary source for accessing information and content online. But Google's ascendancy to one of the most successful technology companies of our time was far from straightforward.

Established as a company in 1998, Google was born into an intense political debate about how we should regulate the budding digital environment. On one side of the debate, there were those arguing we should avoid overregulating and instead leave the digital environment to flourish on its own, trusting in the liberating potential of a participatory, creative, and enlightening online world. On the other side, there were those arguing for strict copyright laws to support the media and entertainment industries, which appeared to be on unsteady ground in the burgeoning digital age. In this political and ideological contest, Google was quickly thrust into the role of principal foe of the media and entertainment industries. Rather than charging for access to content and information like media and entertainment businesses typically do, Google sought to profit from the open structure of the internet and the free flow of information and content online.

*Google Rules: The History and Future of Copyright Under the Influence of Google.* Joanne Elizabeth Gray, Oxford University Press (2020). © Oxford University Press.
DOI: 10.1093/oso/9780190072070.001.0001

Google's founders, Larry Page and Sergey Brin, claim Google originated from one question: "what if we could download and index the entire web?"[1] As it turns out, they could, and they did. Page and Brin built Google by making copies of all the web pages on the internet. This is why Google is often cast as a company that takes other people's information and content, without permission, to sustain an information and advertising empire. Google copies and analyzes other people's websites to provide an internet search index and targeted advertising service. It is also an underlying reason why, over the years, Google has clashed with website owners, news and book publishers, record labels, movie studios, photographers, and others who have claimed that Google has infringed their copyright or that Google is responsible for others doing so. Remarkably, Google has largely prevailed in its many copyright disputes, forging ahead with its indexing activities and its stated mission to organize and provide access to all the world's information.[2]

While forging ahead, Google has also vigorously pursued laws and policies that support its highly profitable business model. In particular, Google has pushed back against the political agenda of the media and entertainment industries and pursued a copyright framework that prioritizes public rights to access and use information and content. In fact, the sustainability of Google's business model depends upon its achieving, in some form or another, its particular vision for copyright.

And so, truly understanding Google's success requires looking beyond the genius of its founders and the eloquence of its technology, and even beyond Google's blockbuster legal disputes. It requires examining the specific copyright settings—and a convergence of legal, political, and ideological conditions—that have facilitated Google's immense growth.

By examining Google in this way, we also gain valuable insights into the current state of digital copyright governance. Copyright law is a public interest issue. As the policy debate continues to evolve, it is important we have a clear understanding of exactly how copyright is functioning in the digital environment and its future trajectory.

Today, Google presides over large portions of the digital environment and is hugely influential in many aspects of society. Taking a close look at Google's relationship to copyright law improves our understanding of the consequences of Google's influence, and it provides a solid basis from which to consider what can and should be done about it.

## COPYRIGHT'S FOUNDATIONAL TENSION: IN SERVICE OF BOTH PUBLIC AND PRIVATE INTERESTS

A fundamental policy tension underpins modern copyright law. On the one hand, the purpose of copyright is to protect and advance the private interests of authors of expressive works. Conventionally, in the copyright context, an "author" is a creator of works subject to copyright protection; works such as music, books, visual art, movies, television shows, and software. Copyright is a quasi-monopoly right, providing authors exclusive rights over a work, chiefly the exclusive right to make copies and to communicate the work to the public. In practice, copyright regimes typically include a variety of other rights and regulations that allow a rightsholder to control and com-modify works. A "rightsholder" is a person or entity that holds rights to a copyrighted work; this might be the work's author or a person or entity that has obtained rights to a work through a license or an assignment. A primary objective of copyright law is to assist rightsholders to control (and receive payment for) the use of their works by other people.

But copyright also has a public interest objective: ensuring social prog-ress through public access to the ideas and information contained in ex-pressive works. To achieve this objective, copyright is limited. It is limited in duration so that after a period of protection, works fall into the public domain; and it is limited in scope so that some uses of works are not exclu-sive to rightsholders. That is, some uses of works without permission from rightsholders—for example, for news reporting or educational purpose—will not be copyright infringement. These uses are typically termed "exceptions" to copyright. So, while copyright provides rightsholders pri-vate property rights, copyright is not a pure private property right, be-cause it also provides rights to the public. Copyright functions as a tool for regulating public access to and use of information and content.

For many, the private interests associated with copyright are the most intuitive: authors *should* be able to control and profit from the works they create. Yet, the public interest objective is not ancillary, it is in fact a foundational justification for the authors' exclusive rights. The Statute of Anne—a statute enacted in the United Kingdom in 1710 that laid the foundations for modern copyright law by granting book authors, rather than book publishers, exclusive rights to reproduce their works—specified its fundamental purpose to be "the Encouragement of Learning."[3] To encourage learning, the Statute of Anne required authors to register their works and to provide copies for inclusion in libraries.[4] The statute granted authors private rights to their works, but also ensured public access to those works.

The principle that copyright regimes should ensure public access to works is based on an understanding that human knowledge and creativity is cumulative. Today's scientists rely on knowledge established generations ago; today's artists utilize ideas, techniques, colors, styles, and processes developed over centuries. All knowledge and all creative practice is at least to some degree cumulative, drawing from and building upon existing resources—technological, historical, social, cultural, and so on—therefore ensuring some public access to these resources ensures knowledge and creativity can continue to progress. The "logic" behind copyright law is that society benefits from creativity and so creativity should be encouraged by providing exclusive rights to authors, but those rights should be limited because too much protection for authors can hinder social progress.[5]

While copyright regimes have increased in both scope and complexity since the Statute of Anne, the dual foundational objectives of copyright endure. For example, the preamble to the World Intellectual Property Organization (WIPO) Copyright Treaty recognizes "the need to maintain a balance between the rights of authors and the larger public interest, particularly education, research and access to information."[6] In recent decades, however, with the advance of digital technologies, the tension between the public and private objectives of copyright law has heightened.

## COPYRIGHT'S FOUNDATIONAL OBJECTIVES
## IN THE DIGITAL AGE

With the growth of the digital environment, copyright law has become omnipresent in our lives. Contemporary copyright regimes have produced, for example, liability for owners of public Wi-Fi networks; a ten-year litigation over a YouTube video of a child dancing to a Prince song; and ambiguity over whether it is legal to do your own car repairs.[7] From everyday social communications to the use of new technologies, digital copyright intersects with many aspects of society. Why does digital copyright have such a broad reach? There are several reasons—political, legal, and historical—but there is also one important practical reason. Characteristically, in order to function, digital technologies will make copies of copyrighted works. All the things that we do each day online, from sending emails, tweeting, reading, sharing content with friends, shopping, gaming, and so on, it all usually intersects with copyright law because it all usually involves a reproduction and/or a communication to the public of some type of copyrighted work—typically images, text, and software code.[8] Consequently, today, the regulatory effect and social consequences of copyright are far reaching.[9] A complex regime of ownership, control, and liability enmeshes the digital environment, an environment that encompasses an ever-increasing portion of contemporary life. Questions of how copyright should function, and how to properly balance the public and private objectives of copyright law, are relevant to more people and in more spaces than ever before.

The conditions of the digital age have also presented major challenges to rightsholders. The traditional business models of the content industries—that is, the dominant entertainment and media industries, such as film, television, book and news publishing, music, and software industries—centers upon *controlling* access to and the use of works.[10] For decades, these industries relied upon an ability to authorize and seek remuneration for any use of a work; be it the sale of a CD, movie ticket, or book, or a subscription cable television service, a video rental, or a software license. The internet and digital technologies, however, diminished the efficacy of this business model. In the digital age, the capacity to copy and share works is not bound by the limits of one's physical resources. I can make a copy of a song and share it with an infinite number of people around the world, with relatively no cost incurred. What's more, the structure of the internet supports models of uncontrolled access and use of works. At its core, the internet is an open system where users can freely access, share, and use information and content.[11] For rightsholders operating in this environment, controlling and charging for access to works can be very difficult.

For the content industries, this lack of control (or more precisely access without permission and remuneration) is the central copyright problem of the digital age. And, despite the broadened social consequences of copyright in the digital environment, and the public interest objective of copyright law, over the past two decades, this "problem" has heavily influenced the digital copyright policy debate.

## DIGITAL COPYRIGHT POLITICS: THE SEARCH FOR A NEW MODEL OF CONTROL

On critical occasions in the history of digital copyright politics, the content industries successfully framed the policy debate in favor of rightsholders. Indeed, their agenda found a firm foothold in digital copyright politics early on. During the 1990s, as internet usage increased, policymakers became increasingly interested in developing a digital copyright regime. In the United States, a 1995 Clinton administration white paper presented a policy framework that would have delivered rightsholders comprehensive control within the digital environment.[12] It essentially proposed that every use of a work, in all digital forms, would require permission from and remuneration to rightsholders.[13] This would be achieved through three key policies: a digital transmission of a work would be considered a distribution of a copy; temporary copies made in the random-access memory (RAM) of a computer would be considered reproductions of a work; and it would be illegal to circumvent a technical protection measure placed on a work to limit its use (known generally as anticircumvention laws).

At the time of publication, the white paper was criticized as biased toward the interests of the content industries. It had been devised by administration staff who had professional connections to US media and entertainment companies, and essentially it presented the content industries' digital copyright agenda: maximum control in the digital environment.[14] The rather tenuous justification offered for such control was that it would encourage rightsholders to make their works available online, which would in turn encourage investment in digital infrastructure.[15]

Activist groups, including library, education, public interest, and consumer organizations, law professors, and industries, including telecommunications, manufacturing, and internet service providers, successfully opposed the white paper (and its associated legislation), arguing the policy proposals gave too much to the content industries at the expense of consumers, internet users, and the emerging technology sector.[16] Nonetheless, the white paper proposals were alive and well when, in 1996, the United States entered the negotiations over the WIPO Copyright Treaty and the WIPO Performances and Phonograms Treaty (known as the Internet Treaties).[17] The white paper policies were embodied in the draft treaties that were used to conduct the negotiations.[18]

The final Internet Treaties did not adopt the US agenda in full.[19] But they did establish that digital transmissions of works would be considered communications to the public under copyright law, and they introduced an anticircumvention obligation, requiring member states to prohibit the interference with any technical protection measures placed on copyrighted works, regardless of the motivation for doing so.[20] WIPO itself describes the purpose of the Internet Treaties as "address[ing] the challenges posed by today's digital technologies, in particular the dissemination of protected material over digital networks."[21] The challenge was not how to reap the social and economic benefits of the emerging digital information and communication networks but how to protect the private property interests of the content industries.[22] While they did not achieve their full agenda, the Internet Treaties could be marked down as a win for the content industries.

A second significant moment in digital copyright politics proceeded from the negotiation of the Internet Treaties: the enactment of the Digital Millennium Copyright Act (DMCA).[23] This legislation implemented the Internet Treaties domestically in the United States and was the subject of extensive industry negotiations. Primarily, negotiations occurred between representatives of the content industries and technology industries, including telecommunications and consumer electronics, along with certain public interest organizations that were concerned copyright laws crafted to give content owners expanded rights might inhibit the development of the digital environment.[24]

In the DMCA negotiations, internet companies and other service providers, along with libraries and educational institutions, lobbied to have safe harbors for online service providers included in the legislation.[25] Safe harbors would ensure, if certain conditions were met, online service providers would be shielded from copyright liability for infringing content posted or communicated by a user. Effectively, for a service provider to avoid liability, the service provider would just need to remove the content from its service upon becoming aware that the content was infringing material.[26] Intermediary safe harbors were justified on the grounds that almost all intermediaries can be used for unlawful purposes, and if they were presumptively liable for every illegal act by a user, many intermediaries would be rendered operationally and financially unviable.[27] Safe harbors were deemed necessary to ensure the continued investment in and development of digital information and communication networks.

Ultimately, the DMCA specified four provisions, providing safe harbor for transitory digital network communications, caching, storage of information at the direction of users, and information-location tools, including directories, indexes, references, pointers, and hyperlinks.[28] Since the enactment of the DMCA in 1998, similar safe harbor regimes have been implemented throughout the world.

The inclusion of intermediary safe harbors within the DMCA brought a measure of balance to the legislation—balancing the interests of rightsholders against the interests of technology companies and internet users. However, as a product of extensive industry-led negotiations, rather than evidence-based policymaking, as Jessica Litman documented, the DMCA lacked a clear articulation of the public interest and was instead "what a variety of different private parties were able to extract from each other in the course of an incredibly complicated four-year multiparty negotiation."[29] The two most influential provisions contained in the DMCA were the anticircumvention protections in line with the requirements of the Internet Treaties and safe harbors for online intermediaries: two provisions to satisfy two powerful industries.[30]

Since the enactment of the DMCA, the content industries have persevered in their pursuit of a maximalist copyright agenda for the digital environment. A major attempt at legislative reform in the United States occurred in 2011 with the Stop Online Piracy Act (SOPA) and the Preventing Real Online Threats to Economic Creativity and Theft of Intellectual Property Act (PIPA). Both acts sought to expand the copyright enforcement obligations of intermediaries by, for example, requiring that service providers, including search engines and digital advertising services like Google, block or stop servicing websites associated even indirectly with any copyright infringement.[31] In 2011, there was also the Anti-Counterfeiting Trade Agreement (ACTA), a multilateral agreement that among other things proposed member states increase or introduce criminal penalties for copyright infringement.[32] Neither SOPA/PIPA nor ACTA were successfully enacted. Undeterred, the content industries have persisted with their agenda—including pursuing policies from the Clinton administration white paper. For example, an early draft of the Trans-Pacific Partnership Agreement proposed categorizing transitory copies as reproductions, and, in 2013, the European Union called for public submissions on the question of whether transitory copies and hyperlinks should be subject to the authorization of rightholders.[33] In 2019, the European Union introduced a new copyright directive that will in effect significantly expand the copyright enforcement responsibilities of online intermediaries. Over the past three decades, in response to the progress of digital information and communication networks, the content industries have relentlessly pursued a copyright policy agenda aimed at controlling and moderating access to information and content.

When each policy proposal is viewed individually, it is evident that the content industries have had inconsistent success in achieving their maximalist digital copyright agenda.[34] Yet, through all their lobbying and campaigning, they have successfully framed the digital copyright policy debate in their favor. The mainstream debate focuses upon the private property rights of the content industries and how their interests can be preserved in the digital environment.[35] While internet intermediaries like Google have challenged this view, by framing the digital copyright debate in their interest, the content industries have largely won the rhetorical and conceptual battle.[36] In the digital copyright debate, the public interest objective of copyright is usually sidelined in favor of private property concerns.[37] Politically, there is generally more concern for exclusive rights than for exceptions and limitations.[38] Rhetorically, more is said of the private interests of rightsholders and less is said of the public interest in accessing information and creative works.

## AN IDEOLOGICAL SETTING: THE LAISSEZ-FAIRE EVOLUTION OF THE DIGITAL ENVIRONMENT

Another factor important to the history of digital copyright law and politics is an ideological one. Neoliberalism, a political ideology that has dominated Western democracies since, approximately, the 1980s, is a political philosophy that proposes the welfare of citizens in a society is best served by private property rights and free markets.[39] While there are varying assessments of neoliberalism in theory and practice, the central guiding principle of neoliberalism is that society should be organized through market transactions.[40]

Within the neoliberal framework, individual liberty is positioned as the most important social and political value.[41] Critically, for the neoliberalist, individual liberty is best achieved through free markets.[42] For the neoliberalist, the freedom to transact and trade in pursuit of one's own economic interests is valued as "a fundamental good."[43] The primary role of the state should be to support free markets, which predominantly involves protecting private property rights.[44] Private property rights are necessary for efficient market transactions because they ensure goods can be traded legitimately and reliably.[45]

Within the neoliberal framework, as a means for organizing society, the market is considered superior to governments on the assumption that governments are less efficient than markets, and they are vulnerable to influence from lobbyists and interest groups.[46] But distrust of government regulation (and faith in market transactions) is also strongly associated with the neoliberal evaluation of liberty. For example, in 1980, free-market economists Milton and Rose Freidman famously wrote:

Our society is what we make it. We can shape our institutions. Physical and human characteristics limit the alternatives available to us. But none prevents us, if we will, from building a society that relies primarily upon voluntary cooperation to organize both economic and other activity, a society that preserves and expands human freedom, that keeps government in its place, keeping it our servant and not letting it become our master.[47]

The neoliberal claim is that government regulation is inefficient and diminishes individual liberty, and, therefore, governments should, where possible, refrain from regulating and instead allow the market to organize society.

Neoliberal reasoning has supported deregulation and privatization policies implemented by governments in Western democracies over the past several decades.[48] Deregulation typically refers to the removal of laws regulating the operation of businesses domestically and internationally. Privatization typically refers to the transfer of public property to private property, for example, the sale of government assets, but it also includes making private organizations responsible for services traditionally provided by public institutions. According to neoliberal ideology, deregulation and privatization policies are liberating and will remove barriers to

trade and economic growth, increasing economic efficiency and productivity.[49] Intellectually, neoliberalism is a philosophy that free markets are
liberating; politically, neoliberalism is a deregulation and privatization
policy agenda designed to limit the size and reach of governments.[50]

In reality, while politicians and industry actors often embrace neoliberal language and concepts, the neoliberal era has not achieved the neoliberal ideal of pure free markets. To varying degrees, markets remain
regulated and Western democracies remain comprised of complex regulatory systems.[51] Nonetheless, despite not diminishing the number and
scope of regulatory institutions, neoliberal policies have had the effect of
shifting certain regulatory responsibility from public to private actors,
through models of self-regulation.[52] Espousing neoliberal ideas about the
inefficiencies of government regulation and the efficacy of free markets,
governments have given private organizations various powers to regulate
their own industries and practices.[53]

It is within this ideological setting that policies for managing the development of the internet and digital technologies have evolved. For example, in 1995, the US government specified private investment would
"define and guide the development of the Global Internet Infrastructure."[54]
Similarly, the 1997 Framework for Global Electronic Commerce expressed
that the position of the US government was that private sector investment
should lead the development of the emerging "information society."[55] In
the United Kingdom, the Information Society Agenda commissioned
in 1995 supported self-regulation.[56] Essentially, early in the digital age,
policymakers encouraged private actors to manage the development of
the digital environment.

In the United States in particular, an appeal to free markets and the
benefits of technological development have continued to justify an anti-
interventionist approach to the regulation of the technology sector.
Policymakers have sought to permit the technology sector to grow un-
encumbered by government regulation.[57] As Anupam Chander has
documented, "the story of Silicon Valley is not only a story of brilliant
programmers in their garages, but also a legal environment specifically
shaped to accommodate their creations."[58] Where economic and political

conflicts have emerged, for example, stemming from disruptive techno-logical developments, governments have largely continued to encourage industry-led solutions, such as private agreements and self-regulation.[59] Even the DMCA safe harbors were developed with industry cooperation and self-regulation in mind; the United States Senate specifying: "Title II preserves strong incentives for service providers and copyright owners to cooperate to detect and deal with copyright infringements that take place in the digital networked environment."[60]

In this political and ideological setting, while there has yet to be an-other major internet-specific copyright treaty development since the Internet Treaties and the DMCA, through processes of self-regulation and private agreement, industries have continued to negotiate the scope and application of copyright in the digital environment.[61] As a result, today, copyright regimes are comprised of a complex assemblage of laws and private agreements, administered by both public and private actors.

## THE ADVENT OF GOOGLE

Google entered copyright politics several years after the conclusion of the Internet Treaties and DMCA negotiations. Developed from a research project at Stanford University, Larry Page and Sergey Brin incorporated Google in 1998, and Google became a publicly listed company in 2004.[62] Today, however, Google stands center stage in global copyright politics, as a powerful private actor, and a party to some of the most significant digital copyright disputes to date.

Google views copyright from its position as a technology company, one that has developed technologies and services that exploit, harness, and advance digital information and communication networks.[63] In essence, Google's algorithms order and facilitate global access to a vast network of diffuse information.[64] Today, the Google Search index contains over 130 trillion web pages; the Google Books database allows the public to search and view snippets of millions of books; and over one billion hours of YouTube videos are watched each day.[65] Through these services, Google has driven a spectacular increase in the creation and circulation of information and content in contemporary society.

Page and Brin's identification and conceptualization of the issue of internet search, and their anticipation of its future importance, was the critical first step in the company's development. Brin explains:

> Before Google, I don't think people put much effort into the ordering of results. You might get a couple thousand results for a query. We saw that a thousand results weren't necessarily as useful as 10 good ones. We developed a system that determines the best and most useful websites. We also understood that the problem of finding useful information was expanding as the web expanded. In 1993 and 1994, when Mosaic, the predecessor of Netscape, was launched, a "What's New" page listed new websites for the month and then, when more began appearing, for the week. At the time, search engineers had to deal with a relative handful of sites, first thousands and then tens of thousands. By the time we deployed our initial commercial version of Google in late 1998, we had 25 million or 30 million pages in our index . . . That volume requires a different approach to search technology.[66]

Google's PageRank algorithm was key to the search engine's original utility. Not only did Google find and provide access to websites, PageRank also determined their relevance. Put simply, PageRank operates so that the more hyperlinks there are to a website, the higher in the search results that website will be.[67] According to Google, PageRank is an ever-improving democratic process: "sites have been 'voted' to be the best sources of information by other pages across the web. As the web gets bigger, this approach actually improves, as each new site is another point of information and another vote to be counted."[68]

In Google's current search algorithm, PageRank is one of hundreds of variables used to assess the relevance of a website to a search query. According to some reports, Google updates its search algorithm hundreds of times per year.[69] While Google does not disclose the specifics of its current search algorithm—it is protected as a trade secret—the sophistication of the search algorithm is apparent to any user. Of particular significance is the ability for Google's algorithm to understand user intent. For example, the search query "how many people live in NY" will return results related to the terms "population" "demographics" "New York City," and "New York State." Google Search takes into account synonyms and spelling variations, purposeful or erroneous. It is able to understand that the prefix "bio" means "biography" when it is typed with a person's name and "biology" when it is typed with "warfare."[70] Google Search also incorporates user context, providing results relevant to the user's geographical location and previous search history. The speed of service is enhanced by the auto-complete function, which predicts a search query as a user types, and by the instant results feature, which provides search results as the query is typed. Overall, the search results Google returns to a user are heavily curated, according to a complex regime of variables devised by Google in the pursuit of speedily anticipating the needs of its users.

In many ways, Google's advertising service is as impressive as its search technology. AdSense and Google Ads (previously called AdWords) are the company's two key advertising programs that facilitate advertising across Google's platforms and third-party websites. A large portion of Google's advertisers pay on a "cost-per-click" basis, which means Google generates revenue when a user engages with an advertisement.[71] As such, Google is motivated to identify user interests and target advertising accordingly. Google uses two broad methods to target advertising: contextual targeting and interest-based targeting. Contextual targeting involves scanning and analyzing websites, in order to place advertisements relevant to that website's visitors.[72] Interest-based targeting is achieved by collecting information about individual Google users. Google collects personal information provided when individuals use a Google product or service. For example, Google retains users' individual search history and YouTube viewing history.[73] Google also collects information on user devices and locations.[74] Through Google's advertising system, businesses can target specific users with specific products based on Google's understanding of that user's personal interests.[75]

Targeted advertising has driven the success of Google's business, success measured by both reach and profitability. Indicatively, despite an extensive range of products and services, advertising revenue has consistently accounted for at least 85 percent of Google's total revenue per year since 2004.[76] Indeed, Google's lucrative advertising business allows the company to provide the majority of its services to users free of charge. Google Search, News, Images, Books, Maps, Gmail, Calendar, Docs, Sheets, and so forth are all provided to users without a monetary charge.[77]

While Google has produced an imposing array of products and services—including Google Search, Images, News, Books, Maps, Earth, Translate, Scholar, Art, Glass, Fiber, Play, and Drive; Gmail; AdWords and AdSense; Google for Work including Calendar, Docs, and Sheets; Chrome; Google+; Android; and YouTube—search and advertising continue to dominate its business. Worldwide, Google has close to an 85 percent share of the search engine market, and it has one of the largest portion of global digital advertising revenues, at approximately 30 percent.[78] Internet search and targeted advertising remain fundamental to Google's business model.

With this business model, Google has a vested interest in the flow of information and content online. The more information and content that is accessed and shared online, the larger the market is for Google's advertising system. Similarly, Google has a vested interest in a user-friendly internet, and Google openly attributes its user-centric approach as key to its success: "we believe that our user focus is the foundation of our success to date. We also believe that this focus is critical for the creation of long-term value."[79] Google's business model is based on providing highly desirable and useful information and technology to users, for free, and leveraging its closeness to users to sustain a highly profitable global advertising network.

Given this business model, it is unsurprising that Google has clashed with rightsholders. Google represents a structural challenge to the content industries. The continued flow of content and information online is central to Google's business model, but copyright is not—while Google deals in copyrighted content, Google's core business activities do not depend upon a strict copyright regime.[80] Furthermore, Google profits from copying and providing access to copyrighted works, often done so without permission from rightsholders.

Interestingly, when Page and Brin first copied the internet to create their search index, the lawfulness of this action was uncertain at best.[81] As Timothy Wu remarked, "no one really knows whether that copying was legal—whether a massive copyright violation occurred at the birth of the firm . . . As a matter of law, copying generally requires permission, something that Google never asked for."[82] Since it first copied and indexed the internet, Google has continued to not ask for permission to use websites, images, books, news articles, and other content—causing several major legal disputes with rightsholders. When developing its products and services, Google has challenged the laws and assumptions of copyright, pushing for copyright regimes that limit the private property rights granted to rightsholders in favor of public rights to access and engage with information and content.

By providing high-quality technology that facilitates free access to information and content, and by doing it so successfully and ubiquitously, Google is a unique force in the history of digital copyright. Google is a powerful private actor that has tested the foundations of the copyright agenda upheld by the content industries. But it has been over two decades since Google first created its search index, and today the story of Google and copyright is far more complex than a "Google versus the content industries" framing might suggest. Today, the story of Google and copyright is littered with private negotiations between powerful companies, automated enforcement systems, artificial intelligence, and sizable monopoly power. Identifying and safeguarding the public interest in this complex digital copyright landscape is more difficult and more necessary than ever before.

# The Value and Function of Copyright

## *Why the Copyright Debate Matters to Us All*

In a political debate dominated by private industries, the public interest in copyright law is often obscured. But the copyright debate matters to us all. As a tool for regulating access to and the use of information and content, copyright influences cultural conditions. Our culture includes all the information, advertising, art, entertainment, and other media that we come into contact with, and it affects how we understand and engage with the world around us; it influences social, political, and economic conditions. Copyright matters to us all because copyright impacts our daily lives, our cultural conditions, our experience of democracy, and the distribution of power in society.

You might ask, if this is all true, then why is copyright so often presented as an issue mainly relevant to artists and the content industries? Intense and sustained lobbying and campaigning undertaken by the content industries is one part of the answer. For decades, the content industries have doggedly pursued their copyright agenda in political and social fora. But as well, embedded in the copyright orthodoxy are particular ideas and theories that present copyright as a private property right—ideas and theories that underpin many of our current copyright laws, treaties, and legal decisions. While these theories of copyright are not without merit, they

*Google Rules: The History and Future of Copyright Under the Influence of Google.* Joanne Elizabeth Gray, Oxford University Press (2020). © Oxford University Press.
DOI: 10.1093/oso/9780190072070.001.0001

are incomplete. They tend to narrow our understanding of copyright's value and function and marginalize the public interest; and they fail to grapple with the full range of copyright stakeholders, the public in particular, but also stakeholders like Google who do not fit neatly into the authors' private property rights orthodoxy.

When we try to grapple with the new centers of cultural power in contemporary society—when we try to understand, embrace, or challenge organizations like Google—we need a framework of understanding that takes us beyond narrow private property claims. We need a framework that can help us understand the significance of Google's ability to regulate the flow of information globally and the implications for the public interest.

Improving our understanding of the link between copyright and the public interest issues with which it intersects requires thinking carefully about the function of copyright in the digital age. It also requires that we challenge the central assumptions, ideas, and theories that dominate the copyright tradition—exposing in whose interest they operate and why. By doing so, we can more effectively evaluate the influence of Google and the other private actors that dominate the digital copyright debate and, hopefully, formulate laws and policies that are in the public interest, rather than laws and policies that are aimed narrowly at resolving inter-industry disputes.

## THE CONVENTIONAL WISDOM OF COPYRIGHT
## AS A PRIVATE PROPERTY RIGHT

In the conventional copyright narrative, the author of creative works is the primary character—for instance, the painter, songwriter, playwright, or novelist. An author fixes into a tangible format some original, creative expression: the painter paints a watercolor, the musician records a song, the novelist writes a novel.[1] Through copyright law, this work becomes the author's private property. Joined to the author are the companies engaged to promote and disseminate their work—for example, a record label, publisher, distributor, or merchandiser.[2] The personal and economic interests of the author, and associated industries, are positioned as the principal copyright stakeholders. In this conventional narrative, copyright is a property owner's right: the owner has the exclusive right to reproduce their work; to distribute their work; to publish, perform, or communicate their work to the public; and to create and control derivative works. If a third party wishes to use the work, they must seek permission from and typically pay the copyright owner. The author has a rightful claim to own and control their works; private property is an undisputed, natural consequence of authorship.[3]

In this conventional narrative, the public is a collection of individual consumers of creative works—consuming for enjoyment, education, or commentary—existing separately from the author. The public has some limited rights to use copyrighted works such as those provided under a fair use or fair dealings exception, for example, for news reporting or parody. The public's rights are limited because, or so the conventional story goes, it is primarily the author that copyright seeks to reward. Yet, the history of modern copyright tells a somewhat different story; the conceptual dominance of the author's private rights results from a specific political and economic history.

## POLITICALLY CONSTRUCTED CONCEPTS
## OF AUTHORSHIP AND CREATIVITY

In Germany in the eighteenth century, a group of politically and economically motivated writers helped form the concept of authorship conventional to copyright law today. Recognizing an expanding market for book sales, writers began to question their status in the book-making business.[4] At the time, the work of a writer was regarded as that of a craftsman; a writer was a "master of a body of rules, or techniques, preserved and handed down in rhetoric and poetics."[5] Any contribution beyond the tradition of the craft was considered externally derived, from God or muse.[6] Working through external inspiration or craft, rather than personally responsible for their work, a writer was merely a "vehicle of received ideas" and so they did not acquire property rights to the finished work.[7] The writer was considered just one of many responsible for the creation of a book; the writer's contribution commensurate with that of the printer, papermaker, binder, publisher, and so on.[8]

As book dealers' profits expanded, writers became increasingly dissatisfied that they were not earning a living from the sale of the books they wrote.[9] And so, for political and economic ends, the established definition of a writer as craftsman was contested and ultimately transformed. Writers presented a new theory, demoting the craftsmanship component of their work and promoting—and internalizing—the inspiration component.[10] Rather than ideas received from an external source such as tradition or heavenly inspiration, writers said they drew upon a personal, internal source—the "original genius" of the individual writer.[11] This redefinition allowed writers to claim more ownership over their work.[12] As personally inspired authors of original works, as they had so become, writers were entitled to own, control, and be remunerated for their efforts.

The redefinition of authorship brought with it a significant normative change. It brought with it an emphasis on originality over affiliation. Previously, writing was admired for having a strong association with other works: "copying or imitating the great poets and writers that had gone before was considered a worthy objective and, if done successfully, an admirable achievement."[13] But if an author was to claim greater ownership of their work, their work must be original, a product of the author's unique internal inspiration and talents. And so, through political action, undertaken in response to a particular moment in Western economic history, previously highly regarded concepts of craft and affiliation were degraded and ideals of originality promoted.[14]

## SOCIAL, CUMULATIVE, AND APPROPRIATED CREATIVITY

That the concepts of authorship and originality were formed through political processes does not brand them harmful or erroneous. Indeed, it is difficult to point to any legal doctrine that is not politically and historically contingent. Rather, their history suggests they do not deserve a natural law–like status and should be regarded as limited by the purposes for which they were constructed. Because these concepts were developed in order to improve remuneration to authors, they purposefully neglect external factors relevant to creative practice. While creators of expressive works undoubtedly possess and produce works that are a product of their unique talents and view of the world, the concept of a "genius artist" purposefully obfuscates the social, cumulative, and often appropriated nature of creativity.[15]

The evolution of artistic styles throughout human history is evidence of the social, cumulative, and appropriative nature of the creative process. Impressionism, Surrealism, Rococo, Brutalists, and Art Deco—at various times throughout history, different artistic styles have formed and dominated, adopted by artists in response to social, cultural, and technological conditions and through patterns of appropriation. For a more contemporary example, the new millennium has seen a predominance of soulful female pop singers, for example, Amy Winehouse, Adele, and Lorde. Their sounds at once derivative and new, finding value in an association with previous soul and gospel works, as well as via conformity with the conventions of modern pop music. Or K-pop, a consciously derivative genre of popular music that is at once homogenized and manifestly Korean.[16] Copying is also evident in many of the world's "great" art and literary works. Geoffrey Chaucer's *Canterbury Tales* appropriates from Giovanni Boccacio's *The Decameron*.[17] Consider Picasso's Cubist collages.[18] Or *The Waste Land* by T.S. Eliot, *Ulysses* by James Joyce, *The Bridge* by Hart Crane, all of which appropriate from other works.[19]

Music producer Mark Ronson describes how, in the 1980s, the introduction of digital music sampling technology provided a new way for artists to connect with the music and artists from previous generations:

Albums like De La Soul's "3 Feet High and Rising" and the Beastie Boys' "Paul's Boutique" looted from decades of recorded music to create these sonic, layered masterpieces that were basically the Sgt.

Peppers of their day. And they weren't sampling these records because they were too lazy to write their own music . . . they were
sampling those records because they heard something in that music
that spoke to them . . . [and] they instantly wanted to inject themselves into the narrative of that music. They heard it, they wanted
to be a part of it, and all of a sudden they found themselves in pos-
session of the technology to do so, not much unlike the way the
Delta Blues struck a chord with the Stones and The Beatles and
Clapton . . . in music we take something that we love and we build
on it.[20]

What Ronson identifies is an example of the social, cumulative, and
appropriative nature of creativity. The works referenced by Ronson
found their value in their affiliation with previous works. As Ronson
identifies, the value of the album is enhanced rather than diminished
by appropriation and affiliation, forming part of an ongoing social
discourse.[21]

The point is not that creative works are devoid of originality. Creative
works can be at once appropriated and original. Levels of appropriation
and originality vary from work to work, but all creators are constrained
and empowered by the technological, social, and cultural conditions in
which they work.[22] Creative works are shaped by and comment upon the
society and culture in which they are born, and authors work "within and
through existing discourses."[23] As Julie Cohen captures, all creative works
are socially and culturally situated:

A host of cultural and personal factors explains why Alison Krauss
became a bluegrass musician but Sarah Chang became a classical
violinist and Stefani Germanotta became Lady Gaga, why Joshua
Redman became a jazz bandleader rather than a symphony oboist,
why Edward Burtynski photographs epic industrial landscapes
but Cindy Sherman stages pulp fiction tableaux, and why Barbara
Kingsolver's fiction draws on Native American culture but that of Ian
McEwan mines the disaffections of the British upper-middle class.[24]

Rather than emanating exclusively from an internal, unknowable source, creative practice is the product of real experiences, responsive to real social and cultural conditions.[25] Creative works, by their very nature, take from and give back to the creator's environment. Creative practice is always, to some extent, appropriated and cumulative because creative practice is culturally situated. The author's cultural environment inescapably influences their creative practice. In other words, creative practice is shaped by conditions of access to existing ideas and resources because creativity occurs through experimentation with the resources and ideas to which we have access.[26]

Recognizing creativity as a cumulative process, tied to conditions of access to existing knowledge and resources, challenges the dominance of the private property claim that underlies the conventional account of copyright, and it conceptually affirms the continued importance of copyright's foundational public access objective. Copyright is aimed at benefiting authors, but it is also aimed at benefiting the public by providing access to resources necessary for creative practice.

The concepts of authorship and originality central to the copyright orthodoxy purposely obscure the social and cultural aspects of creative practice and, in turn, the public interest objective of copyright. Over time, this obfuscation has been reinforced by key theoretical justifications for copyright: the labor, personality, and economic incentive theories.[27] Products of the liberal and neoliberal traditions, these theories have proven pervasive and enduring, informing conventional understandings of the value and consequences of copyright that dominate the copyright policy debate.

## AUTHORS' RIGHTS: THE LABOR AND PERSONALITY THEORIES OF COPYRIGHT

Two theories of copyright most directly support the concepts of authorship, originality, and private property that dominate in the copyright orthodoxy: the labor and personality theories. Both theories lead to the conclusion that authors *deserve* private property rights. Labor theorists reason authors are entitled to reward for their efforts. Personality theorists reason authors should be entitled to own and control their works because they are personally and psychologically connected to them. Both approaches continue to inform copyright law and politics today, justifying a prioritization of private property rights.

## Labor Theory: The Liberating Nature of Private Property

The labor theory of intellectual property is based on the Lockean theory of property rights. Philosopher John Locke proposed that when a person applies their labor to goods held in common, they may obtain a private property right.[28] Justin Hughes explains, "our handiwork becomes our property because our hands—and the energy, consciousness, and control that fuel their labor—are our property."[29] If construed simply, Locke's theory appears to apply neatly to intellectual property: intellectual labor mixes with knowledge from the public domain to create a new work, just as physical labor mixes with physical materials. The normative proposal is that labor is deserving of reward. It is deserving of reward because labor creates value or because labor is unpleasant.[30]

An alternative interpretation of Locke's value theory of labor derives from Locke's natural law ethical theory.[31] In this explanation, the value of labor does not result from physical or intellectual efforts but from a natural law obligation to preserve one's own life. This natural law gives a person the right to work and produce, to do what is necessary to live.[32] Adam Mossoff suggests, "productive labor is a moral activity because it sustains human life and the goods that result from productive labor are of value because they sustain human life."[33] Viewed in this way, Locke's normative claim is not about rewards deserved for effort but rather about the right to create the conditions necessary to live. Following this reasoning, an expressive work—a piece of art, a song, a book—is the product of an author's labor, and ownership of it supports individual liberty and self-preservation. Under this interpretation, as Stewart Sterk identifies, "the principal attraction of Lockean labor theory is its emphasis on respect for personal autonomy, affording each person an equal opportunity to pursue his own vision of the good life."[34]

The claim that laws should be crafted to provide opportunity for individuals to pursue conditions facilitative of a good life is uncontroversial, yet, within the Lockean framework, it is unclear why private property rights are specifically necessary. While the ability to own and control property is an important liberty in contemporary life, modern capitalism also features experiences of inequality and exclusion that private property rights can exacerbate. In 2015, Credit Suisse published research showing half of all household wealth globally is owned by the top 1 percent of wealth holders.[35] In 2015, the Organisation for Economic Co-operation and Development (OECD) reported that across OECD nations, "wealth inequality is much larger than income inequality due to financial assets that are very unequally distributed and mainly accrue to top income and top wealth households."[36] In a world where wealth is heavily concentrated, legal regimes that support private property rights do not alone ensure a good living for all. As well, there are alternatives to private property that may reward authors and support good living, including public recognition, a substantial fee, or ongoing financial support. Enduring, exclusive private properties rights are not clearly or inevitably justified in the Lockean account.[37] Understanding why private property rights are privileged (yet underjustified) within the Lockean framework requires historical context.

In the seventeenth century, Locke's classical liberalism was a radical political philosophy. Locke delivered a theory of individual liberty in opposition to monarchical control: through private property rights, he sought to liberate individuals and societies from systemic, theocratic inequality. Stanley Brubaker emotively depicts: "Locke's story of the right of property is also the story of man's coming into his own, his coming into his own mind, freed from the irrational claims of Revelation. Thus, Locke's theory of property is nothing less than a story of man's Enlightenment."[38] The historically specific centralized system of property control Locke sought to reform made private property necessary to Locke's framework. Locke promoted principles of individualism and private property for political

reform and for social and economic liberation. In contemporary political and economic conditions, however, these values do not necessarily
serve the same goal as Locke conceived. And if they do not, or if they do
not do so to the same extent as they did centuries ago, arguably there is a
substantial gap in the theory's justification for and prioritization of private
property rights.

## Personality Theory: Private Property for Self-Actualization

As a supplement to labor theory, providing support for the specific requirement of private property, personality theory is one possible gap
filler.[39] German theorist Immanuel Kant distinguished literary works
from other forms of property. Kant proposed a book is both a physical object and a personal communication by an author to the public.[40]
Although a physical book can have many owners, the communication belongs exclusively and inalienably to the author. Georg Wilhelm
Friedrich Hegel extended these propositions. For Hegel, the human existence is characterized by an internal will seeking external reality, and
personality is the manifestation of one's will.[41] Hegel wrote, "free will, in
order not to remain abstract, must in the first instance give itself reality;
the sensible materials of this reality are objects, i.e., external things."[42] For
Hegel, property embodies an individual's will and personality and so has
a profound connection with the human experience.[43] The author creates
a work that manifests their personality and to it they have an irrevocable
bond. In the personality framework, private property is specifically necessary; it is a uniquely suitable means of control, necessary "for self- ac-
tualization, for personal expression, and for dignity and recognition as
an individual person."[44]

The personality and labor theories of intellectual property encourage us
to be attentive to the value of intellectual labor and to the personal significance of a creative work to its author. A study by Jeanne Fromer found all
authors tend to share certain beliefs about their works—for example, they

all view their work as deeply personal, they believe strongly in the integrity of their work, and they have expectations of "reputational benefits."[45] Fromer argues that because these beliefs are widely held and critically important to most authors, consideration of them in copyright policy creates "expressive incentives to creators" and increases the legitimacy of copyright law.[46] Undoubtedly, many authors of creative works feel personally connected to their work. Copyright laws, however, reach beyond the minds of individual authors.

There are important social and cultural considerations relevant to creativity that the labor and personality models largely neglect. How do conditions of access fit into this framework? These theories say little of copyright law's public interest objective, and they do not clearly account for the actors and interests beyond authors or rightsholders that modern copyright regimes implicate. With such shortcomings, the copyright orthodoxy has required support from an additional theory of copyright—an economic theory.

## AN ECONOMIC THEORY OF COPYRIGHT: PRIVATE PROPERTY FOR MARKET TRANSACTIONS

The economic incentive theory of copyright takes the copyright tradition further than do the labor or personality theories, including both private property and access considerations. It provides an economic model of market transactions and offers a utilitarian justification for copyright. Within this framework, copyright is understood as incentivizing creative practice and operating within a system of individual producers and consumers making rational production and consumption decisions. Like the authors' rights theories, the central propositions from this approach continue to influence copyright law and politics. Yet, again like the authors' rights theories, this approach is not equipped to deal with the full range of variables relevant to contemporary copyright regimes.

## The Economic Model—Copyright as an Economic Incentive

Within the economic incentive framework, copyright is understood as addressing the problem of public goods: goods that are nonrivalrous and nonexcludable.[47] Creative works are nonrivalrous because use by one person does not limit use by others.[48] To illustrate, if I were to drink wine and listen to music, the wine is rivalrous but the music is not. Once drunk, the wine is gone and cannot be enjoyed by anyone else. The music, however, once played, may be enjoyed again by me or others. Creative works are also nonexcludable because once a work is made available to the public it can be difficult to prevent continued access. Nonrivalrous and nonexcludable works are by their nature easily copied and shared; and, critically for creative works, they can be copied and shared at a cost less than the cost incurred by the author of the work. This is because the author must invest in both the production and distribution of the work, while the copier need only invest in the distribution.

The economic model of copyright suggests that if there is a supply of low-cost copies of a work, the amount price-sensitive consumers are willing to pay for the work will fall, potentially to a price that is below the author's cost of production. Consequently, if an author anticipates that they will not be able to recoup the cost of their production, they may decide not to produce their work.[49] In this scenario, copyright intervenes and addresses the nonexcludable nature of a creative work: copyright introduces a legal restriction on copying, granting authors the exclusive right to make and distribute copies. This exclusive right allows authors to price their goods above the cost of production. A price above the cost of production yields the author a profit and creates an economic incentive to produce works.

The economic incentive created by copyright occurs at the cost of access to works by consumers. When authors price their works at a price higher than the cost of production, those consumers who are willing to pay more than the cost of production, but not the price set by the author, are labeled a deadweight loss (because, given the nonrivalrous nature of a creative work, they too could have consumed the work without exhausting it).[50] The deadweight loss is deemed an allocative inefficiency. However, the price mechanism should direct production to wherever demand is strongest and will prevent authors from pricing their works too high. The desire for maximum profit will be balanced against the desire to minimize the deadweight loss. More simply, authors will make pricing decisions based on their understanding of consumers' willingness to pay for their product. Social welfare is maximized when rational, self-interested market participants efficiently allocate resources in response to a price mechanism. In this case, social welfare is measured by levels of wealth (for authors) and consumption (by the public).[51] A high level of incentive and low deadweight loss is an efficient allocation of resources and provides the greatest good for the greatest number of people.[52]

In this economic model, creative works are commodities—property—to be owned and sold on the market. In a market system, strong and enforced private property rights are necessary because producers and consumers rely on private property rights when making decisions to sell or purchase goods.[53] Accordingly, the economic model suggests copyright lawmakers should seek to secure for authors enough private property rights to incentivize the production of creative works and to support market transactions.[54] In this way, the economic incentive theory of copyright falls squarely within the neoliberal framework, prioritizing private property, efficiency, and market exchange.[55]

That authors are rational decision makers, only willing to create if the expected return from the sale of their work exceeds the expected cost of production, is a fundamental premise of the economic incentive theory of copyright.[56] Yet, this assumption fails to hold up against even light scrutiny. The limitless quantity of digital creative production occurring today is evidence that an economic reward is not essential for incentivizing creative practice. Remixes, gifs, memes, blogs, fan-made music videos, fan fiction, and open source software are all examples of contemporary creative production undertaken without the guarantee of an economic reward.[57]

As an unpredictable social and cultural experience, creative practice cannot be wholly reduced to market transactions. Human behavior, and

therefore creative practice, is contingent upon and constrained by social, economic, and technological conditions, and is complex, reactive,
and unpredictable.[58] As a reductionist and abstract model, the economic
incentive approach cannot account for the social, cultural, and personal conditions and experiences incentivizing and informing creative
practice.[59]

The economic model of copyright also suffers from broader problems
of utilitarianism: it seeks to maximize aggregate welfare (and in this
model social welfare is measured by wealth and consumption levels)
without regard for actual conditions of access.[60] As Martha Nussbaum
explains, "individual citizens' lives are not merely inputs into a glorious
social total or average. It matters how each is placed. Notoriously, utilitarian views approve results that augment the social total or average,
even when they give some people extremely miserable lives."[61] If copyright policy is reduced to the pursuit of economic efficiency and wealth
maximization, measured in the aggregate, it will not account for the
distribution of that wealth or distribution of access to information and
content.

Importantly, the limitations of the economic model do not diminish its utility entirely. Creative works do have economic value, and
copyright does have an economic function. Copyright commodifies
works and provides an opportunity for authors to earn revenue
from their work in a market economy. Jane Ginsburg evocatively
submits: "filthy lucre may not have spurred the first endeavor; many
new creators hunger for exposure over income. But to *remain* a creator requires material as well as moral sustenance."[62] By allocating private property rights, copyright assists creators to participate in market
transactions—copyright commodifies creative works, facilitating their
sale and distribution.[63]

In a study of the creative practices of over fifty artists and scientists,
Jessica Silbey found that intellectual property laws seldom play an important role in the initiation of a creative work, but they do assist in their
commercial development and distribution.[64] The economic model of

copyright may inaccurately assume copyright incentivizes creative practice, and it may overemphasize the importance of private property rights
to creative practice, but it does identify the economic function of copyright: commodification for market transactions.

Identifying the economic function of copyright as *commodification* rather than *incentive* is a small but important clarification because
it permits us to dispense with the notion that copyright is necessary to
incentivize creative practice while still acknowledging the important economic function of copyright. However, if we view copyright through
a purely economic lens, we are still left with a prioritization of private
property rights and without a clear articulation of the public interest. But,
fear not, the idea that copyright is a public interest issue, critical to social, cultural, and political conditions is not without theoretical support.
A cultural theory framework helpfully broadens our understanding of
copyright and assists us to place the public interest at the center of the
copyright law and policy debate.

## A CULTURAL THEORY OF COPYRIGHT

The cultural theory of copyright provides a normative framework diverging
from the authors' rights and economic incentive theories and challenging
the orthodoxy of copyright as a private property right.[65] Rather than a
justification for private property rights, within the cultural theory framework, copyright is understood as regulating participation in processes of
meaning-making. Cultural theorists advise lawmakers should strive to
create a diverse and participatory culture. In a diverse and participatory
culture, all people are provided opportunity for participating in processes
of meaning-making, which promotes human flourishing and strengthens
democratic political systems. And, as we will see, placing copyright within
a cultural context facilitates an understanding of the interests of a broad
range of copyright stakeholders, including creators and rightsholders, the
public, and (for better or worse) the interests of powerful private technology companies like Google.

## Human Flourishing, the Social Human,
## and a Cultural Democracy

Within the cultural theory framework, consideration for authors' economic and noneconomic interests—including those articulated by the labor, personality, and economic theories—forms part of a broad evaluation of the role copyright plays in contemporary society and its relationship to activities fundamental to our existence as social and creative beings. The cultural theory framework encompasses both of the foundational objectives of copyright law—protecting and advancing the private interests of authors of expressive works and ensuring the continued advancement of knowledge and creativity through public access to the ideas and information contained in expressive works. Like economic incentive theory, within the cultural theory account copyright is an instrument. It is an instrument for regulating the production and circulation of information and ideas, and for distributing cultural power.[66]

Cultural theory suggests copyright laws should be crafted to achieve cultural conditions that support human flourishing.[67] William Fisher explains that the cultural theory framework

> proceeds from the propositions, sometimes associated with the Aristotelian tradition of moral philosophy, that there exists such a thing as human nature, which is mysterious and complex but nevertheless stable and discoverable, that people's nature causes them to flourish more under some conditions than others, and that social and political institutions should be organized to facilitate that flourishing.[68]

Human flourishing is to some degree a subjective concept, but it can be broadly defined as living "within an optimal range of human functioning," which includes happiness, resilience, behavioral flexibility, and growth in personal and social resources.[69] Within the cultural theory framework, an ideal society is one in which all persons will have the opportunity to experience optimal functioning.[70]

An important assumption within the cultural theory of copyright is that people are innately social.[71] We experience our lives through social relationships, interacting personally, professionally, politically, and creatively. Our decisions, our identity, our political, economic, religious, and ethical beliefs are all informed by our social relationships and our socially constructed view of the world.[72] In other words, they are shaped by cultural conditions—all existing information and ideas, and the social processes of meaning-making.[73] A culture is the product of social activities in which ideas, information, and opinions are formed and shared.[74] Our culture is present in all facets of our lives, and it shapes our understanding of the world: "almost like the weather, the flow of information defines the basic tenor of our times, the ambience in which things happen, and, ultimately, the character of a society."[75]

In our deeply social lives, information and ideas, our cultural conditions, can empower or constrain.[76] Cultural representations challenge or reinforce stereotypes, social and economic hierarchies, values and desires. Ideas in our culture shape our political opinions, our understanding of the choices we have available to us, and the expected outcomes of those choices.[77] Our culture is a powerful force in our lives—and the people and organizations that have the ability to influence our culture can exert power over us. They can shape our understanding of the world, our choices and expectations.[78] Given this influence—the influence of the ideas that circulate in our culture—and given that power can be exercised by influencing cultural conditions, cultural theorists suggest we should strive to create a cultural democracy. In a cultural democracy, all individuals are given a meaningful opportunity to contribute to our culture.[79]

A cultural democracy contains a diversity of cultural representations, produced by a diversity of voices. Jack Balkin suggests that in a cultural democracy, "everyone—not just political, economic, or cultural elites—has a fair chance to participate in the production of culture, and in the development of the ideas and meanings that constitute them and the communities and sub-communities to which they belong."[80] Cultural theorists posit that we should seek to participate in the "semiotic shaping" of our own subjectivity and in the "semiotic shaping of others' subjectivity."[81] Through democratic participation in meaning-making, we improve our ability to make meaningful choices about our own existence, facilitating human flourishing and supporting a democratic culture.[82]

A highly diverse and participatory culture also supports democratic political systems.[83] Democratic governance is more than an electoral process that counts the static political preferences of individuals, it is also

> an ongoing process of rational preference formation. This process involves public deliberation of important public issues conducted by an involved and informed citizenry. Under ideal speech conditions, this public deliberation would be open to numerous and diverse competing views and arguments. Participation would be as free as possible from hierarchical relations of power, either public or private . . . Participation and diversity are thus seen as essential conditions for the democratic political process: they ensure that all relevant information, views, arguments, and options are placed before the public, considered and deliberated, and they cultivate an empowered sovereign citizenry.[84]

Diversity and participation drive experiences of human flourishing, but they are also important to our social and political conditions: a democratic system is enriched by a diverse and decentralized culture.[85] In this way, cultural theory is concerned with social welfare; however, unlike the economic incentive theory, the measures of social welfare are not levels of wealth and consumption but diversity and participation.[86] Rather than observing patterns of creative practice and consumption in the aggregate, the cultural theory approach requires an analysis of what is being produced, who is producing it and how equitably it can be accessed and engaged.[87] It calls for an examination of material, political, and cultural conditions.

## Cultural Theory, Creativity, and Copyright

In the cultural theory account, creativity is not a wholly unknowable wonder. It is a social experience shaped by our culture, technology, history, economy, and so on, and it is an intrinsic feature of human nature.[88] Madhavi Sunder explains, "cultural theory takes as a starting point that human beings are creative and cultural, continually seeking to make and remake our world, contributing to commerce and culture, science and spirituality."[89] As we make and remake our world, we draw upon and contribute to our culture. In this context, creativity takes on new significance. Rather than an outcome valuable only to an individual or to society in the aggregate, creativity is also valuable as a process that can support human flourishing.[90]

Given the relationship between creative practice and human flourishing and of cultural conditions to democratic political systems, cultural theorists suggest copyright regimes should support opportunities for participation in meaning-making. Rebecca Tushnet, argues:

> respect for creativity, and for the possibility that every person has new meaning to contribute, should be at the core of our copyright policy. Instead of monetary rewards or even artistic control of how works are transmitted to others as our highest value, we should aim for policies that maximize participation—even when that changes the mix of economic winners and losers. Economic reward and control rights are likely to be part of the proper balance, but only part.[91]

In this way, the cultural theory approach to copyright recognizes copyright's economic function and the private interests of authors but suggests the central objective of copyright policy should be to foster the conditions of a cultural democracy.[92]

An obvious criticism of the cultural theory approach is that it is paternalistic, demanding government intervention to craft laws that influence our behavior in accordance with a preordained vision of optimal human functioning.[93] While a valid assessment to some degree, it is not uniquely true of cultural theory. All political and economic structures require intervention to sustain their forms. Governments make choices regarding the allocation of resources and state coercion in order to create and enforce laws. Even (or perhaps especially) property rights are not a singular, static phenomenon. Private property rights in all circumstances result from political choices.[94] All rights and obligations under the law are, as Jack Balkin captures, "a terrain of struggle in a world of continuous change—a site of ongoing controversies, a battleground where the shape and contours of the terrain are remade with each victory."[95]

Copyright in particular embodies a multiplicity of choices. Despite the conventional account, copyright is not a natural property right. It is a selection of rights and regulations governing ownership, control, access, liability, and so forth. Copyright is a selection of politically constructed and contested choices. The challenge for those concerned with crafting copyright law in the public interest is controlling which actors are permitted to influence these choices. Private actors, including from both the content and technology industries, have a long history of influence over modern copyright law, and, while the cast of actors may have changed, as this book on Google shows, their influence has not declined in the digital age.

## Why the Cultural Theory Approach to Understanding Copyright Is the Right Approach for the Digital Age

Just as Locke's labor theory suited the political and economic conditions of the time in which it was formulated, the cultural theory approach befits current times. The complexities and far-reaching consequences of copyright in the digital environment require a broad framework of analysis. The authors' rights and economic incentive theories of copyright set narrow parameters— they frame copyright as an issue mostly relevant to the markets for creative works. Yet, contemporary copyright is not simply an authors' rights regime. Copyright implicates actors beyond authors and rightsholders, and, more than ever before, copyright regimes regulate the flow of information and distribution of power within societies and economies.

Many cultural theory accounts argue for the potential of digital technology to serve the goals of a cultural democracy—diversity, participation, and human flourishing. The shift from an industrial to a digital information economy has permitted a wider variety of works to be produced, distributed, and consumed, works that previously would not have been created or distributed if left to the discretion of the dominant media and entertainment companies.[96] The internet provides substantial opportunities for participation in the creation and circulation of meaning, disrupting older concentrations of cultural power.[97] In the digital environment potentially everyone is a creator, distributor, and user of information and ideas.

Yet, digital technologies have also altered the relationship between copyright enforcement and everyday creative expression. In the physical world, copyright owners are less able to enforce their rights. If someone plays a David Bowie song at a dinner party, it is unlikely the performance will come to the attention of a rightsholder. Upload a video of the dinner party to YouTube and the video is likely to be algorithmically blocked or monetized by a record company or publisher that holds rights to Bowie's original work. Enforcement is often the default response in the digital environment. So too is commodification. In a digital environment that is awash with advertising, experiences of noncommercial cultural activities are the exception.

There is a powerful conflict at the core of the digital copyright experience. Digital technology offers new avenues for participation, diversity, equality, and autonomy, but it also brings with it new and more efficient ways to enforce copyright, censor content, restrict participation, and commodify culture.[98] Sonia Katyal summarises:

> This new surveillance exposes the paradoxical nature of the Internet: It offers both the consumer and creator a seemingly endless capacity for human expression—a virtual marketplace of ideas—alongside an insurmountable array of capacities for panoptic surveillance. As a result, the Internet both enables and silences speech, often simultaneously.[99]

Google occupies a central position in this conflict. Through its provision of technology and its facilitation of public access to information and content, Google has the capacity to be an agent of human flourishing. At the same time, as a dominant information provider that is in control of large portions of the digital environment, Google also has the capacity to restrict participation and diversity. Google has the capacity to be an agent for or against the common good, as envisaged by cultural theorists.

As we will see, Google has challenged the old centers of cultural power and many of the tenets of the copyright orthodoxy. But, as a global information provider, Google is a new and powerful entity with the capacity to regulate our culture. Google controls the information that we see when we search the internet. In a global, networked society, more than ever, information is a strategic resource.[100] As an increasingly important resource, the actors that own information and those that own the infrastructure that facilitates access to it—actors like Google—are exceptionally powerful. Google is a new center of cultural, social, and political power in contemporary society.[101]

## CONCLUSION

When we think of copyright law, we must not limit ourselves to notions of creators' rights and the potential for profiting from creative practice. These things matter, but they are not all that matters. Copyright is one of the key tools for regulating our cultural conditions with broad implications for the functioning of democratic social and political systems. As the old and new cultural industrial powers continue to clash over copyright, each seeking a regulatory regime that suits their interest, we must not lose sight of the public interest. The democratic potential of the internet and digital technologies can easily be overridden by the centralization of cultural power into the hands of new powerful private interests.[102] When we examine Google's activities and agenda, we must bear this in mind. Google is a powerful, motivated, and cashed-up stakeholder in a critical debate that matters to us all.

# "Innovate First, Permission Later"

## Google's Copyright Policy Agenda

Google cares about copyright—a lot. Upon opening its first office in Washington, DC, in 2005, Google confirmed the key policy issues for the company were net neutrality, copyright, fair use, and intermediary liability.[1] Google explained its political mission was to "defend the Internet as a free and open platform for information, communication and innovation."[2] Between 2012 and 2016, Google spent over USD 82 million lobbying the US government, and, according to disclosure reports, during that period, Google most frequently lobbied on issues of intellectual property law.[3] As well, Google is one of the most active lobbyists within the European Union, declaring 207 meetings with European Commission officials between 2014 and 2018 and spending over EUR 6 million on lobbying in 2017 alone.[4]

What is it that Google seeks when it lobbies lawmakers on issues of copyright? What is Google's vision for copyright law? The first and probably least surprising thing to say about Google's copyright agenda is that Google approaches copyright law from the perspective of an innovator. As governments from around the world have sought to amend, reform, and introduce new copyright laws for the evolving digital environment, Google consistently appeals to the social and economic benefits of the internet and technological innovation. Google argues that the advent of the digital environment rendered the conventional account of copyright

*Google Rules: The History and Future of Copyright Under the Influence of Google.* Joanne Elizabeth Gray, Oxford University Press (2020). © Oxford University Press.
DOI: 10.1093/oso/9780190072070.001.0001

inappropriate and calls for a transformed view, one that is sensitive to the relationship between innovation and rights to access and use information and content. Google proposes that for society to benefit from technological progress and the free flow of information in the digital environment, authors' private rights must be limited and public rights strengthened.

## GOOGLE'S INNOVATION IDEALISM

Google presents technological innovation as a democratizing force—enriching lives economically, socially, and politically. Google asserts digital technologies have

> democratized communication and creation of information. Capabilities that were once available only to the largest corporations are now available to businesses, political movements, governments, and individuals alike. There is no longer a need to manage servers, updates, and patches; instead, users simply refresh their browser.[5]

According to Google, "every year, it gets clearer that the web helps lead to more successful businesses, stronger economies, more vibrant towns, and more prosperous communities."[6] For Google, the unremitting march of technology is a positive force in contemporary society.

Google regularly emphasizes the social value of its own products and services. Google posits that "a well functioning society should have abundant, free and unbiased access to high quality information" and, therefore, facilitating internet search is "an unusually important task."[7] Google describes Google Books an undertaking in expanding human knowledge and YouTube a tool for social justice;[8] Brin explains:

> While it may have been known for its "lolcats" videos several years ago, YouTube is now used for citizen engagement (such as interviews with President Obama), documenting human rights violations (such as in Tunisia, Egypt, and Libya), full-length movies, education, and

much more . . . The ability to easily publish video has leveled the playing field between the select few and the rest of the world in terms of being able to communicate using this powerful medium.[9]

As a technology company that provides access to information and content, Google presents itself as a benevolent entrepreneurial endeavor.

Google's co-founder, Larry Page, claims to have had benevolent entrepreneurial aspirations from a young age. Google biographer, Ken Auletta, describes a conversation with Page:

> "I realized I wanted to invent things, but I also wanted to change the world," Page once said. He became convinced that in order to effect scientific change he needed to start a business. Inventing things, he once said, "wasn't any good; you really had to get them out into the world and have people use them to have any effect. So probably from when I was about 12, I knew I was going to start a company."[10]

Page's mix of both grand scientific and commercial ambition captures something intrinsic to Google. Google articulates lofty social justice goals and espouses the social benefits of innovation and the free flow of information online. Google develops products that facilitate access to and engagement with information and technology. Google claims to provide access to these products freely and indiscriminately.[11] Yet, Google is a private company, unabashedly amassing immense wealth by systematically profiting from the use of information online. Google's rhetoric and practices exhibit a heady blend of both public and private values.

Google's distinctive socially conscious entrepreneurialism aligns with what Richard Barbrook and Andy Cameron identified in 1996 as the Californian ideology.[12] Barbrook and Cameron describe the Californian ideology as a "contradictory mix of technological determinism and libertarian individualism," emerging from "a bizarre fusion of the cultural bohemianism of San Francisco with the hi-tech industries of Silicon Valley."[13] In the Silicon Valley context, the unlikely combination of cultural

bohemianism and capitalistic entrepreneurialism occurs through "a profound faith in the emancipatory potential of the new information technologies."[14] In Silicon Valley, there is nothing more sacred than the power of
technology combined with the power of enterprising individuals; a mix of
technological determinism and economic liberalism is the Silicon Valley
religion.[15]

A philosophical mix of technological determinism and economic liberalism is apparent in Sergey Brin's assertion that technological innovation
is inherently virtuous:

> The Internet, mobile phones, and other technologies are having
> profound effects on the spread of information and the lives of
> people worldwide. It's a virtuous circle, with the information rev-
> olution directly accelerating the pace of technical development as
> inventors and entrepreneurs benefit from the increased demand for
> new products, the opening of new markets and dramatic gains in
> productivity.[16]

A political consequence of mixing economic liberalism and technological determinism is distain for government regulation.[17] If technological innovation produces democratic outcomes, enriching the
lives of individuals and improving economies and societies, surely it
should remain free from government interference.[18] Indeed, Google has
stated, "in an increasingly data-driven digital world, it is essential that
policymakers both minimise regulatory impediments to not only digital
based businesses models, but also to traditional businesses that are increasingly using digital technologies."[19] Government regulation, it seems,
risks stifling virtuous market and technological forces. In this way, the
Californian ideology is similar to the neoliberal framework: both con-
clude free markets are preferable to government regulation. And this
ideology, that is a strong belief in the positive powers of free markets and
unbounded innovation, strongly influences Google's copyright policy
framework.

## IN A DIGITAL ECONOMY, COPYRIGHT
## IS ECONOMIC POLICY

As more and more of our daily transactions are connected to the digital environment, Google urges policymakers to consider copyright as an economic policy issue.[20] Google argues, in a digitally connected world, economic growth requires reformed copyright laws that support continued technological innovation. In 2011, Google submitted to the Irish government that if Ireland were to implement "a flexible copyright regime that enables and encourages new technologies," the digital economy would be key to Ireland's economic recovery.[21] In 2013, Google submitted to the Australian government that copyright reforms had the potential to unlock AUD 600 million in productivity gains.[22] Google reasoned "more flexible, technology-neutral copyright laws" could unlock this potential, specifically in the areas of education, research, libraries, cultural institutions, and digital services.[23] In 2015, Google warned Australia's Productivity Commission that without copyright reform "there is far less scope for new Australian businesses capitalising on the next wave of innovation, unlocking new investments and economic growth."[24] In Hong Kong, Google linked the adoption of a copyright exception for parodies to economic policy, submitting "a parody exception will bolster its status regionally and internationally as a critical place to do business because of its free flow of information."[25] For many years now, throughout the world, Google has presented to policymakers arguments for reforming copyright laws for economic gains.

A central assumption within Google's copyright-as-economic-policy framework is that the digital environment is critical to the way in which modern economies function. In 2008, Google urged the European Commission to recognize that the internet is not simply a tool for entertainment but is a "central communication means in personal and professional life" and provides citizens with "a diversity of information and public services."[26] Google argues that today "the internet is the critical infrastructure of the digital economy."[27] For this reason, Google posits that today "copyright is no longer simply an issue of cultural or creative policy, but rather is a core part of innovation policy."[28] Google seeks to expand our understanding of the consequences of copyright beyond the interests of the content industries. For Google, copyright is a "public interest" issue because it impacts innovation, economic development, and the services we access in our day-to-day lives.

Indeed, that copyright law regulates technological innovation is another important assumption in Google's copyright policy framework. Google points to the way digital technologies copy copyright subject matter in order to function:

> The innovative technologies that underpin the development of the digital economy depend on making and transmitting multiple copies of content in which copyright subsists, which means they are themselves deeply affected by copyright law.[29]

Copyright law, Google argues, intersects directly with innovation because "the very nature of the Internet involves the making and dissemination of copies of information, whether it be through web search where Internet pages must be copied and stored in order to be indexed, through emails, or even watching an online video of a government press conference."[30] Google emphasizes that "internet tools make multiple copies in order to deliver the kinds of essential services we now take for granted in our lives."[31] Which means, "for the first time in history, nonconsumptive or everyday activities, occurring billions of time a day throughout the world, give rise to potential copyright liability."[32] Google's position is that copyright "rightly acts to prevent business models that free ride on the work of prior creators . . . [and] oversteps its purpose, and harms innovation, when it enforces rigid constraints to stifle productive and reasonable new uses of copyrighted works."[33] For Google, the central copyright problem of the digital age is ensuring copyright regimes do not stifle technological innovation.

Google argues that copying for innovative new technologies "should not unreasonably run afoul of laws designed by earlier lawmakers with no concept of digital technology."[34] Google also claims that the imposition of traditional copyright arrangements upon new internet-based businesses is effectively the imposition of a copyright tax, in the form of money and time spent trying to "navigate complex licencing and legal processes."[35] Google also asserts that a "lack of clarity within copyright law together with the high risk nature of a potential breach" will constrain innovation and investment in new technologies.[36] For Google, the copyright tradition is an ever-present threat to innovation.

Google calls for policymakers to create a "regulatory environment that allows for new business models, new ways for consumers to enjoy creative content, new ways to bring content to market, and new ways of advancing knowledge through research."[37] Google advises:

> In protecting copyright, the law must not create a culture of "permission first, innovate later" for technology innovators. Such a culture threatens to chill socially beneficial innovation that helps content owners, creators and consumers alike . . . The copyright framework needs to have the space to allow for the creation of transformative innovations that legislatures do not anticipate.[38]

An "innovate first" culture is core to Google's legal and economic agenda. Google explains, "the importance of an environment—social and regulatory—that fosters innovation is central to Google's story. When Google started as a project of two friends from Stanford University, they didn't have to ask anyone's permission to develop an Internet search engine."[39] Prioritizing innovation above all else, through its rhetoric and practices, Google does not readily adopt the default position that permission from rightsholders must be obtained to use information and content in the digital environment.

## COPYRIGHT AND CREATIVITY—VALUING INNOVATION OVER TRADITION

Inasmuch as Google concerns itself with creative practice, Google focuses on new patterns occurring in the digital environment; the social,

user-generated, and nonprofessional forms that are typically disseminated on digital platforms such as YouTube, Instagram, and Facebook.
Google argues these new forms of creative practice should be valued and
warns that traditional copyright laws can favor established industries and
stifle these new modes. Google explains: "content *creation* is no longer
the sole preserve of 'professional' creators: professionally produced content from traditional sources competes and interacts with user generated
content shared via social networking sites, blogs and video and photo-
sharing sites."[40] The content industries, Google describes, "now co-exist
with a larger creative community" and "content *consumption and en-*
*gagement* is no longer a one way street: consumers are interactively engaged, responding to content and in that process generating new cultural
genres."[41] When it comes to creative practice, Google asks us to value
everyday social digital production along with traditional media, art, and
entertainment.

In a new environment featuring user-generated content and creativity,
according to Google, the conventional categorization of and dichotomy between authors and consumers is called into question.[42] Google describes,
"the model of a professional media sector delivering content to passive
consumers has been replaced by a model where the lines between creation
and consumption of content have been blurred."[43] In 2013, Google submitted to the European Commission that the European Union copyright
system was unsuited to contemporary creativity and inconsistent "with
society's legitimate expectations."[44] Google called for policymakers to

work toward a copyright law that is well suited for 99% of the works
being made and 99% of the uses being made. Creation is now
everyone's daily activity. The vast majority of works are created by
amateurs, are ephemeral in nature, and are not created with any
view toward commercial exploitation. Similarly, the vast majority
of all uses whether in the form of copies or communications—are
personal in nature, as individuals upload and share photographs on
Instagram or text messages on WhatsApp.[45]

According to Google, "in the world of digital creativity and automatic copyright, we are all rights-holders, we are all users, and we are all distributors" and relying on outmoded categorizations "unhelpfully perpetuates the 'them-versus-us' division that has proved so inimical to the development of a unified approach to removing barriers to innovation and creativity."[46] In Google's assessment of copyright and creativity, the "original genius" style of creativity must now share the stage with a global output of social, interactive, and noncommercial creative practice.

## WHAT, THEN, SHOULD POLICYMAKERS DO? "BALANCED" COPYRIGHT FOR THE DIGITAL AGE

Google argues the social and economic conditions of the digital age—including new patterns of creativity and the critical role of digital technologies—necessitate a copyright regime in which private property rights are properly balanced against public rights to access and engage with information and content.[47]

In 2016, as a large group of nations attempted to negotiate a controversial new free trade agreement, the Trans-Pacific Partnership Agreement (TTP), Google commended the draft agreement for its approach to copyright.[48] Article 18.66 of the TPP stipulates:

> Each Party shall endeavour to achieve an appropriate balance in its copyright and related rights system, among other things by means of limitations or exceptions . . . including those for the digital environment, giving due consideration to legitimate purposes such as, but not limited to: criticism; comment; news reporting; teaching, scholarship, research, and other similar purposes; and facilitating access to published works for persons who are blind, visually impaired or otherwise print disabled.[49]

According to Google, "the TPP balances the interests of copyright holders with the public interest in the wider distribution and use of creative works" and "promotes a regulatory environment that is well placed to support the innovative technologies that underpin the digital economy."[50] But what does "balanced copyright" mean in real policy terms? In Google's formula for balanced copyright, two policies are key—a flexible fair use exception and safe harbors for online intermediaries. Google asserts these provisions are the "pillars of the United States copyright framework that enable it to cope with the challenges of rapid technological advance" and that they provide "a safety valve for what would otherwise be overly broad copyright protection."[51] For Google, balanced copyright requires creating legal space for developing and delivering digital technologies without risk of triggering copyright infringement.

## A FLEXIBLE FAIR USE EXCEPTION—THE GOLD STANDARD FOR BALANCED COPYRIGHT

Invariably, copyright regimes establish that some uses of works without permission from (or remuneration to) rightsholders are fair and do not constitute copyright infringement. In most jurisdictions, the uses that are deemed fair are established in a static list—to be subject to the exception, the use must fall within a category of uses expressly specified by statute.[52] By comparison, in the United States, rather than a static list, the Copyright Act sets out a nonexhaustive list of factors a court must consider in a fair use determination.[53] The first factor is "the purpose and character of the use, including whether such use is of a commercial nature."[54] This factor seeks to uncover whether the use of the work is transformative or simply supersedes the original work.[55] The second factor is "the nature of the copyrighted work."[56] This requires consideration of factors such as whether the copied work was published or unpublished, expressive or factual.[57] The third factor is "the amount and substantiality of the portion used in relation to the copyrighted work as a whole."[58] This requires consideration of whether the portion of the work copied was necessary for the purpose and character of the use.[59] The fourth factor is "the effect of the use upon the potential market for or value of the copyrighted work."[60] When deciding whether a use is fair, US courts will consider all four factors weighed together and "in light of the objectives of copyright," which is to "promote the Progress of Science and useful Arts."[61]

Google has advocated for the adoption of a US-styled flexible fair use exception in jurisdictions throughout the world. Google argues that a flexible exception is necessary in the context of the evolving digital environment.[62] Google explains:

> No matter how forward thinking or careful legislators are, they cannot predict the future. This has always been true, but the consequences of this truth are more pronounced now because the rapid pace of technological innovation brought about by the Internet and digital tools has radically collapsed the time lines for the development of new and innovative goods and services and business models that support them. Put simply, the most appropriate way for effectively and efficiently regulating in a dynamic environment is through a principles-based approach. Static laws that attempt to establish for all time the rules governing technological and market innovation will inevitably remain permanently out of date and impede innovation.[63]

This is why, for Google, a flexible exception is preferable to a static exception. Flexible exceptions "are inherently able to adapt to changing technologies and uses without the need for constant legislative intervention," whereas, Google argues, "static exceptions will always lag behind the current state of innovation."[64] If, like Google, innovation is your first priority, legal flexibility is key for ensuring rapidly evolving new technologies are not constrained by established, static laws.

As policymakers in jurisdictions throughout the world have debated whether they should replace their static fairness exception with a flexible one, Google has loudly refuted the common critique that static exceptions are advantageous because they provide more legal certainty than do flexible exceptions.[65] Google points to its own business activities and argues it relies on the US fair use exception with considerable certainty:

> Google's product counsels routinely make decisions in relation to the permissibility of new products and product features that require them to consider fair use. This requires them to consider the competing fairness factors . . . As with many other legal assessments they make, this requires a careful examination of the factual issues and balancing and weighing of relevant matters having regard to the established legal tests. In the vast majority of cases, Google's product counsels are able to form clear views on whether particular products or features are permissible. Nor is this experience limited to Google: major US media companies routinely rely on fair use without any apparent difficulties.[66]

Furthermore, Google stresses that even if static exceptions offer increased certainty it "comes at the direct cost of innovation and ultimately economic growth."[67] Google maintains, "innovation, culture and creativity are inherently dynamic," and, consequently, in order to flourish they require flexible copyright laws.[68] Google argues, static laws are "not capable of adapting to changes in technologies, consumer uses or business practices"[69] and they "enshrine existing business models, and create a barrier to innovation."[70] For Google, it is not worth putting innovation at risk in pursuit of legal certainty.

Google claims that in the United States the flexible fair use provision has offered "room within the framework of copyright law for many of the Internet technologies that have been so crucial to stimulating creativity, free expression, and economic growth in recent years."[71] Google posits that the thriving technology sector in the United States is confirmation of the benefits of a flexible exception: "no country in the world can compete with the U.S. for the most innovative search technologies, social networks, video and music hosting platforms, and for the sheer generation of the most jobs and wealth in the Internet domain."[72] Google argues that in the United States entrepreneurs can "take an informed risk, knowing that if your innovative product serves a genuinely new need and doesn't unfairly harm the people whose work you copied, then it will be on the right side of the law."[73] A flexible exception, Google argues, creates "breathing room for creation and technical innovation."[74]

For Google, another advantage of the US fair use exception is that it allows courts to consider the consequences of copyright broadly, balancing the interests of both rightsholders and the public. Google argues it permits lawmakers to find "a balance between the monopoly rights of the original creator, and the socially and economically beneficial output of subsequent creators or innovators" and that in the United States the "body of fair use law is shaped by a long history of inquiry into the central motivating factors for creation of new works and protections of the public interest."[75] According to Google, its own fair use cases embody this objective: "the fair use cases in which Google has been involved are precisely those where litigation has served a broad public interest in advancing the law in the face of new technologies."[76] As we will see, in its litigations over its search index and Google Books in particular, Google has evoked public interest arguments to successfully mount fair use defenses against claims of copyright infringement.

Google also argues that fair use benefits rightsholders by supporting the development of new markets for the sale and distribution of works.[77] Google submits, "the development and growth of the US technology sector has not been at the expense of the content industries."[78] Google argues, "creators have nothing to fear from flexible, dynamic copyright exceptions . . . new platforms, tools and services are enabling cheaper, easier and better ways to create, distribute, and promote content, and to make a living from it."[79] Google asks us to trust in the power of technological innovation to yield benefits for all.

Google also posits that, "the idea that fair use somehow reduces copyright owners' rights is belied by the regular practice of large U.S. media companies applying fair use in their every day commercial decisions."[80] For example, Google suggests, "Viacom, Inc., a very large, litigious media company . . . relies heavily on fair use for its popular 'Daily Show with Jon Stewart' and 'The Colbert Report.' "[81] Fair use, according to Google, provides "critical protections to cultural producers"[82] and should not be "dismissed as a derogation of authors' rights," when in fact it is a provision for permitting "legitimate re-use."[83] According to Google, because it secures public rights to access and engage with information and content, a flexible fair use exception "should be regarded as an essential tool for all authors to create and innovate."[84] By Google's assessment, be it new technologies, economic gains, or creativity, a flexible fair use exception offers benefits for all.

## SAFE HARBORS FOR ONLINE INTERMEDIARIES— THE SECOND PILLAR OF BALANCED COPYRIGHT

The purpose of intermediary safe harbors is to limit the potential liability of online intermediaries for acts of copyright infringement that occur on their platforms because of the actions of their users.[85] In principle, they do so in order to ensure copyright liability does not unduly impede the functioning of digital infrastructure and services. Unsurprisingly, given Google's business structure, safe harbors are the second major constituent of Google's copyright policy framework. Google posits, "the existence of robust and well defined 'Safe Harbours' for online intermediaries is another crucial pillar of the legal regimes that supports technological innovation and free expression in the US."[86] For Google, one of the world's largest "intermediaries," intermediary safe harbors provide a necessary limit on copyright liability, encouraging innovation and investment in digital technologies.

To qualify for safe harbor under the US DMCA, an intermediary must meet the statutory definition of a service provider, satisfy conditions of eligibility, and satisfy the requirements of the relevant safe harbor provision. The DMCA includes four provisions providing safe harbor for: transitory digital network communications, caching, storage of information at the direction of users, and information location tools including directories, indexes, references, pointers, or hyperlinks.[87] A service provider is defined as "a provider of online services or network access, or the operator of facilities therefor."[88] The conditions of eligibility include the implementation of a termination policy for repeat infringers and the accommodation of technical measures used to identify or protect copyrighted work.[89] All four safe harbors apply to Google. Google relies on Section 512(a) for its broadband service Google Fiber, Section 512(b) for its caching functions, Section 512(c) for services such as YouTube and Gmail, and Section 512(d) for its internet search services.[90] Google maintains, "none of these services could exist in their current form without the DMCA safe harbors."[91]

Both Section 512(c) and Section 512(d) stipulate that the service provider must not "receive a financial benefit directly attributable to the infringing activity" where a service provider has the "right and ability to control" the infringement, and the service provider must not have "actual knowledge" of infringing material or activities or awareness of "facts or circumstances from which infringing activity is apparent." Additionally, "upon obtaining such knowledge or awareness," the service provider must act "expeditiously to remove, or disable access to, the material."[92] Because of this requirement to remove or disable access to infringing content upon obtaining knowledge or awareness of infringing material, the DMCA safe harbors are commonly termed a "notice and take-down" model.

According to Google, a key strength of the notice and take-down model is its flexibility and scalability. Google explains:

A key to the effectiveness of the notice-and-takedown process has been its adaptability to all kinds of OSPs [online service providers]. For smaller startups, the costs of implementing a notice-and-takedown system are reasonable, especially when compared to the unpredictable (and potentially enormous) costs of litigating with individual rightsholders one by one. For larger OSPs like Google, serving billions of users, the notice-and-takedown process helps focus efforts to combat infringement into a manageable process.[93]

Furthermore, Google claims the notice and take-down system has proven to be adaptable to "innovative new technologies," supporting the "most successful cutting-edge online services, including social networking, instant messaging, and live video streaming."[94] Google maintains that without safe harbor these technologies would have faced "ruinous copyright liability based on the misdeeds of a tiny minority of users."[95] Google contends, "the safe harbor framework is crucial not only to Google's many online products and services, but to the growth of the Internet."[96] Safe harbors allow companies to deliver digital platforms and services safe in the knowledge that if they remove content upon becoming aware that it is infringing material, they will not be liable for copyright infringement.

Google argues intermediary safe harbors also benefit rightsholders as they provide "stringent guidelines for providing and responding to notices of infringement," creating "business certainty for internet companies, and a clear and swift process for content owners."[97] Google asserts the notice and take-down system benefits rightsholders by providing "a cheaper and more efficient way to remove infringing content from the Internet quickly without the need for lawyers and court actions."[98] Safe harbors provide guidelines by which intermediaries and rightsholders can act cooperatively to efficiently remove infringing material from the internet.

Google also argues safe harbors have benefited rightsholders by supporting the development of new online distribution platforms:

> the DMCA has created a plethora of new opportunities for creators to find and engage their audiences. Platforms like YouTube, Flickr, Instagram, Facebook, Twitter, and SoundCloud are just a few of the mechanisms by which musicians, photographers, and video creators are reaching audiences, developing careers, selling their works, and publicizing their events . . . Before the development of these platforms, creators had far fewer ways to reach global audiences, and most of those avenues often required creators to sign away their copyrights (and much of the value that derived from them) in exchange for distribution.[99]

For Google, the notice and take-down system provides an effective and efficient means for enforcing copyright, while also benefiting creators and the public by supporting innovation within the digital environment.

In jurisdictions throughout the world, Google has advocated for the adoption of safe harbors that mirror the DMCA provisions. For example, in 2010, through the Asian Internet Coalition, Google urged the Hong Kong government to adopt intermediary liability provisions that closely followed the DMCA. The Asian Internet Coalition proclaimed, "by following closely the DMCA provisions, we can also take advantage of the wealth of case law that has been established on the application and interpretation of the DMCA by US courts."[100] In 2013, commenting on proposed amendments to Thailand's copyright laws, the Asian Internet Coalition suggested the Thai government look to the DMCA for guidance, stating, "the DMCA has notable safe harbour provisions which protects Internet Service Providers from the consequences of their users' actions, but at the same time legitimately addresses copyright infringement."[101] Google has also argued that Australia's safe harbor regime presents a "serious impediment to the growth of Australia's digital economy"[102] because it does not provide protection for activities such as "transmitting data, caching, hosting and referring users to an online location."[103] On the world stage, Google consistently acts as a powerful supporter of DMCA-styled intermediary safe harbors.

In Europe, where the correct formulation of intermediary responsibilities has been hotly debated for several years, Google has fought strongly against reforms. In 2013, the European Commission launched a public consultation as part of "on-going efforts to review and modernise EU copyright rules."[104] The European Commission sought comments on whether hyperlinks and transitory copies made in the process of viewing a web page, including on a screen and in a cache, should be subject to the authorization of rightsholders.[105] Google was highly critical of the proposal, stating, "The notion that under EU law the question of whether copies (which are *invisible to users*) should trigger new permissions or payments highlights that the copyright system is liable to being abused with overbroad claims."[106] Google again argued transitory copying is fundamental to the functioning of the digital environment and that in a system that depends upon "the making and dissemination of copies of information," assessing liability by using the principles that apply to the ownership of a physical work puts the law "at odds with current technology."[107] Certainly, it would put the law at odds with many of Google's technologies.

Google also took issue with the proposition that hyperlinks could be subject to the authorization of rightsholders. Google argued, "links are merely pointers, addresses, like footnotes, and are naturally out of the copyright regime as they do not reproduce a work or make it available."[108] Google warned:

> If the trillions of links online were to be accompanied by trillions of licenses, information would not circulate smoothly anymore and the very existence of the Web would be undermined. And copyright law would be contrary to the very structure of the Web itself.[109]

Google urged the commission to recognize that "behind the technical legal question . . . lies a very important socio-economic issue." [110] Of course, for a company born from the digital age, one built from copying and linking to information, such a policy could be catastrophic.

Google is also not supportive of a "notice and stay down" model for intermediary safe harbor.[111] Broadly, under a notice and stay-down regime, in order to qualify for safe harbor, after an initial infringement notice, intermediaries must continue to remove infringing content as it reappears on their platform, without a requirement for additional notices from the rightsholder. Google argues implementation of a notice and stay-down policy "would impose an extraordinary burden on OSPs to monitor all content available through their services."[112] Google also asserts effective implementation of a notice and stay-down system is not feasible because an intermediary

> would need to know whether the ownership of a specific piece of content has changed or whether the content was licensed for the subsequent use. The OSP would also need to make a legal (and contextual) determination as to whether the posting of allegedly reappearing content was a fair use or covered by another copyright exception.[113]

Consequently, according to Google, it is "both legally and technically difficult to imagine that a 'staydown' obligation could feasibly be imposed on all OSPs that are covered by the DMCA safe harbors."[114]

In 2019, the European Union introduced copyright reforms that will bring the jurisdiction's intermediary liability regime closer to a notice and stay-down system. Under Article 17 of the new copyright directive, while there is no explicit obligation to monitor for infringement, "online content sharing service providers" will become directly liable for the copyright infringement of their users. Article 17 specifies that "online content sharing service providers perform an act of communication to the public or an act of making available to the public . . . when it gives the public access to copyright protected works or other protected subject matter uploaded by its users," and therefore they must obtain an authorization (a license) from rightsholders.[115] Under Article 17, Google (and other intermediaries) may be liable for the copyright infringement of users, without the need for a notice from a rightsholder.

Google fought strongly against the directive, initiating a #SaveYourInternet campaign, warning that the change "threatens to shut down the ability of millions of people in Europe to upload content to platforms like YouTube" and that it will result in Europeans being "cut off from the latest cultural moments being created and shared on the Internet."[116] A touch of hyperbole? Perhaps. Although it is not yet clear exactly how it will be applied in practice when the directive becomes law at the national level among EU member states, what is certain is that it will substantially alter Google's responsibilities and motivations as an intermediary operating in the region.

To avoid liability for acts of infringement by users, we can expect to see Google negotiating licensing deals with rightsholders and more actively monitoring and enforcing copyright across its platforms. The biggest unanswered questions for those concerned with the public interest—for those concerned with securing a diverse and participatory culture—is with whom will Google negotiate? YouTube CEO Susan Wojcicki herself warned the reforms could result in YouTube only hosting content from large media and entertainment companies. According to Wojcicki, "It would be too risky for platforms to host content from smaller original content creators, because the platforms would now be directly liable for that content."[117]

## GOOGLE'S PLAN FOR ADDRESSING "PIRACY"—LEAVE IT TO INNOVATION!

In response to continuous calls from the content industries that more must be done to prevent and punish the illegal consumption of entertainment online, Google consistently argues that a combination of market and technological forces will yield the best outcomes. Google views piracy as a market supply problem that can be solved by "new business models and a free marketplace for legal purchasing of content."[118] Google argues that "consumers will play by the rules if they are offered high quality content that is convenient to purchase and competitively priced."[119] In order to encourage the development of such services, Google suggests strengthening copyright exceptions and limitations such as fair use and intermediary safe harbors.

For Google, copyright exceptions and limitations are effective policy instruments for combating piracy because they encourage the development of innovative content distribution services. In 2016, Google submitted to the US Copyright Office that "platforms like iTunes, Netflix, Amazon, Hulu, Google Play, Spotify, and Deezer ... By providing access to convenient and legitimate content offerings to users in markets all around the world ... offer the most effective method of fighting piracy."[120] Google suggests that rather than introducing "overly harsh regulation to combat piracy," governments should "adopt copyright exceptions that allow the market, new technologies and new creativity to evolve."[121] Google argues it is exceptions to copyright rather than stronger copyright laws that will solve the problem of internet piracy.

Along with the implementation of exceptions and limitations to copyright, Google claims piracy can be curbed through policies that restrict the flow of money to websites dedicated to online piracy. Google proposes, "'follow the money' strategies ... play a critical role in the effort to fight piracy online."[122] Accordingly, Google participated in the development of Best Practices and Guidelines for Ad Networks to Address Piracy and Counterfeiting, which assist advertising networks to "maintain and post policies prohibiting websites that are principally dedicated to engaging in piracy or counterfeiting from participating in the ad network's advertising programs."[123]

The third component of Google's approach to piracy is the implementation of automated content-identification technology, such as Content ID, Google's rights management program on YouTube. Content ID allows rightsholders to monetize and block or track videos containing their works that are uploaded to YouTube. Google boasts, "Content ID represents a thoughtful and eminently practical solution to piracy, as well as a new and growing revenue stream for rights holders."[124] Google also claims "Content ID is good for users . . . When copyright owners choose to monetize or track user-submitted videos, it allows users to remix and upload a wide variety of new creations using existing works."[125] Through Content ID, Google offers proof that innovation and cooperation, rather than expanded copyright laws, is a fruitful approach to copyright enforcement.

Yet Google cautions that while useful for enforcing copyright, there is a "real possibility that identifiers and or permissions markers carry wrong, misleading, or out-of-date information, for instance wrongful attribution of covering works which are in the public domain."[126] Google explains that content-identification technologies can "reduce transaction costs," but they can "never address all of copyright's complexities and subtleties."[127] In particular, Google notes that content-identification technologies cannot identify "videos which are covered by an exception, and thus require no licensing."[128] Google urges policymakers to "keep in mind the need for mechanisms to protect fair use remixes from being blocked or being 'licensed' by rightsholders who have no proper claim on them."[129] Google advises content-identification systems should be considered "a supplement to, not a substitute for, fair use."[130]

Google strongly opposes copyright enforcement measures that block access to digital services, such as internet filtering or site blocking. Google argues "filtering will not achieve much in preventing copyright

infringement online, with the ability for users to encrypt their communications rendering filters totally ineffective."[131] At the same time, Google
warns filtering technologies can degrade internet quality:

> Packet-filtering and analysis is a process that requires a larger amount
> of processing power and network reconfiguration. It risks degrading
> the quality and users' experience for perfectly legitimate online serv-
> ices, raising serious concerns for competition and innovation.[132]

In a 2014 submission to the Australian government, Google described site-
blocking as a "blunt and ultimately ineffective instrument for addressing
online piracy."[133] Google cautioned, "it is imperative that policies designed
to address online piracy do not inadvertently stifle the explosion in innovation that has opened up new opportunities for creators and creative
industries."[134] Always, for Google, innovation must be prioritized.

## CONCLUSION

As the debate over the correct copyright policy formulation for the digital environment has played out over many years throughout the world,
Google has forcefully resisted the conventional wisdom of copyright as
purely an author's private property right. Google points to important economic and social consequence of copyright and argues copyright should
be understood as a policy instrument that regulates technological innovation. Google calls for limitations on the scope of copyright and strengthened public rights to access and engage with information and content. In
particular, Google submits that strong exceptions and limitations prevent
a "permission first, innovate later" culture from stifling socially beneficial
technological innovation. Google also argues copyright exceptions and
limitations are critical for ensuring access to and democratic participation
in the creation of information and content.

Google has an obvious vested interest in its copyright agenda. As
Google continues to innovate and acquire companies that develop digital

technologies, Google needs strong and reliable exceptions to copyright and limitations on liability. As well, through its advertising service, Google profits from people accessing, creating, and sharing information online. Google's copyright policy framework incorporates social and economic considerations, but nonetheless its parameters are set according to Google's private interests.

Google's copyright agenda is also driven by an unwavering faith in the power of innovation and entrepreneurialism. Google assumes free markets and innovation can solve all problems. Consider, for example, Google's argument that the best policy for curbing piracy is strong copyright exceptions and limitations. Effectively, Google is arguing that rather than introducing regulation, policymakers should leave it to market and technological forces to solve the economic issues facing the media and entertainment industries. While the "free" market and technological innovation might produce great new services for consumers, there is no assurance that they will at the same time ensure vibrant, diverse, and participatory creative sectors throughout the world.[135] The philosophical underpinnings of Google's framework can lead to an overemphasis of innovation and wealth creation and a lack of consideration for actual cultural conditions.

In the copyright policy debate, Google is a powerful voice speaking directly to politicians, industries, and the public about the benefits of innovation and public rights to access and engage with information and content. But regardless of any invocations of broad social and economic benefits, or the public interest, Google is also operating for its own interest and to great financial success. And, in the context of such tremendous success, there has been no shortage of dissenters, opponents, and disbelievers willing to challenge Google's positions on copyright.

# Google vs. The Copyright Tradition

## *Litigating "Innovate First, Permission Later"*

When developing technologies and acquiring companies, rarely is Google constrained by tradition. Google typically takes an *innovate first* approach to its business. An approach that has triggered numerous high-profile copyright disputes, including over Google's use, without permission, of copyrighted content in Google Search, Google Images, Google Books, YouTube, and its phone operating system, Android. Essentially, the release of each new Google product or service has brought with it legal challenges; parties contesting the legitimacy of Google's activities, some seeking to win on principle, many pursuing financial gain.

More often than not, in its US copyright litigations, Google has successfully defended its activities, primarily relying on fair use and intermediary safe harbor. Both provisions are central to Google's copyright policy agenda and to its legal strategy. Interestingly, what we see in this legal history is that, generally, Google has secured, at least with respect to its own activities, its vision for copyright. What we also see is Google's deep dependency on its particular view of how copyright should function in the digital environment. Without the favorable legal decisions that it has obtained over the years, Google would not be the company it is today. With each win, Google took a step forward, legitimized and emboldened.

*Google Rules: The History and Future of Copyright Under the Influence of Google.* Joanne Elizabeth Gray, Oxford University Press (2020). © Oxford University Press.
DOI: 10.1093/oso/9780190072070.001.0001

Google's immense wealth affords it a near inimitable capacity to withstand multiple, extensive copyright litigation; and Google exhibits a keenness to pursue copyright disputes on principle, seeking to establish precedent that is favorable to its copyright agenda. Of course, these cases do not stand alone in US copyright jurisprudence. They are contributions to a larger body of law involving varying litigants and outcomes that have shaped digital copyright in the United States. Nonetheless, what we see in Google's litigation history is a company consistently and unrelentingly promoting a progressive copyright agenda, arguing for expanded or strengthened public rights to access and engage with content in the digital environment.

But the consequences of Google's copyright litigation history are more than doctrinal or rhetorical. Google's disputes over search, images, and books in particular have allowed Google to privately accumulate extensive data resources that Google uses to fuel its information empire. At its core, Google's US copyright litigation history is a story of a company pushing technological and legal boundaries, amounting wins to enormous private benefit, in the process of becoming one of the most significant technology companies of our time.

## COPYING THE ENTIRE INTERNET

To generate its search index, Google uses the "Googlebot," a program that crawls the internet and gathers information about websites.[1] When the Googlebot scans a website, it copies, analyzes, and stores textual information on Google's servers. Google also stores full copies of a website's HTML code in its cache index. When a user searches the internet using Google Search, Google's algorithm searches the information stored on its servers in order to retrieve and present hyperlinks to relevant websites. Search results also make available for viewing cached copies of websites. Google does not obtain express prior permission from website owners to scan and copy their websites. To exclude a website from Google Search, a website owner must include the robots.txt code in their website's HTML code. The robots.txt code, together with other meta tags, will instruct the Googlebot to exclude either the full website or specific web pages from the Google index.[2] When Google became a publicly listed company in 2004, it also became a more visible litigation target for those who questioned the legality of this system of automated copying and indexing of websites.

## TESTING THE LEGALITY OF AUTOMATED COPYING OF WEBSITES—*FIELD V. GOOGLE*

In 2004, Blake Field, a US attorney, created a personal website and on it published a collection of his own poetry.[3] When building his website, Field was aware of Google's automated indexing and caching and of the robots.txt exclusion protocol, but chose not to include the code in his website design.[4] Subsequently, the Googlebot included Field's website in Google Search. When this occurred, Field sued Google, claiming that each time a Google user viewed cached versions of his website Google directly infringed Field's exclusive reproduction and distribution rights.[5] Despite Google and other search engines having provided cache indexes for several years, Field's challenge initiated the first ruling on the legality of this activity under US copyright law.[6]

In 2006, a US District Court for the District of Nevada found there was no direct infringement by Google because it was the user, not Google, who created a copy of Field's website when accessing Google's cache index.[7] The District Court considered Google's conduct to be "automated, non-volitional . . . [and] in response to a user's request."[8] Furthermore, the District Court reasoned Google was protected from liability through Section 512(b) of the US Copyright Act, which provides safe harbor for system caching by online service providers.[9] This finding was particularly significant as it required a broad view of the safe harbor provision for caching. At the time, it was generally unclear whether the safe harbor provision for caching was intended to cover the type of search engine caching undertaken by Google or whether it was intended to apply only to proxy caching, a technical

process that can reduce bandwidth use and improve network performance.[10] In its case against Field, Google obtained a small but significant victory in support of its caching practices.

The District Court also found Google had an implied license to reproduce and distribute Field's works.[11] The District Court reasoned the ability
to opt out of indexing and caching was known by Field and with this
knowledge he chose not to include the necessary instructions in his website design.[12] While the decision has had no lasting effect on the doctrine
of implied license, it was notable for the District Court's implicit support
of an "opt-out" rather than "opt-in" copyright arrangement. It deviated
from the convention that rightsholders do not need to actively assert
their rights to enjoy copyright protection.[13] By requiring Field to opt out
of Google Search, the District Court required Field to actively assert his
copyright. Again, a small but significant conceptual victory for Google's
search engine practices.

In its resounding rejection of Field's claims, the District Court also
found Google's use of Field's work was a fair use. In its fair use analysis, the
District Court relied upon *Kelly v. Arriba Soft Corp* (*Kelly*) of the US Court
of Appeals for the Ninth Circuit.[14] In *Kelly*, the Ninth Circuit held the use
of thumbnail-sized copies of photographs for a search engine index was
a transformative fair use. The Ninth Circuit reasoned a search engine's
purpose is to improve access to information, a purpose fundamentally
different from the original purpose of a photo, which is artistic expression.[15] Applied to the facts in *Field*, the District Court found Google's use
of Field's works was transformative: the original purpose of Field's poetry
was artistic expression and entertainment, whereas Google's cache index
serves purposes such as providing access to content when the original is
unavailable, allowing users to monitor changes to websites over time and
facilitating analysis of the results of a search query.[16] The District Court
also reasoned Google's for-profit status did not weigh against a fair use
finding because "the transformative purpose of Google's use is considerably more important, and . . . weighs heavily in favor of a fair use finding."[17]
Google's innovative technology that improved public access to knowledge
prevailed over an author's private property claim.

In *Field*, through fair use, intermediary safe harbor, and implied license, Google easily survived an initial challenge to its use of rightsholders' works in its search engine. As a newly incorporated company, Google could progress with some confidence that, at least in the United States, with the robots.txt protocol in place, Google's automated copying of the entire internet without prior express permission from website owners, was not copyright infringement.

## A SECOND TEST—*PARKER V. GOOGLE*

In 2004, Gordon Parker, the author of an e-book titled *29 Reasons Not to Be a Nice Guy*, sued Google for copyright infringement.[18] Parker had posted an excerpt from his e-book to USENET—an internet bulletin board system in which users post and search for information. The Googlebot copied the USENET posts, and they were included in Google Search.[19] In his claim, Parker sought to establish Google's automated indexing and caching, as well as hyperlinks to his work and excerpts from his work displayed in Google Search results, constituted direct copyright infringement.[20]

In 2006, the US District Court for the Eastern District of Pennsylvania rejected Parker's claim on the grounds that Google was neutral in the transmission of Parker's work and so there was not the required volition or causation necessary to establish direct infringement.[21] The District Court stated:

When an ISP automatically and temporarily stores data without human intervention so that the system can operate and transmit data to its users, the necessary element of volition is missing. The automatic activity of Google's search engine is analogous. It is clear that Google's automatic archiving of USENET postings and excerpting of websites in its results to users' search queries do not include the necessary volitional element to constitute direct copyright infringement.[22]

Citing the decision in *Field,* the District Court also found the safe harbor for system caching protected Google from liability.[23]

Although Parker's challenge to Google was weakened by what the District Court described as a "rambling Complaint," the decision in *Parker* was significant to Google inasmuch as it again saw Google easily surviving a rightsholder's challenge to its search engine activities.[24] With straightforward wins in both *Field* and *Parker*, it was becoming clearer that under US law, Google would not be found liable for copyright infringement when copying content across the internet for its search index, without the prior permission of rightsholders. In *Perfect 10*, however, Google was to face a far less rambling and far more substantial challenge to its search engine activities. In *Perfect 10*, features of Google's search engine service would come under much greater scrutiny—Google would have to defend its decision to copy and display photos without permission from rightsholders.

## COPYING OTHER PEOPLE'S PHOTOS— *PERFECT 10 V. GOOGLE*

Google's search engine includes an image search function, Google Images. In 2004, when its dispute with Perfect 10 commenced, Google Images drew upon a database of thumbnail images—small, low-resolution images—that Google created by copying images from websites across the internet, without the express prior permission from rightsholders. Google displayed the thumbnail images to Google users in search results, along with links to the websites hosting the full-sized image.[25] The thumbnail images Google created were stored on its servers, along with textual information about the images.[26] Both the images and textual information were also stored in Google's cache.

When displaying image search results to users, Google employs the website design techniques "in-line linking" and "framing." In-line linking directs a browser to show information stored in different locations.[27] Framing affects how in-line content is displayed, for example, by applying borders, scroll bars, or text.[28] In other words, in-line linking and framing are methods for displaying in the one browser window content hosted on various websites.

Perfect 10 operates an adult website that provides access to photos of nude models for a subscription fee. At the time of the initial claim, in addition to its subscription service, Perfect 10 was also licensing its photos to a third party who then sold the photos to mobile phone users.[29] In its complaint against Google, Perfect 10 alleged the inclusion of thumbnail versions of Perfect 10's photos in Google's search indexes, along with in-line linking to websites hosting full-sized photos, and Google's cache of websites hosting full-sized photos, constituted copyright infringement.[30] Perfect 10 claimed Google had directly infringed Perfect 10's exclusive display and distribution rights.[31]

## In-Line Linking—What Does It Mean to Serve Content over the Internet?

In 2007, the US Court of Appeals for the Ninth Circuit held in-line linking to full-size images was not a direct infringement of Perfect 10's display right.[32] To reach this conclusion, the Ninth Circuit decided the lower court's analysis of the "server test," which defines display as "the act of *serving* content over the web—*i.e.*, physically sending ones and zeros over the internet to the user's browser," was consistent with the language of the US Copyright Act.[33] The Ninth Circuit explained:

> a computer owner that stores an image as electronic information and serves that electronic information directly to the user . . . is displaying the electronic information in violation of a copyright holder's exclusive display right . . . Conversely, the owner of a computer that does not store and serve the electronic information to a user is not displaying that information, even if such owner in-line links to or frames the electronic information.[34]

As Google did not directly display a copy of Perfect 10's images, but rather provided instructions directing a user's browser to refer to another website's content, Google's in-line linking to Perfect 10's images was not an infringement of Perfect 10's display right.[35]

In accordance with this analysis, the court also found Google's in-line linking was not an infringement of Perfect 10's exclusive distribution right. The court reasoned that distribution requires an act of "actual dissemination" of a copy, and, as "Google did not communicate the full-size images to the user's computer, Google did not distribute these images."[36] Effectively, in its decision on in-line linking, the Ninth Circuit viewed Google's linking in the context of the technical processes involved in browsing the internet and concluded these activities did not fall within the scope of an author's exclusive rights—an important victory for Google and anyone using in-line linking in their website design. As well, with the issue of in-line linking so decided, the likelihood that Google's search service could be held liable for copyright infringement was further diminished.[37]

## But What About Those Thumbnail Copies?!

The server test did, however, render Google's display of thumbnail images as an exercise of Perfect 10's exclusive display rights.[38] Google had stored on its own servers and served directly to users copies of Perfect 10's photos.[39] Yet, the Ninth Circuit found Google's use was fair.[40] In its fair use analysis, the Ninth Circuit emphasized the need to explore each fair use factor in the context of the purpose of copyright—to promote the progress of science and useful arts—and to weigh the results against the objective of serving "the welfare of the public."[41]

In its fair use analysis, the Ninth Circuit found Google's use of thumbnails to be "highly transformative," transforming a photo from a work of entertainment into a reference tool.[42] The Ninth Circuit stated:

Although an image may have been created originally to serve an entertainment, aesthetic, or informative function, a search engine transforms the image into a pointer directing a user to a source of information. Just as a "parody has an obvious claim to transformative value" because "it can provide social benefit, by shedding light on an earlier work, and, in the process, creating a new one," *Campbell*, 510 U.S. at 579, 114 S. Ct. 1164, a search engine provides social benefit by incorporating an original work into a new work, namely, an electronic reference tool. Indeed, a search engine may be more transformative than a parody because a search engine provides an entirely new use for the original work, while a parody typically has the same entertainment purpose as the original work.[43]

High regard for a search engine indeed.

In accordance with the finding in *Kelly* that "even making an exact copy of a work may be transformative so long as the copy serves a different function than the original work,"[44] the Ninth Circuit held that the transformative nature of Google's use was not diminished by the fact that Google copied Perfect 10's photos in their entirety.[45] In addition, the Ninth Circuit stated it was "mindful" of the US Supreme Court's direction in *Campbell v. Acuff-Rose Music* (*Campbell*) that the more transformative a new work is, the less significant are other factors.[46]

This consideration also impacted the Ninth Circuit's appraisal of the commercial elements of Google's activities—its AdSense business—and any potential superseding uses. Perfect 10 claimed Google's thumbnails negatively impacted on its ability to profitably license its photos to mobile phone users because Google's thumbnails were a direct substitute for this product.[47] But the Ninth Circuit specified that in a fair use analysis any superseding or commercial uses must be weighed against the transformative use, the purpose of copyright, and the public interest.[48] The Ninth Circuit concluded that the highly transformative nature of Google's search engine and the public benefits of a search engine that substantially improves access to information online outweighed any commercial impact.[49] Accordingly, the Ninth Circuit concluded the first fair use factor weighed heavily in favor of fair use.[50] The Ninth Circuit also argued for "the importance of analyzing fair use flexibly in light of new circumstance."[51]

Despite taking other people's images and making exact copies of them, without prior permission, in *Perfect 10*, Google was not found liable for copyright infringement.

## A PUBLIC INTEREST DEAL

Together, the decisions in *Field, Parker,* and *Perfect 10* were important moments in Google's commercial history. They legitimized Google's copying of the entire internet. Google's search engine was deemed a so-cially beneficial new technology that did not illegally encroach upon the exclusive rights provided to rightsholders by copyright law. An implicit deal had been struck. The public gained an important tool that would in-crease access to information at a scale never before seen. In return, Google gained databases of full copies of websites and images from across the internet—databases to which only Google has full access—and Google was free to continue to develop its search and advertising services. It was, apparently, a deal (almost) everyone could live with. And one Google would seek to make again, only next time regarding millions of books.[52]

## IF WE CAN COPY WEBSITES AND IMAGES,
## THEN WHY NOT BOOKS?

According to Sergey Brin and Larry Page, they first formulated their book digitization concept as students at Stanford University: they envisioned a fu-ture where digital libraries were common, made possible by a "web crawler," which would scan and index the content of entire books, "determining any given book's relevance and usefulness by tracking the number and quality of citations from other books."[53] In 2002, Google began developing its book-scanning technology and forming relationships with libraries and publishers.[54] In 2004, Google entered into an agreement with Oxford University's Bodleian library, the first of several agreements struck that year, granting Google permission by the library to scan its full collection.[55]

There are two divisions within Google Books. The Google Books Partner Program sees Google scan, or incorporate scans of books provided by publishers, into the Google Books database, with the express permission of publishers.[56] Within this division, Google displays excerpts from the book (relevant to a user's search query) and provides links for purchasing the full book, along with bibliographic information about the book.[57] Under the second division, the Google Books Libraries Project, Google scans books held in library collections.[58] The libraries are provided with a digital copy of each book for cataloging and preservation purposes, and the books are made available to the public for searching and excerpts of the books are displayed in Google Books search results.[59] The copyright status of books within the library collections varies; some are in the public domain, while others remain under copyright protection, and the majority are out of print.[60] Within the Libraries Project, Google does not obtain permission from rightsholders to copy or display books, and it does not compensate rightsholders.[61]

In 2005, Google was sued by the Authors Guild, a writers' organization that advocates for "the copyright and contractual interests of published writers."[62] The Authors Guild claimed Google was "engaging in massive copyright infringement" by copying works held in libraries without the permission of copyright holders.[63] The Authors Guild alleged Google was required to gain permission from rightsholders to scan books held in libraries, and by not doing so Google was infringing rightsholders' electronic rights.[64] The Authors Guild sought damages and injunctive and declaratory relief.[65]

In an initial response to the suit, Google publicly expressed confidence that its use of the books was fair. Susan Wojcicki, who was at the time the vice president of product management at Google, stated the "Library Project is fully consistent with both the fair use doctrine under U.S. copyright law and the principles underlying copyright law itself."[66] Google's chief executive officer, Eric Schmidt, also stated:

The program's critics maintain that any use of their books requires their permission. We have the utmost respect for the intellectual and

creative effort that lies behind every grant of copyright. Copyright
law, however, is all about which uses require permission and which
don't; and we believe (and have structured Google Print to ensure)
that the use we make of books we scan through the Library Project is
consistent with the Copyright Act, whose "fair use" balancing of the
rights of copyright-holders with the public benefits of free expression
and innovation allows a wide range of activity, from book quotations
in reviews to parodies of pop songs—all without copyright-holder
permission.[67]

Regardless of any apparent legal certitude, at the time, it was far from clear
that copying full books for a search index fell within the parameters of fair
use. As the Second Circuit would ultimately state, Google's use of the library books unquestionably tested "the boundaries of fair use."[68]

## Perhaps Making Full Copies of Books Is Pushing Things Too Far? A Proposed Settlement (2008)

Plausibly, tacit legal uncertainty accounts for Google's initial decision to
pursue a settlement with the Authors Guild. In 2008, after three years
of legal proceedings and negotiations, the parties sought court approval
for a settlement agreement that included all books registered with the
US Copyright Office or published in the United Kingdom, Australia,
or Canada.[69] The settlement provided Google permission to continue
its book digitization, in return for various forms of compensation to
rightsholders.[70] For example, Google agreed to pay rightsholders a percentage of revenues earned from subscription fees, electronic sales, and
advertising.[71] The agreement also established a "Book Rights Registry," responsible for maintaining a database of rightsholders and for distributing
revenues.[72] The agreement required Google to implement an "opt-out"
policy, facilitating the exclusion of books from all or some of the proposed
uses at the request of a rightsholder.[73]

In 2011, the US District Court for the Southern District of New York rejected the proposed settlement. The District Court suggested the parties change the agreement from an opt-out to an opt-in arrangement.[74] The District Court considered the opt-out policy to "expropriate rights of individuals involuntarily" and to produce a system in which "if copyright owners sit back and do nothing, they lose their rights . . . class members who fail to opt out will be deemed to have released their rights even as to future infringing conduct."[75] The District Court reasoned that it could not release Google from liability for future acts of infringement.[76]

Following the rejection of the settlement, the Authors Guild sought class certification for a class including any US resident holding a copyright interest in a book copied by Google. However, in 2013, the Court of Appeals for the Second Circuit remanded the case to the District Court for consideration of Google's fair use defense.[77]

## Google Books Is a Fair Use of Authors' Works—The District Court Decision (2013)

In 2013, the District Court agreed with the Authors Guild that Google's digital copies, stored on its servers, provided to libraries and displayed in search results, without the permission of rightsholders, was prima facie an infringement of the rightsholders' exclusive reproduction, distribution, and display rights.[78] However, the District Court held Google's use was fair.[79]

In the years since the original complaint, Google had continued its book-scanning, partnering with libraries and publishers worldwide. By the time the District Court considered Google's fair use defense in 2013, Google had scanned more than twenty million books, each available to the public for full-text searches and for view either in full or in snippets.[80] In its opinion, the District Court recognized that Google Books had become an "essential research tool" providing "a new and efficient way for readers and researchers to find books" and to undertake data-mining activities.[81] The District Court acknowledged the contribution of Google

Books to preserving, reviving, promoting, and expanding access to books, particularly for the print-disabled and other "traditionally underserved populations."[82]

In its fair use analysis, the District Court held Google's use of the books was highly transformative, transforming "expressive text into a comprehensive word index that helps readers, scholars, researchers and others to find books."[83] The District Court also held the display of snippets of the books in search results was a transformative use, relying on the Ninth Circuit's decisions in *Perfect 10* and *Kelly*, as well as *Bill Graham Archives v. Dorling Kindersley* (*Bill Graham Archives*) of the US Court of Appeals for the Second Circuit. In *Bill Graham Archives*, the Second Circuit held the display of copies of Grateful Dead tour posters in a Grateful Dead biography was transformative.[84] The District Court reasoned that the display of snippets was transformative because Google was using snippets of text to direct users to books.[85]

The District Court held Google's for-profit status did not weigh against fair use; because Google did not sell digital copies of the books and was not running advertisements on Google Books web pages, Google was not engaging in directly commercializing the books.[86] Furthermore, the District Court concluded any commercial benefit enjoyed by Google must be considered in the context of the other educational purposes of Google Books.[87] The District Court similarly rejected the argument that Google Books served as a market replacement for books and instead held "Google Books enhances the sale of books to the benefit of copyright holders."[88]

The District Court found the amount and substantiality of the portion of books used by Google, to weigh only slightly against fair use: Google had copied the works in full, however, copying the entire work was necessary in order to facilitate full-text searches of books.[89] Viewed in light of the purpose of copyright law, the District Court concluded Google's use of the books was a fair use, providing "significant public benefits" and advancing "the progress of the arts and sciences, while maintaining respectful consideration for the rights of authors."[90]

## Copying for a Searchable Database Is a Quintessentially Fair Use—The HathiTrust Decision (2014)

In 2008, several of the libraries participating in Google Books collaborated to create the HathiTrust Digital Library (HDL), a joint repository of digitized books, including the books provided to the libraries by Google for preservation and archiving purposes.[91] The HDL provides public access to its database of digital books, permitting users to conduct full-text keyword searches. The results returned to users include the number of times the search term appears in a book and page numbers, however, unlike Google Books, HDL search results do not include snippets of text from the books.[92] The Authors Guild sued the HathiTrust, seeking a declaration that digitizing books without permission from rightsholders was copyright infringement and an injunction preventing the reproduction, distribution, display, or delivery of books to Google for digitization without permission.[93]

The Second Circuit, however, rejected the Authors Guild's claims, holding that copying entire books for the purpose of full-text searching was a fair use, stating, "the creation of a full-text searchable database is a quintessentially transformative use."[94] For Google, this decision meant the question of whether digitizing books without the permission of rightsholders, for use in a search index, was largely resolved prior to the Authors Guild's appeal in 2015.

## Displaying Snippets Is Fair Too—The Second Circuit Decision (2015)

With the HathiTrust case decided, when the Authors Guild appealed the District Court's 2013 Google Books decision, the central question for the appellate court was whether Google's display of snippets of books was also a fair use. In their appeal, the Authors Guild argued Google's copying of books in full, and the display of snippets, was not transformative because it produced substitutes for their works.[95] The Authors Guild also argued

Google's for-profit status precluded a fair use finding.[96] Additionally, the Authors Guild claimed the use of books in search technologies, including snippet displays, infringed rightsholders' exclusive derivative rights.[97]

In 2015, the US Court of Appeals for the Second Circuit rejected the Authors Guild's arguments, affirming the District Court decision.[98] The Second Circuit assessed Google's book-scanning and display of snippets of copyrighted books without the permission of rightsholders, against the historical objectives of copyright. The court expressed that "while authors are undoubtedly important intended beneficiaries of copyright, the ultimate, primary intended beneficiary is the public, whose access to knowledge copyright seeks to advance."[99] The public interest in access to information would be key to the court's assessment of Google's fair use claim.

In its first factor analysis, the Second Circuit concluded Google Books' purpose is to "provide otherwise unavailable information about the originals."[100] The Second Circuit explained, "the purpose of Google's copying of the original copyrighted books is to make available significant information *about those books*, permitting a searcher to identify those that contain a word or term of interest,"[101] and the snippet view feature "adds important value to the basic transformative search function."[102] According to the Second Circuit, the snippet view provides a reader "just enough context surrounding the searched term to help her evaluate whether the book falls within the scope of her interest (without revealing so much as to threaten the author's copyright interests)."[103] The Second Circuit concluded Google's copying and display of snippets of books was a transformative use, providing information about books rather than providing a substitute for or derivative of the original work.[104]

In its decision, the Second Circuit asserted the importance of transformativeness to a fair use determination: "transformative uses tend to favor a fair use finding because a transformative use is one that communicates something new and different from the original or expands its utility, thus serving copyright's overall objective of contributing to public knowledge."[105] The Second Circuit rejected the Authors Guild's argument that Google's for-profit status should preclude a finding of fair use, stating that in cases where there is a "convincing transformative purpose and absence of significant substitutive competition with the original," this argument had been "repeatedly rejected."[106] The court also assessed that as the snippets displayed to readers were of a "fragmentary and scattered nature," Google did not "reveal matter that offers the marketplace a significantly competing substitute for the copyrighted work."[107] The Second Circuit reasoned the ability to search a book for words or phrases is not a substitute for the original work, and while the snippet view may cause some loss of sales, "some loss of sales does not suffice to make the copy an effectively competing substitute."[108]

The Second Circuit rejected the Authors Guild's claim that Google Books infringed the exclusive derivative right in "the application of search and snippet view functions to their works."[109] The court concluded an author's copyright does not include all information about a work, for example, information regarding how often a word or phrase is used in a work.[110] The Second Circuit explained the underlying reasoning for the derivative right is that "an author's right to control and profit from the dissemination of her work ought not to be evaded by conversion of the work into different forms" and that "nothing in the statutory definition of a derivative work, or of the logic that underlies it, suggests that the author of an original work enjoys an exclusive derivative right to supply information about that work of the sort communicated by Google's search function."[111]

In late 2015, the Authors Guild unsuccessfully petitioned the US Supreme Court to review the Second Circuit's decision.[112] Google had achieved another significant copyright law win—a win for its business activities and a win for its copyright agenda.

## The Significance of the Google Books Decision

The Google Books decision makes a significant contribution to an ongoing shift in the application of the US fair use doctrine.[113] Where courts might once have deemed commercial factors critical to fair use, the Google Books decision helped to consolidate a shift away from commercial considerations and towards transformativeness. For example, in 1985, the US Supreme Court in *Harper & Row v. Nation Enterprises* stated the fourth fair use factor, the effect on the market, was "undoubtedly the single most important element of fair use."[114] In 1990, in *Stewart v. Abend*, the Supreme Court again stated the fourth factor was the most important factor in a fair use analysis.[115] It was not until *Campbell* in 1994 that the US Supreme Court made its significant articulation of the importance of transformative works. In *Campbell*, the Supreme Court stated:

> Although such transformative use is not absolutely necessary for a finding of fair use . . . the goal of copyright, to promote science and the arts, is generally furthered by the creation of transformative works. Such works thus lie at the heart of the fair use doctrine's guarantee of breathing space within the confines of copyright . . . the more transformative the new work, the less will be the significance of other factors, like commercialism, that may weigh against a finding of fair use.[116]

The Google Books decision fortifies the *Campbell* approach.

The Google Books decision is often and rightly celebrated as a win for public access to information. When Google prevailed in its litigation, the whole world won access to millions of books. Full libraries of books are available online and free for all to search. What is less frequently remarked upon, however, is the fact that with this decision Google again received an immense private benefit. Again, a deal was struck. The public gained the valuable ability to search and view snippets of millions of books, and in return Google gained exclusive *full* access to those books, again adding a new and highly valuable resource to its information stockpiles.

## GOOGLE'S OBLIGATION TO MONITOR FOR COPYRIGHT INFRINGEMENT—*VIACOM V. YOUTUBE*

Undoubtedly, the outcomes in *Field, Parker, Perfect 10,* and *Authors Guild* were overwhelmingly favorable to Google. Under US law, Google was vindicated as a socially beneficial digital service provider. However, since 2007, Google had been fighting a copyright matter on another front, against another media entity, regarding its newly acquired video hosting platform, YouTube. YouTube was founded by Chad Hurley, Steve Chen, and Jawed Karim in 2005 and acquired by Google in 2006 for a reported value of USD 1.65 billion.[117]

In 2007, Viacom International (Viacom), a global media organization that produces and distributes content for television, film, radio, and online, sued YouTube and Google alleging they were liable for copyright infringement for videos posted to YouTube containing works owned by Viacom.[118] In its complaint, Viacom alleged "direct and secondary copyright infringement based on the public performance, display, and reproduction of approximately 79,000 audiovisual 'clips' that appeared on the YouTube website."[119]

### Was YouTube Entitled to Intermediary Safe Harbor?

Google sought protection from liability under Section 512(c) of the US Copyright Act, which provides safe harbor for internet service providers against copyright infringement occurring from the storage of infringing material by a user. Section 512(c) shields a service provider from infringing activities of its users if several requirements are met. Firstly, the service provider must not have "actual knowledge" of infringing material or activities or awareness of "facts or circumstances from which infringing activity is apparent," known as red flag knowledge. Additionally, upon obtaining actual or red flag knowledge, the service provider must act "expeditiously to remove, or disable access to, the material." The provision also requires that the service provider must not "receive a financial benefit directly attributable to the infringing activity" where a service provider has the "right and ability to control" the infringement.[120]

Viacom claimed Google was disqualified from protection under Section 512(c) because YouTube had actual knowledge and was aware of facts and circumstance from which infringing activity was apparent and failed to act expeditiously to remove the infringing videos.[121]

## Viacom: YouTube Knew All About Its Users' Infringement!

Viacom asserted YouTube was aware infringing videos were uploaded to YouTube by users and YouTube in fact welcomed the practice, because they knew users came to YouTube to watch infringing videos and that is how YouTube sought to build its user base and increase its advertising revenue.[122] Viacom stated:

> YouTube's founders single-mindedly focused on geometrically increasing the number of YouTube users to maximize its commercial value. They recognized they could achieve that goal only if they cast a blind eye to and did not block the huge number of unauthorized copyrighted works posted on the site. The founders' deliberate decision to build a business based on piracy enabled them to sell their start-up business to Google.[123]

Viacom cited internal correspondence between YouTube employees to show YouTube's knowledge of specific infringements. For example, Viacom cited an email sent between YouTube staff prior to a meeting with sporting league personnel, requesting the removal of infringing Premier League broadcast footage from YouTube.[124] Viacom also cited email correspondence between the YouTube founders in which they discussed their obligation to remove Bud Light television commercials; in the emails, Steve Chen suggested delaying the removal of the videos.[125]

Viacom claimed YouTube received a financial benefit directly attributable to the infringing activity by selling advertising placements throughout

YouTube.[126] Viacom also asserted YouTube had the right and ability to control the activity because YouTube was able to remove videos and terminate accounts at its discretion and often did so for videos containing hate speech and violent or pornographic content, thus exercising "the ultimate editorial judgment and control over the content available on the site."[127] Viacom also argued YouTube could have conducted keyword searches to identify and remove infringing content, or block it before it was uploaded.[128] As well, Viacom noted YouTube had the ability to control infringement through its community flagging policy, under which YouTube users could flag infringing content, but YouTube chose to abandon the policy.[129] Similarly, Viacom argued YouTube had the ability to find and remove infringing content through digital fingerprinting or content identification technology but had chosen not to implement the technology uniformly across YouTube.[130]

## Google: YouTube Has No Obligation to Monitor for or Investigate Infringement!

In response, Google argued that US copyright law does not place on service providers an obligation to investigate and ascertain the copyright status of a work. Google argued that when creating the DMCA safe harbor provisions, "Congress decided that copyright holders, rather than service providers, should bear the primary responsibility for pursuing unauthorized uses of copyrighted materials."[131] Google asserted, "the statute expressly provides that a service provider need not monitor its service for possible infringement to obtain safe-harbor protection."[132]

Google also asserted Viacom used YouTube to promote its content in a manner that made it impossible for YouTube to know whether videos were infringing.[133] For example, YouTube provided evidence showing Viacom uploaded content anonymously as part of stealth marketing campaigns, it used techniques to diminish the quality of some of its clips so that they appeared to be made by fans, it purposely leaked content, and, on one occasion, it expressly decided infringing clips of *The Daily Show* and *The*

*Colbert Report* could remain on YouTube believing "their presence on YouTube was important for their ratings as well as for their relationship with their audience."[134]

In addition, Google claimed it did not have control over the infringing activity because control over a system does not equate to control over a particular infringing activity.[135] Google insisted "Congress presupposed that service providers would have control over their systems" and that the right and ability to control infringing activity requires more than an ability to remove or block access to content.[136] Google argued, "the DMCA's control inquiry is specific, not general," requiring control over the "particular infringing activity at issue."[137]

## No Duty to Monitor—The District Court Decision (2010)

In 2010, the US District Court for the Southern District of New York held YouTube was entitled to safe harbor under Section 512(c).[138] Critical to the decision was the question of whether the statutory language "actual knowledge" and "facts or circumstances from which infringing activity is apparent" (red flag knowledge) should be understood to mean a general awareness of infringement or actual knowledge of specific and identifiable infringements.[139] The District Court concluded knowledge of specific and identifiable infringements of individual items is required for disqualification from safe harbor.[140] The District Court described the application of the DMCA safe harbor principle as "clear and practical," placing the burden on rightsholders to identify the infringement and not imposing on service providers an obligation to investigate and verify infringing material.[141]

The District Court determined that while YouTube was generally aware of the presence of infringing videos on its platform, "general knowledge that infringement is 'ubiquitous' does not impose a duty on the service provider to monitor or search its service for infringement."[142] The District Court found YouTube had satisfied the statutory requirements and was entitled to safe harbor because YouTube had engaged a designated agent

who swiftly removed clips, including the clips named in the suit, upon receiving notification from rightsholders.[143]


## But Did YouTube Have Actual Knowledge of Infringement? The Second Circuit Decision (2012)

In 2012, the US Court of Appeals for the Second Circuit vacated the
District Court's decision. The Second Circuit affirmed the District Court's
holding that both actual knowledge and red flag knowledge refer to specific and identifiable infringements.[144] However, the court explained the
two forms of knowledge are not specific versus generalized knowledge,

> but instead between a subjective and an objective standard. In other
> words, the actual knowledge provision turns on whether the pro-
> vider actually or "subjectively" knew of specific infringement, while
> the red flag provision turns on whether the provider was subjectively
> aware of facts that would have made the specific infringement "ob-
> jectively" obvious to a reasonable person.[145]

The Second Circuit held that a "reasonable jury could find that YouTube
had actual knowledge or awareness of specific infringing activity on its
website."[146] The Second Circuit considered the internal company correspondence cited by Viacom to raise "a material issue of fact regarding
YouTube's knowledge or awareness of specific instances of infringement"
and remanded the case to the District Court in order to determine whether
YouTube had specific knowledge of the clips-in-suit.[147]


## The Path to a Settlement

On remand in 2013, the District Court found Viacom had failed to provide "proof that YouTube had knowledge or awareness of any specific
infringements of clips-in-suit."[148] Viacom sought to appeal the District

Court's decision; however, in 2014, the parties agreed to a confidential settlement.[149]

Despite settling with Viacom, and although this case forms part of a broader interplay of US litigation over a service provider's duty to monitor for copyright infringement, Google claims *Viacom* a victory and as an important contribution to intermediary liability law in the United States. In a 2016 submission to the US Copyright Office, citing *Viacom*, Google asserted the standard for requiring actual knowledge of specific infringement, appropriately avoided placing "overly burdensome demands on OSPs to make unilateral judgments regarding potentially infringing material" and added, "the consistent case law has aided in the effectiveness of the statute in promoting innovation online."[150] Ultimately, the outcome in *Viacom* was largely consistent with Google's copyright agenda, in particular with Google's heavy reliance on intermediary safe harbors and Google's assertion of their importance to innovation in the digital environment.

## COPYING ORACLE'S API—*ORACLE V. GOOGLE*

In 2010, Google became once again in the spotlight over a major copyright dispute, this time with the computer software company, Oracle Corporation. So far, Google has not prevailed in this case, and for that reason it is an outlier in Google's US copyright litigation history. However, Google's dispute with Oracle also fits neatly into this history because once again Google finds itself in the position of rightsholder foe, attempting to place limitations on authors rights and mounting a fair use argument to justify its copying of another's work.

### The Java Platform and Google's Android

In 1996, Sun Microsystems released Java, a computer programming platform that facilitates the "development of portable, high-performance applications for the widest range of computing platforms."[151] Put simply, the Java platform enables computer programmers to create applications that can run on multiple devices. Java is widely used by software developers, providing a "standard for developing and delivering embedded and mobile applications, games, Web-based content, and enterprise software."[152]

When developing its phone operating system, Android, which today runs across more than two billion devices worldwide, Google held discussions with Sun Microsystems regarding Google licensing and modifying the full Java platform for Android; however, the companies were unable to finalize an agreement, and, ultimately, Google developed its own software, using the "Java language."[153]

The Java language contains words, symbols, and a set of prewritten programs that execute commands.[154] The set of prewritten programs is called the application programming interface (API).[155] When Google developed Android, the Java API had 166 "packages," divided into six hundred "classes," including six thousand "methods," which "is very close to saying the Java API had 166 'folders' (packages), all including over six hundred pre-written programs (classes) to carry out a total of over six thousand subroutines (methods)."[156]

Each method or subroutine contains declaring code and implementing code. Declaring code is the method's name or title, and the implementing code is the code that performs the method's task. The declaring code does not perform a command itself, rather, declaring code directs a computer to execute the method's implementing code. Programmers using the Java platform use the declaring code to operate the subroutines or methods.[157]

## So, What Exactly Did Google Copy?

For Android, Google used the Java language to "design its own virtual machine via its own software and to write its own implementations for the functions in the Java API that were key to mobile devices."[158] Essentially, Google copied the names and functions of thirty-seven packages; however, it wrote its own implementing code.[159] Google explained it copied the names and functions of the thirty-seven packages so that Android would be interoperable with other Java-based applications.[160]

In 2010, Oracle acquired Sun Microsystems and sued Google seeking close to USD 10 billion in damages.[161] Oracle claimed Google's copying of the thirty-seven packages from the Java API constituted copyright infringement.[162] The parties agreed Google's use of the Java language, Google's virtual machine, and the implementing code did not infringe Oracle's copyrights, but they disputed whether Google was allowed to use without permission the same names, the same functions, and the same organization of the thirty-seven packages in the Java API—referred to in the litigation their "structure, sequence and organization."[163]

## No Copyright Protection for the Java API—The District Court Decision (2012)

In 2012, the US District Court for the Northern District of California held the Java packages contain creativity and originality, but the parts of the Java API that were copied by Google were not protected by copyright.[164] The District Court held the declaring code copied by Google was a method of operation, as the declaring code is used to operate the implementing code.[165] Section 102(b) of the US Copyright Act provides that methods of operation are not afforded copyright protection.[166] The act stipulates:

> In no case does copyright protection for an original work of author-ship extend to any idea, procedure, process, system, method of op-eration, concept, principle, or discovery, regardless of the form in which it is described, explained, illustrated, or embodied in such work.[167]

Accordingly, the District Court specified:

> no matter how creative or imaginative a Java method specifica-tion may be, the entire world is entitled to use the same method

specification (inputs, outputs, parameters) so long as the line-by-line implementations are different . . . The method specification is the *idea*. The method implementation is the *expression*. No one may monopolize the *idea*.[168]

The District Court concluded, "yes, it is creative. Yes, it is original. Yes, it resembles a taxonomy. But it is nevertheless a command structure, a system or method of operation."[169]

In addition to finding the declaring code a method of operation, the District Court also held two additional principles precluded copyright protection for the Java API. First, the District Court relied upon the merger doctrine, which establishes that when there is only one way of expressing something that expression is not copyrightable.[170] Second, the District Court relied upon the principle that names and short phrases are not protected subject matter.[171] For these reasons, the District Court dismissed Oracle's claim and held "the particular elements replicated by Google were free for all to use under the Copyright Act."[172]

## Oracle's API Is Protected by Copyright—The Federal Circuit Decision (2014)

In 2014, the US Court of Appeals for the Federal Circuit reversed the District Court's decision.[173] The Federal Circuit had jurisdiction on appeal because the original complaint included allegations of patent infringement, and the Federal Circuit has jurisdiction over cases that involve a patent claim. When hearing cases that ultimately do not include a patent claim, such as this one, the Federal Circuit applies the law from the circuit in which the case originated, which in this case was the Ninth Circuit.[174]

The panel of the Federal Circuit held Google had copied protected elements of the Java API.[175] The Federal Circuit reasoned excluding a computer program from copyright protection on the grounds that it is a method of operation would create a far too broad exemption because "computer programs are by definition functional."[176] The Federal Circuit agreed that the declaring code was a method of operation but nonethe-less could contain expression that is protected by copyright.[177] The Federal Circuit considered that Section 102(b) does not deny copyright protection to a work that has a functional element, rather, Section 102(b) requires courts to separate protected expression from unprotected functional components.[178]

To identify whether Google copied protected expression in the Java API, the Federal Circuit employed the "abstraction-filtration-comparison" test established in *Computer Associates International v. Altai* of the US Court of Appeals for the Second Circuit.[179] The test requires a court to separate the program into structural parts, to filter out all nonprotected components, and, finally, to compare the remaining components with the program accused of infringement.[180] The Federal Circuit explained the filtration step is critical and requires considering whether the copying was "dictated by considerations of efficiency, required by factors already external to the program itself, or taken from the public domain—all of which would render the expression unprotectable."[181]

The Federal Circuit rejected the District Court's finding that the declaring code names copied by Google were not protected by copyright. The Federal Circuit held the words and short phrases copied by Google were protected expression because "the manner in which they are used or strung together exhibits creativity."[182] The Federal Circuit also found the merger doctrine did not apply to the declaring code, for Sun Microsystems had available to it unlimited different ways of writing the declaring code copied by Google.[183] Critically, the Federal Circuit emphasized that cop-yright subsistence had "to be evaluated at the time of creation, not at the time of infringement," and so it was not relevant whether Google had only the one option when it copied the work, relevant to the analysis were the options available to Sun Microsystems when it created Java.[184]

With regard to Google's copying of the structure, sequence, and organi-zation of the packages, the Federal Circuit explained that it was "well es-tablished" that copyright protection extends to the literal (for example, the source and object codes) and the nonliteral (for example, sequence, struc-ture, organization, and user interface) features of a computer program.[185]

The Federal Circuit asserted that an original work that serves a function qualifies for copyright protection "as long as the author had multiple ways to express the underlying idea."[186]

As it was undisputed that Java's API structure and organization of packages involved creativity and originality, with multiple options for structure and organization, the Federal Circuit concluded the declaring code and the structure, sequence, and organization of the API packages copied by Google were subject to copyright protection, and while "Google may employ the 'package-class-method' structure . . . Google, like any author, is not permitted to employ the precise phrasing or precise structure chosen by Oracle."[187]

In its decision, the Federal Circuit rejected interoperability arguments presented by Google, stating,

> Google was free to develop its own API packages and to "lobby" programmers to adopt them. Instead, it chose to copy Oracle's declaring code and the SSO [structure, sequence, and organization] to capitalize on the preexisting community of programmers who were accustomed to using the Java API packages. That desire has nothing to do with copyrightability. For these reasons, we find that Google's industry standard argument has no bearing on the copyrightability of Oracle's work.[188]

However, the Federal Circuit suggested interoperability might prove relevant in a fair use analysis and remanded the case back to the District Court for a jury to decide on the validity of Google's fair use argument.[189]

## Google's Copying Was a Fair Use—A Jury Decision (2016)

In 2015, Google petitioned the US Supreme Court to review the Federal Circuit decision; however, Google's petition was denied, leaving in place for now the Federal Court's holding that APIs can be subject to copyright protection.[190] After the Supreme Court's denial, Google removed the thirty-seven packages from the Android platform.[191]

Yet, in 2016, in what has been described as "one of the most momentous fair use jury trials in U.S. history," a jury found Google had "shown by a preponderance of the evidence that its use in Android of the declaring code and their structure, sequence, and organization from Java" was a fair use.[192] In an order denying Oracle's request to set aside the jury's decision, District Judge William Alsup offered insight into the jury's reasoning, explaining:

> With respect to transformativeness, our jury could reasonably have found that (i) Google's selection of 37 out of 166 Java API packages (ii) re-implemented with new implementing code adapted to the constrained operating environment of mobile smartphone devices with small batteries, and (iii) combined with brand new methods, classes, and packages written by Google for the mobile smartphone platform—all constituted a fresh context giving new expression, meaning, or message to the duplicated code.[193]

Judge Aslup also concluded that "avoiding cross-system babel promoted the progress of science and useful arts—or so our jury could reasonably have found."[194]

## The Jury Was Wrong—The Federal Circuit Decision (2018)

In 2018, the case returned once again to the Federal Circuit on appeal. The jury decision was reversed by the same panel that decided the 2014 appeal.[195] The court found as a matter of law, Google's copying was not a fair use. Critical to the court's decision was its reasoning that Google's use was not transformative because both uses serve the same purpose, Google had not changed the message of the expression, and use of the declaring code in a smartphone was not use in a new context.[196] The court also considered Google's commercial use to weigh heavily against a fair use finding and that Google's use of the Java API had resulted in substantial market harm.[197]

In 2018, Google filed for a rehearing of the case in front of the full Federal Circuit panel, and, in early 2019, Google petitioned for a review of the decision by the US Supreme Court. As Peter Menell has remarked, so far, Google's dispute with Oracle has "contributed to, rather than quelled, confusion surrounding API copyright protection."[198] Whether Google will ultimately prevail in this case is highly uncertain. But its dispute with Oracle highlights Google's remarkably consistent reliance on fair use as a tool for legitimizing its activities. If, by chance, Google does finally win against Oracle, it will be the latest in a series of cases in which Google has vigorously defended and secured its vision for copyright.

## CONCLUSION

Over the past two decades, Google has employed its extraordinary wealth to pursue copyright litigation on principle, gaining decisions that accord with its commercial interests and copyright agenda. When deciding in Google's favor, while courts may not have explicitly accepted Google's "innovate first, permission later" philosophy, they have exhibited a willingness to apply limits on copyright, supporting Google's position that in the digital setting some copying without permission is necessary.[199] In these decisions, courts have decided Google did not need the explicit permission of rightsholders to copy websites, books, images, and code, and they have also limited Google's liability for copyright infringement occurring on its platforms.

In these cases, lawmakers have confronted the question of where to draw the boundary between public and private rights. Repeatedly, the line has been drawn to limit exclusionary rights in favor of public rights. Redrawing the line is significant, but so too are the rhetorical and ideological implications. Posing the question of where the boundary of exclusive rights exists pushes back against rhetoric and ideology presented by the content industries that frames copyright as private property. Overall, throughout Google's copyright litigation history, US courts have evaluated the public benefits of Google's services and embraced public interest arguments over private property claims. Very possibly, illuminating a path to public interest outcomes in contemporary copyright lawmaking is Google's most valuable contribution to the digital copyright tradition.[200]

Undoubtedly, the public has benefited from the outcomes in Google's copyright disputes. Google's digital services increase opportunities for participation in meaning-making and broaden access to information and content globally. But Google's gains are also considerable. Not only has Google attained legal decisions that have legitimized its activities, but through several of these decisions, Google also amassed considerable informational resources. Google has been allowed to generate immense databases of information—including copies of websites, books, videos, and images—data to which only Google has unfettered access that it uses to continue to innovate and enhance its range of digital services. Both gains, the legal decisions and informational resources, have driven Google's colossal commercial and technological ascension in the digital environment.

# The Problems of Google News in Europe

As Google has grown beyond its US borders, it has had to confront far less accommodating legal and political environments. One of Google's most high-profile battles over copyright outside of the United States has been over its news aggregation service, Google News. Under the 2019 EU copyright directive, news publishers are provided a right to be paid for the use of their works in the digital environment. Derisively called the "link tax" by its critics, essentially the new right compels online services providers, such as Google, to pay news organizations for indexing and linking to news articles. The policy is in fact squarely aimed at Google. It is the latest move in a long history of European lawmakers seeking to regulate Google in order to support European news organizations. Unfortunately for Google, in this particular policy debate, public interest justifications for using other people's content without their permission have generally been met with suspicion and hostility.

When navigating its way through the problems of Google News in Europe, Google has sought to appeal to the power of innovation, reframing disruption as opportunity, and doing everything it can to re-sist burdensome regulation. But in Europe, evidently, an appeal to free markets resonates less strongly than it does in the United States, and

*Google Rules: The History and Future of Copyright Under the Influence of Google.* Joanne Elizabeth Gray, Oxford University Press (2020). © Oxford University Press.
DOI: 10.1093/oso/9780190072070.001.0001

European lawmakers appear quite willing to take action to regulate Google. Yet, like their US counterparts, European lawmakers also have a habit of approaching copyright policymaking as inter-industry conflict. Repeatedly, European lawmakers have acted as though their primary responsibly is to mediate between "big tech" and "big media." A strong and instrumental articulation of the public interest remains largely absent from the mainstream debate, and policymakers encourage industry actors to cooperate and negotiate.

In its negotiations over Google News in Europe, as one of the world's largest technology companies, Google has at its disposal a range of tools it can employ to protect its interests and pursue its agenda. Indeed, the history of Google News in Europe shows Google leveraging its wealth, market power, and technological capabilities to compel and entice news publishers to work within Google's system and according to Google's copyright framework.

## AGGREGATING NEWS ARTICLES

Google's search engine includes the news aggregation service, Google News. For Google News, Google scans and indexes news articles published online globally. The Google News home page lists news articles that are algorithmically grouped by subject (for example, "top stories," "sports," "technology"). Users of Google News can conduct keyword searches of the news database and search results display the article headline, the name of the newspaper or media organization that published the story, a thumbnail image of a photograph taken from the article, and, until late 2017, Google also displayed a short snippet from the article known as the story "lead." The news headlines are hyperlinks, linking users to the website hosting the full article. News publishers can opt out of Google News using the robots.txt exclusion protocol.

Generally, Google does not acquire permission from or remunerate news publishers for the use of their works in Google News. Google maintains that its news aggregation activities do not require permission from rightsholders because they fall outside rightsholders' exclusive rights. Google asserts news headlines and snippets are not protectable subject matter, that Google News is an information location tool and so qualifies for intermediary safe harbor, and that Google's use of the news articles is a fair use. Google also argues that news aggregation expands markets for news content—Google News increases the speed and ease of finding news and directs traffic to newspaper websites, contributing to the vitality of the news industry in the digital economy. Google claims that "through Search and News, we send over 10 billion visits, for free, to publishers globally each month. We're proud of that, and those readers represent real revenue opportunities for the publishers."[1]

Many news publishers, however, vehemently reject Google's position. News Corporation's Rupert Murdoch has asserted, "to aggregate stories is not fair use. To be impolite, it is theft."[2] News publishers claim that rather than clicking through to read full articles, readers simply scan the headlines and story leads on Google News, and so Google News is a substitution for their products. The data to support this claim is contentious. A study undertaken in 2013 found evidence of a substitution effect: the study found text snippets and images satisfied the requirements of some readers, reducing click-through rates.[3] However, a 2015 study, which included a review of eight unique studies undertaken between 2011 and 2015, found that while news aggregators do have a substitution effect, they also have a market expansion effect, and, overall, news aggregation services produce a net positive effect in terms of traffic to newspaper sites.[4]

Nonetheless, with palpable hostility, in jurisdictions throughout Europe, news media organizations have sued Google for copyright infringement, seeking to compel Google to pay for the use of their articles in Google News. They have also lobbied European legislatures, in some cases successfully, for the introduction of a sui generis copyright or neighboring right that requires Google to pay news media for the use of their work in Google News.

### THE PROBLEMS OF NEWS MEDIA IN THE DIGITAL AGE

To properly understand the dispute over Google News in Europe, it must be placed within its economic context. With the advent of the digital environment, the organizations that dominated the news media market in the twentieth century experienced a steep decline in advertising revenues, and they have struggled to establish robust business models for the digital economy.[5] Indicatively, a 2017 Pew Research study found that including both print and digital platforms, the weekday circulation of US daily newspapers fell 8 percent in 2016, "marking the 28th consecutive year of declines."[6]

News organizations have faced increased competition from internet-based news businesses, internet users, and social media, and their business models have been undermined by a loss of control over content online. Seth Lewis explains:

> for much of the twentieth century, both the business model and the professional routines of journalism in developed nations were highly stable and successful enterprises because they took advantage of scarcity, exclusivity, and control. In the local information market, news media dominated the means of media production, access to expert source material, and distribution to wide audiences—which translated to tremendous capital, both in gatekeeping authority and economic power.[7]

The digital environment disrupted this previously stable and successful industry. In the digital environment, media is easily produced and easily distributed, and, once released online, it is difficult to control access to it. In a world of digital information and communications, advertising and sales revenues declined, while the costs associated with producing professional journalism remained high: digital technologies may significantly reduce the cost of distributing content, but they do not reduce the costs required to produce high-quality journalism.[8]

Overall, a combination of stable production costs and emaciated revenue streams caused a severe decline in profitability within the news
media industry in recent decades. A 2016 Reuters Institute and University
of Oxford *Digital News Report* summarized, throughout the world, "we
see a common picture of job losses, cost-cutting, and missed targets as
falling print revenues combine with the brutal economics of digital in a
perfect storm."[9]

The economics of news journalism in the digital age is a complex
public interest issue. On the one hand, the internet and digital technologies have significantly increased access to news content and participation
in its creation. They have given individuals seeking to engage with and
speak on issues of news and public affairs the tools and platforms to do so.
On the other hand, if the institutions that produce high-quality, rigorous
journalism are left to erode, there is a social loss: our culture suffers if
high-quality journalism is abandoned in favor of low-quality, unreliable
information sources.[10]

A conceptually satisfying and efficacious answer to the question of how
to fund high-quality news journalism in a digitally connected world remains elusive.[11] Over the years, news organizations and many European
lawmakers have set their eyes upon Google. They have sought to compel
Google to pay for its use of news content, presenting various policy
proposals in a protracted battle over the issue of news aggregation. Google,
while willing to invest significant resources to support the news industry,
has remained steadfast in its opposition to policies that require it to pay
for aggregating news articles.

If assessed against Google's copyright framework, Google's position
is unsurprising. Placing news aggregation within the scope of exclusive
rights of authors stands at odds with Google's copyright philosophy and the
decisions Google has obtained in its US copyright litigation history. Indeed,
the contest over news aggregation strikes near to the heart of Google's business model. If using news content in a search index requires permission
from and remuneration to rightsholders, what are the implications for
other types of content? Conceivably, Google views this issue as an attack
on its vision for copyright, one that could, if further applied, threaten the

economic viability of Google's search indexing business. Conceivably, along with a potentially onerous financial burden, Google fears a slippery slope of expanding rights—expanding the requirements for permission from and remuneration to rightsholders in the digital environment. This is perhaps why Google has responded so strongly and in a variety of ways—as the following examples attest—in its contest over Google News in Europe.

## AGENCY FRANCE PRESSE—UNITED STATES

French news agency, Agency France Presse (AFP), licenses news photography and articles to third parties, including "newspapers, wires, web sites, aggregators, companies, governments, national and international agencies, and data services like Lexis-Nexis," and AFP owns the copyright to all its images and articles.[12] In 2005, AFP filed suit against Google in the District Court of the District of Columbia, claiming Google willfully infringed the copyrights in AFP's photographs and news stories by "reproducing and publicly displaying APF's photographs, headlines, and story leads" in Google News. AFP sought a preliminary and permanent injunction and statutory damages of approximately USD 17.5 million.[13]

In response, Google asked the District Court to dismiss AFP's claims on the grounds that the works copied by Google were not subject to copyright protection.[14] Google argued news article headlines are "terse factual phrases" and copyright does not protect facts or "words and short phrases such as names, titles and slogans."[15] AFP countered that story headlines and leads are critical for capturing readers' attention and "are qualitatively the most important aspects of a story."[16]

In April 2007, AFP and Google agreed to a confidential settlement.[17] While the details of the settlement were not made available to the public, in August 2007, Google announced it had in place a licensing agreement with AFP, Associated Press, Canadian Press Association, and the United Kingdom Press Association granting Google permission to host content on Google News.[18] In the announcement, Google explained:

Because the Associated Press, Agence France-Presse, UK Press Association and the Canadian Press don't have a consumer website where they publish their content, they have not been able to benefit from the traffic that Google News drives to other publishers. As a result, we're hosting it on Google News.[19]

Google biographer Ken Auletta suggests the agreement was an acknowledgment by Google that organizations like the AFP that syndicate rather than publish news articles (organizations that cannot directly benefit from increased website traffic that results from content being included in Google News) were particularly problematic for Google.[20] However, as Auletta noted, "solving one problem created another."[21] When other news organizations sought similar deals, they found Google's willingness to seek permission and pay for the use of content in Google News to be strictly limited.

## COPIEPRESSE — BELGIUM

In 2006, Copiepresse, a Belgian copyright collection society representing Belgian publishers of French and German language press, filed suit against Google in Belgium, claiming Google's inclusion of its members' articles in Google News and in Google's cache index, without permission, were acts of copyright infringement.[22] In May 2011, a Belgian Court of Appeals found in favor of Copiepresse. The court held article headlines and leads are protected elements of copyrighted works and cannot be reproduced without the permission of rightsholders.[23] The court stated:

> Contrary to what Google maintains, "Google News" is not a "signpost" which allows cybernauts to find press articles on a specific subject matter more efficiently, but is a slavish reproduction of the most important sections of the inventoried articles.[24]

The court also rejected Google's argument that by not implementing the robots.txt exclusion protocol Copiepresse members had granted Google an implied license to include their articles in Google News and Google's cache. The court held an opt-out copyright system was "incompatible with the requirement of explicit permission which is inherent to copyright."[25]

The court stated a copyright holder is not "deprived of his rights simply because he has neglected to implement a technological process" and that such a theory was comparable to the theory that it may be legal to steal from a house because an owner left open the door.[26] The court concluded, "the authors' explicit, unequivocal and prior permission is required before Google can exploit the articles."[27] The court also stated, "the reproduction right is exclusive and absolute. The emergence of an information society does not prevent that authors can benefit from a high level of protection."[28]

The court also found Google's caching was outside of the scope of Directive 2001/19, which excludes from liability copies "which are transient or incidental and an integral . . . and essential part of a technological process."[29] The court held Google's caching was not functionally necessary to its service, it was not for the purpose of improving processing speeds, and it was not a temporary, transient reproduction.

Consequently, the court ordered Google to:

> remove from the *Google.be* and *Google.com* sites, more specifically from the "cached" links on "Google Web" and from the "Google News" service, all the articles, photographs and graphic representations from the Belgian publishers of the French and German-speaking daily newspapers, represented by Copiepresse . . . under penalty of a fine for non-performance of € 25,000.00 per day of delay.[30]

Complying with the order, Google removed the Belgian newspaper articles from both Google News and Google Search. Two months later, in July 2011, Google announced that it had received permission from Copiepresse to include articles in Google Search, with the assurance that Copiepresse would not enforce the court-ordered fines.[31] One Belgium publisher described the delisting from Google Search as "brutal."[32] Copiepresse may have won the case, but the decision advantaged Google: the Belgian publisher could not have it both ways, if inclusion of their articles in Google

News required their permission, then so too did inclusion in Google Search.

The following year, Google and Copiepresse announced an end to their litigation. The parties confirmed they had in place a private agreement under which Google and Copiepresse would "partner on a broad range of business initiatives."[33] Google explained:

> Instead of continuing to argue over legal interpretations, we have agreed on the need to set aside past grievances in favour of collaboration. This is the same message we would like to send to other publishers around the world - its much more beneficial for us to work together than to fight.[34]

The agreement included an arrangement for Google to assist in the promotion and distribution of Copiepresse content through mobile platforms, AdWords, YouTube, and other social media.[35] It also included an advertising commitment that guaranteed advertising revenue to Copiepresse publishers.[36] However, Google stated explicitly that despite these arrangements it would not be licensing content from Copiepresse for Google News. Google explained, "we continue to believe that our services respect newspaper copyrights and it is important to note that we are not paying the Belgian publishers or authors to include their content in our services."[37] Google had managed to win in principle and forge a business partnership with its foe.

## FEDERAZIONE ITALIANA EDITORI GIORNALI — ITALY

In 2009, in response to a complaint from Italian Newspaper Publishers Federation, Federazione Italiana Editori Giornali (FIEG), Italy's competition authority initiated an investigation of Google News. The FIEG complained that Google's policy for automatically excluding from Google Search websites that opt out of Google News effectively prevented publishers from controlling how their articles were used. In its investigation, the competition authority sought to determine whether this policy created "distortive effects on the online advertising market."[38] In 2012, the investigation concluded upon Google changing its policy to directly address the FIEG complaint—by retaining articles excluded from Google News in the Google Search index.[39]

In 2016, Google announced that it had in place an agreement with FIEG to promote and distribute FIEG content through Google platforms such as Google Play Newsstand and YouTube. As part of the agreement, Google also agreed to establish a EUR 12 million digital innovation fund for FIEG to use to advance the distribution and protection of online content, knowledge transfers and training, a YouTube video strategy, and use of Google Analytics.[40] Again, Google quelled hostility through a strategic deployment of its technology, market position, and wealth.

## LEISTUNGSSCHUTZRECHT FÜR PRESSEVERLEGER—GERMANY

In 2013, Germany's copyright laws were amended to introduce a *sui generis* right for press publishers—Leistungsschutzrecht für Presseverleger— granting press publishers an exclusive right to make their articles available to the public for commercial purposes.[41] The right is waivable, expires one year after first publication, and does not apply to single words or short snippets.[42] The objective of the law is to require news aggregators to obtain a license to display excerpts of news articles.[43] Google immediately responded to the enactment of the legislation by implementing an opt-in policy for Google News—requiring German publishers to provide Google permission to use their content, free of charge—otherwise Google would exclude articles from Google News.[44]

German publisher organization, VG Media, opted in on Google's terms, but filed an antitrust complaint claiming Google had forced VG Media to waive its rights.[45] While the German competition authority did not open a formal proceeding against Google, in October 2014, Google announced that it would no longer display snippets of news articles or thumbnail images in Google News for websites published by members of VG Media.[46] Google stated:

> We regret this legal process because every publisher has always been able to decide whether and how its content is displayed in our services. Against the background of this complaint, we will no longer display snippets and thumbnails of some well-known websites such as bild.de, bunte.de or hoerzu.de, ie those publishers organized in VG Media. For these pages, we will only show the link to the article and its header.[47]

After two weeks of not including article snippets in Google News, VG Media announced that reduced website traffic had put "major economic pressure on members" and requested Google commence displaying article excerpts without requiring remuneration.[48]

## DIGITAL PUBLISHING INNOVATION FUND—FRANCE

In 2012, several French newspapers lobbied the French government for the introduction of legislation similar to Germany's Leistungsschutzrecht für Presseverleger.[49] The French government encouraged French publishers to work with Google to come to an agreement, advising that if an agreement was not reached, it would introduce a law compelling Google to remunerate rightsholders for the use of their articles in Google News.[50] During the negotiations, in a letter to the French government, Google warned that if the legislation was introduced Google would simply de-index French websites from Google News.[51] Ultimately, an agreement was negotiated and the policy abandoned.[52]

The agreement included a EUR 60 million innovation fund for digital publishing initiatives and an advertising agreement aimed at improving French publishers' advertising revenues through Google's advertising services.[53] Eric Schmidt described the agreement as evidence that "through business and technology partnerships we can help stimulate digital innovation for the benefit of consumers, our partners and the wider web."[54] Once again, through a business and technology partnership, along with a EUR 60 million payment, Google avoided the application of copyright laws antithetical to its interests.

## ARTICLE 32 OF THE LEY DE PROPIEDAD INTELECTUAL—SPAIN

In 2014, the Spanish government introduced a copyright law similar to but stronger than Germany's Leistungsschutzrecht für Presseverleger. Like the German law, the objective of the Spanish law—Article 32 of the Ley de Propiedad Intelectual—is to compel news aggregators to pay news publishers for displaying excerpts of news articles. Unlike the German law, the Spanish right is inalienable, so that Spanish publishers cannot choose to waive their right and opt in to Google News without compensation.[55] Also unlike the German law, the Spanish law is a copyright exception, conditional upon remuneration to rightsholders.[56] Silvia Scalzini summarizes, the law "establishes the right to obtain an equitable, unwaivable and collectively managed remuneration for publishers and other right holders" for quotations published in newspapers or news websites, for the purposes of forming public opinion, information, or entertainment.[57]

In December 2014, prior to the law coming into effect, Google announced the closure of Google News in Spain.[58] Google stated:

> This new legislation requires every Spanish publication to charge services like Google News for showing even the smallest snippet from their publications, whether they want to or not. As Google News itself makes no money (we do not show any advertising on the site) this new approach is simply not sustainable. So it's with real sadness that on 16 December (before the new law comes into effect in January) we'll remove Spanish publishers from Google News, and close Google News in Spain.[59]

Google described the situation as a "lose-lose for everyone" and explained that it would continue to talk to publishers and policymakers in the hope that they could restore Google News in Spain.[60]

The impact of the policy in Spain remains unclear. A study commissioned by the Spanish Association of Periodical Publications—Asociación Española de Editoriales de Publicaciones Periódicas—investigating the impact of the law and the closer of Google News in Spain found an overall reduction in traffic to Spanish news sites of 6 percent, reaching 14 percent for smaller publications. The authors of the study concluded the law was harmful for publishers, competition, consumers, and innovation.[61] Yet a 2017 study found the law did not significantly impact news media website reach, but it did correlate with "an increase in audience fragmentation, defined as a reduction in the audience overlap of news media sites."[62] For Google, however, the benefits of closing Google News in Spain were clear—Google avoided capitulating to a policy that did not align with its economic interests or copyright agenda.


## DIGITAL NEWS INITIATIVE—EUROPEAN UNION

In 2015, Google announced the Digital News Initiative (DNI), which included a EUR 150 million digital innovation fund for 'stimulating and supporting innovation in digital journalism within the news industry in Europe.'[63] The DNI operates in partnership with established European news publishers including: *The Guardian* (United Kingdom), the BBC (United Kingdom), *The Economist* (United Kingdom), *La Stampa* (Italy), *El País* (Spain), *Die Zeit* (Germany), *Der Spiegel* (Germany), *Frankfurter Allgemeine Zeitung* (Germany), *Les Échos* (France), and NRC Media (The Netherlands).[64]

Through the DNI, over a three-year period, organizations and individuals applied for funding to support projects that use technology in an innovative way to "support a more sustainable news ecosystem."[65] David Drummond described the DNI as an undertaking in industry collaboration, commending the initiative as responsible for "some of the greatest practitioners in journalism sitting down for the first time with some of the best brains at Google to figure out how our industries can work more productively together."[66]

In 2017, the DNI announced funding for more than 250 projects from 27 countries in Europe. One example of a funded project is the German start-up, Spectrum, which aims to "build an artificial intelligence engine to help publishers communicate directly with readers—and distribute content—on a 1:1 basis through instant messaging apps."[67] Through the DNI, Google has also introduced Player for Publishers, a YouTube player customized for news publishers, and the Accelerated Mobile Pages (AMP) project.[68] The AMP is an open source HTML code framework developed to improve the speed of mobile internet, with a particular focus on optimizing press publishers' mobile content for speed and usability.[69] According to Google, the objective of AMP is to "protect the free flow of information by ensuring the mobile web works better and faster for everyone, everywhere."[70]

Through the DNI, Google has taken a long-term strategic approach to the issue of news aggregation, effectively acting as a de facto state by intervening to help resolve an industry-level economic problem. And, of course, at the same time shifting the focus away from copyright law and toward innovation as the solution to the economic problems of news media in Europe.

## EUROPEAN COMMISSION COPYRIGHT DIRECTIVE—EUROPEAN UNION

Despite Google's extensive efforts to resist changes to copyright law that would compel it to remunerate news media organizations for the use of their content in Google News, since 2016, the European Commission has recommended the introduction of an auxiliary copyright for press publishers, similar in objectives to the German and Spanish policies.[71] The European Commission explains:

The organisational and financial contribution of publishers in producing press publications needs to be recognised and further encouraged to ensure the sustainability of the publishing industry. It is therefore necessary to provide at Union level a harmonised legal protection for press publications.[72]

Unsurprisingly, Google has responded negatively to the European Union policy, stating:

The proposal looks similar to failed laws in Germany and Spain, and represents a backward step for copyright in Europe. It would hurt anyone who writes, reads or shares the news—including the many European startups working with the news sector to build sustainable business models online. As proposed, it could also limit Google's ability to send monetizable traffic, for free, to news publishers via Google News and Search. After all, paying to display snippets is not a viable option for anyone.[73]

Google argues a better approach to supporting European publishers is through innovation: "innovation and partnership—not subsidies and onerous restrictions—are the key to a successful, diverse and sustainable news sector in the EU."[74]

Amid the policy debate, in 2017, Google announced design changes to Google News.[75] Google claims it did so to "make news more accessible and easier to navigate."[76] Within the new format, Google no longer displays snippets of news articles. This change is a highly significant development in the history of Google News in Europe. Google's display of snippets is central to nearly all of the legal disputes and policy responses to news aggregation. No longer displaying snippets neutralizes a critical component of the news media's case against Google. Viewed in light of Google's long history of problems over Google News, Google's decision appeared as an attempt by Google to put an end to the issue—before legal or policy decisions over news aggregation encroach upon Google's business model any further.

In 2017, Google also announced the implementation of several initiatives to support subscription news business models.[77] These initiatives include Google using its machine learning algorithms and data to assist publishers to target potential subscribers.[78] Google explains, it will be "exploring how Google's machine learning capabilities can help publishers recognize potential subscribers and present the right offer to the right audience at the right time."[79] This intervention is also significant. It shows Google is still motivated to support the news media industry—again employing its market position and vast resources. Arguably, however, what we also see in Google's support of subscription business models is an attempt by Google to shift the financial burden of funding journalism from Google to consumers.

Despite Google's design changes and support for subscription business models, in 2019, when they voted to adopt the new copyright directive, the European Parliament voted for the introduction of an auxiliary copyright for European press publishers.[80] In the final text of the directive, the right applies to online uses of press publications by information society service providers; it expires two years after publication; and it does not apply to acts of hyperlinking, to uses of "individual words or very short extracts of a press publication" or to private or noncommercial uses by individuals.[81] The final directive also includes a requirement that authors of works incorporated in a press publication receive an "appropriate share" of any additional revenues that press publishers receive as a result of the new directive.

The amended directive does not, however, provide guidance on what would qualify as a noncommercial use, which has implications for how the policy will be applied in practice. For example, it is unclear whether a personal blog that hosts and receives payment for advertisements would qualify as a commercial website. If it did, the law would have a much broader impact upon how news is used and shared online, beyond large online service providers such as Google. Similarly, it is unclear exactly how many words will qualify as a very short extract. The exception for hyperlinks also raises questions. In a news index, what use is a hyperlink without some kind of extract? Often, when hyperlinking to a news article, internet users—commercial actors and individuals alike—utilize some kind of reference to the source to provide potential readers with an indication of the article's substance. With these questions left unanswered it is unclear what shape this policy will eventually take once it is introduced by all EU member states.

The European Union's copyright directive is the most forceful step taken so far to compel Google to remunerate press publishers in Europe. Yet, given Google's history with the policy in other markets and its approach to Google News in Europe generally, it is reasonable to have doubts about the policy's potential efficacy, at least as applied to Google. In Europe, Google has faced extraordinary pressure from news organizations and legislatures over Google News. These efforts have forced Google to implement a number of defensive and offensive strategies to defend its interest and copyright policy agenda. Google has invested substantial financial and technological resources to support the news media industry in Europe, and it continues to make changes to its services and practices—removing snippets from Google News and supporting subscription models the latest among many. As the policy is introduced by European nations, we should not be surprised if Google shuts down Google News in Europe, and Google has indicated it may well do so. But it is also quite possible that Google will negotiate an agreement with the major news organizations that enables Google to aggregate and share their news articles without requiring a substantial hit to Google's bottom line or copyright agenda.

## CONCLUSION

Copyright infringement claims, antitrust complaints, and legislation expanding the scope of copyright have largely failed to compel Google to pay news organizations for the use of their works in Google News. Employing its market power and technological and financial resources, Google has successfully compelled and enticed news media organizations to work within Google's networks (for advertising, promotion, and technological benefits) and within Google's copyright framework. Indeed,

Google's ability to resist the application of laws not in its interest—and its ability to compel rightsholders to work within its system—reveal Google's impressive capacity to influence copyright in practice, even in the face of great economic and political hostility. Evidently, Google's unwavering faith in innovation, along with its deep pockets and technical prowess, give Google the ability to turn adversary into business partner.

But should we be satisfied with these outcomes? Certainly, the complete disruption of the publishing industry as a result of unrestrained technological innovation is undesirable. The future of journalism is a high-stakes public interest issue. The quality of the information we have access to has implications for democracy political systems. The public interest lies in having access to reliable, diverse, and considered information sources, and in the context of journalism, in the security of institutions and individuals that are capable of holding power to account. But the public interest does not necessarily equate with the interests of legacy news organization. The public interest aligns more closely with the interests of journalists— ensuring journalists can undertake high-quality journalism. This requires a sustainable economy for new media, but it does not necessarily require that we protect large, established publishers.

In the amended European copyright directive, there is a glimmer of recognition of the value of journalists. Authors must receive an "appropriate share" of any additional revenues publishers receive as a result of the policy. But the publishing industry is still the central focus of the political debate, and there is no thorough articulation of why journalists are recognized. Policymakers appear fixated on the interests and agendas of the dominant industries actors. The lack of a clear articulation of the public interest in this policy debate is perhaps why the new copyright directive remains so contentious. Treating copyright policymaking as industry mediation will often result in policies that attend to the interests of the organizations powerful enough to influence individual policymakers. A novel approach to resolving the issues confronting news media in the digital environment might be to start the policy formulation process with a clear and thorough evaluation of the public interest. With that in place, we can then evaluate policy proposals and stakeholder claims according to how they impact the public interest, including their impact upon our culture and our democracies.

As it stands currently, the new EU copyright directive is just imprecise enough to leave room for continued industry negotiation. Which places into the hands of industry actors, actors who have no formal obligation to act in the public interest, the power to determine how these new rights and regulations operate in practice.

# Google's Private Copyright Rule-Making and Algorithmic Enforcement

We have entered the era of artificial intelligence. Algorithms and machine learning systems regulate our interactions in the digital and physical world on a day-to-day basis. Over the past decade, Google has developed a range of algorithmic tools it uses to deter copyright infringement, enforce copyrights, and remunerate rightsholders. They include automated systems for processing copyright infringement notices on a large scale; signals in Google's search algorithm aimed at removing and demoting websites associated with copyright infringement from search results; and Content ID on YouTube.[1] Indeed, across its platforms, Google has created an elaborate system of private copyright rules and algorithmic enforcement. For those concerned with the quality of cultural participation and distribution of power in the digital environment, the sheer scale of this system—along with its features and flaws, its inaccuracies and in-built biases—should be a source of deep unease.

*Google Rules: The History and Future of Copyright Under the Influence of Google.* Joanne Elizabeth Gray, Oxford University Press (2020). © Oxford University Press.
DOI: 10.1093/oso/9780190072070.001.0001

## LARGE-SCALE ALGORITHMIC NOTICE AND TAKE-DOWN

In accordance with the requirements for intermediary safe harbor, Google removes content from its platforms at the request of rightsholders. Since 2015, the rate of content removal requests due to copyright infringement claims has increased sharply. Between 2001 and 2012, Google received a total of 531,397 removal requests.[2] In 2015 alone, Google received notices to remove 558 million web pages from Google Search.[3] In 2017, Google began processing 75 million notices per month.[4]

What explains the colossal increase? One part of the answer is that over the past decade, rightsholders have developed highly efficient processes for sending take-down notices on a large scale and, at the same time, Google has developed its own processes for efficiently responding to notices.[5] The content industries employ professional rights management companies to carry out large-scale copyright enforcement, and Google employs automated processes for responding to copyright infringement notices from rightsholders.[6] Together, the automation and professionalization of notice and take-down processes in copyright enforcement has created "technological feedback loops," facilitating a rapid rise in copyright infringement notices and the removal of content from Google's platforms.[7]

The majority of copyright infringement notices received by Google are processed without human review, through "trusted member" programs.[8] Google offers the Trusted Copyright Removal Program (TCRP) for Google Search and the Content Verification Program (CVP) for YouTube.[9] Both TCRP and CVP provide rightsholders tools for bulk submissions of notices. Google states TCRP is offered to "copyright owners who have demonstrated a proven track record of submitting accurate notices and who have a consistent need to submit thousands of webpages each day."[10] There is a similar standard for admission to the CVP.[11] For Google Search, approximately 95 percent of take-down requests come via trusted member programs, and Google claims that with these programs in place, it typically only takes Google six hours to process a request.[12]

A 2016 University of California Berkeley and Columbia University qualitative and quantitative study of notice and take-down systems found Google's highly efficient process for enforcing the copyright claims of rightsholders without human review suffers problems of inaccuracy and overinclusiveness.[13] The study found 28.4 percent of the 108 million take-down requests studied had questionable validity.[14] Some notices failed to comply with the statutory requirements for a take-down request, others fell within the scope of fair use, and others related to subject matter that did not fall within the DMCA regime.[15] With no human review, Google's automated system for processing requests may be high speed and large in scale, but it is also a blunt instrument, making mistakes at a similar size and pace.[16] Importantly, the 2016 study also found very few removals are disputed by the subjects of the take-down notices.[17] The authors suggest that generally users subject to a take-down request lack the knowledge and capacity to effectively respond to Google's copyright enforcement actions.[18]

Google argues that overall the notice and take-down regime "strikes the right balance between the needs of copyright owners, the interest of users, and our efforts to provide a useful Google Search experience."[19] However, the high rate of notices with questionable validity and the infrequent rate of counter notifications suggest Google's automated system for processing copyright infringement notices on a large scale prioritizes enforcing rightsholder claims over accuracy. It prioritizes private property rights of copyright owners at the expense of public rights to access and engage with information.

## BEYOND NOTICE AND TAKE-DOWN: SANITIZING SEARCH

Google also takes action to remove content from its platforms without notice from rightsholders. Google explains: "Google does not want to include any links to infringing material in our search results, and we make significant efforts to prevent infringing webpages from appearing."[20] These efforts include factoring into its search algorithm undisclosed signals to

exclude websites associated with copyright infringement from appearing
in search results and a policy for demoting websites associated with copyright infringement in search-result rankings.[21] Google explains:

> Thanks to the efforts of Google's engineers, the vast majority of
> media-related queries that users submit every day return results that
> include only legitimate sites ... Although the vast majority of media-
> related queries yield clean results, there are some infrequent queries
> where the results do include problematic links. For these "long-tail"
> queries, Google collaborates with copyright owners to address the
> problem in a few ways. First, Google has developed state-of-the-art
> tools that allow rightsholders and their enforcement agents to submit
> takedown notices efficiently at high volumes (tens of thousands each
> day) and process those notices, on average, within six hours. Second,
> Google then uses those notices to demote sites for which we receive
> a large number of valid takedown notices, making them less visible
> in search results.[22]

Effectively, Google uses notices received from rightsholders, processed
without human review, to determine the "legitimacy" of websites and
their position or availability in Google Search results.

Google also removes terms associated with piracy from its auto-
complete function and provides prominent advertising space to "legitimate" content providers, to ensure that when a user searches for media
and entertainment content, links to rightsholders' sites are visible to internet users.[23] Within its advertising network, Google implements policies
for denying advertising revenue to websites that infringe intellectual property rights. Google claims it has "zero tolerance for copyright-infringing
ads in Search, and has dedicated considerable human and engineering resources across the company to develop and implement measures to root
out infringing ads."[24]

Google also prohibits participation in its AdSense, DoubleClick, and
AdWords programs by websites hosting unauthorized content.[25] Google
reports:

Since 2012, we have blacklisted more than 91,000 pages from our AdSense program for violations of our copyright policy, the vast majority of which were caught by our own proactive screening processes. We have also terminated over 11,000 AdSense accounts for copyright violations in that time.[26]

And of course, Google adheres to the Best Practices and Guidelines for Ad Networks to Address Piracy and Counterfeiting, which aim to deny advertising revenue to websites that sell counterfeit goods or engage in copyright infringement.[27]

What we see in these policies, none of which are directly required by legislation, is that across its platforms Google is self-regulating and enforcing copyright on behalf of rightsholders.[28] Google, in negotiation with rightsholders, acts as a private copyright rule-maker and enforcer, curating the quality of information and content available online according to the private interests of the content industries.

## FURTHER BEYOND: CONTENT ID ON YOUTUBE

In 2007, Google announced it had partnered with Walt Disney Co., Time Warner Inc., and EMI to implement digital fingerprinting technology on YouTube.[29] Google's technology is an automated content identification system, providing music, film, and television rightsholders control and monetization options over content uploaded to YouTube. Rightsholders submit to YouTube reference files of their work, along with metadata identifying the work. When a user uploads a video to YouTube, it is scanned against the database of references. If a match is found, the user receives a Content ID claim and the claimant's preselected preferences are applied to the video. The claimant can preselect to block videos, monetize videos, mute the audio, or receive viewership statistics. If monetization is selected, the claimant receives a share of revenue received by YouTube for advertisements run against the video.[30] Google claims Content ID has more than 75 million reference files in its database, from more than 9,000 participating rightsholders, including "network broadcasters, movie studios, songwriters, and record labels" who have collectively claimed over 800 million videos through Content ID.[31]

Content ID has become the primary tool for managing copyright on YouTube. Google reports 99.5 percent of sound recording copyright matters, and 98 percent of all copyright matters on YouTube are "resolved" through Content ID.[32] Google explains, in practice "Content ID automatically identifies the work and applies the copyright owner's preferred action without the need for intervention by the copyright owner in all but 0.5 percent of cases."[33] Google also reports that over 90 percent of Content ID participants opt to monetize videos and claims the music industry "generates 50 percent of its revenue on YouTube from monetizing fan uploads."[34] According to Google, since its implementation, Google has paid rightsholders USD 3 billion through Content ID.[35] Google suggests that through Content ID, Google has developed a new business model for the content industries, replacing the conventional practice of permission and remuneration with a system of advertising royalties.[36]

In principle, Content ID benefits rightsholders, YouTube users, and the public. Content ID benefits rightsholders by providing a system in which they can monetize and earn revenue for use of their work in the digital environment, with low transaction costs. Transaction costs associated with licensing works are eliminated when Content ID automatically matches videos with rightsholders and applies their predetermined course of action.[37] YouTube users benefit from Content ID through a reduced risk of copyright liability. By incentivizing rightsholders to let videos remain publicly available in exchange for advertising royalties, the public benefits from an increased availability of content.

In practice, however, the benefits of Content ID accrue mainly to rightsholders. This is because Content ID systematically designates rules of use based on unilateral and unverified claims of ownership by rightsholders, and it operates on the presumption that rightsholders have exclusive rights to a work and so copying or sharing for any purpose requires their permission. Viewed in one way, Google has effectively created a compulsory licensing regime under which Content ID approves infringement prior to it occurring.[38] Alternatively, Content ID can be understood as a system of "second-level" copyright agreements, that is, through its terms of service Google executes nonexclusive licensing agreements that it has negotiated with rightsholders on behalf of users.[39] Whatever the precise legal form, through Content ID, Google has established a system of copyright enforcement in which infringement is assumed, permission is mandatory, and licenses are preemptive.

The Content ID algorithm permits rightsholders to overstate the rights held in a work and is not sensitive to exceptions and limitations to copyright. For instance, Content ID removed from YouTube a keynote speech by Harvard University law professor Lawrence Lessig, in which Lessig plays a snippet of the song *Lisztomania* by the band Phoenix, for which record label Liberation Music held the rights to the sound recording in New Zealand.[40] Professor William Fisher similarly had a video removed— a lecture on the topic of copyright subject matter in which Fisher plays snippets of cover versions of Jimi Hendrix, Joe Cocker, Santana, and Stevie Ray Vaughan songs.[41] In 2015, YouTube user Benjamin Ligeri filed a claim against Google, Viacom, Lions Gate Entertainment, and Egeda Pirateria claiming Content ID had incorrectly attributed ownership of his parody of the film *The Girl with the Dragon Tattoo* and his critique of the 2014 *Teenage Mutant Ninja Turtles* remake.[42] Ligeri criticized Content ID for favoring "the larger copyright holders that make use of its Content ID system over smaller creators."[43]

Content ID restricts uses that may not fall within an exception but nonetheless an author would typically tolerate. An author might tolerate an infringement because they do not want to make the effort to enforce their rights or they might see value in the infringement—for example, they might believe it helps to promote their own work.[44] By preemptively licensing works, Content ID removes the possibility for tolerated uses. For example, in 2013, hundreds of videos containing video game reviews and playthroughs were subject to Content ID claims.[45] Game reviews and playthroughs are typically tolerated by game developers because they are recognized as important components of the video game economy, serving to market and promote new products within the gaming community.

However, when Content ID was applied to the reviews and playthroughs on YouTube, it identified in-game music, trailers, and other video content and applied the predetermined choices of a variety of rightsholders.[46] Game developers, seeking to have the reviews and playthrough videos restored, had to ask YouTube users to dispute the Content ID claims in order to establish which rightsholder Content ID had attributed ownership of the video.[47]

Devised around orthodox notions of authorship and originality, Content ID is inept at dealing with complex structures of production and ownership common in the digital environment.[48] As Michael Soha and Zachary McDowell documented, Content ID's treatment of the Harlem Shake dance meme that achieved global popularity in 2013 exemplifies this attribute.[49] The dance meme emerged from an amateur video of several friends dancing to an electronic dance music (EDM) song by the artist Baauer. The video inspired thousands of re-enactments, at one point reaching close to 4,000 uploads to YouTube per day.[50] As the Content ID database contained a reference file of the audio track, the Content ID algorithm attributed ownership of *all* Harlem Shake videos to Baauer, permitting his record label to monetize over one billion streams.[51] Further complicating matters was the fact that Baauer's EDM song contained music samples, including two used without permission.[52] Content ID effectively permitted one rightsholder to monetize the work of thousands of different people based on an unverified unilateral ownership claim. Soha and McDowell explain the traditional concept of authorship in copyright law, which is "already on shaky ground with EDM music, seems to fall short when attempting to encapsulate the large collections of digital labor that go into Internet memes . . . [which] are rapid, ethereal, produced by often anonymous nodes through networked practices that transform as they replicate."[53] Content ID is insensitive to the complexities of social digital production, the types of everyday creative practice that Google argues policymakers should value equally with traditional media.

Google has publicly acknowledged that Content ID may be used to unilaterally overstate or incorrectly declare ownership, that it has the potential to dilute established limitations and exceptions to copyright, and that it can "never address all of copyright's complexities and subtleties."[54] Google has expressed that Content ID should be considered "a supplement to, not a substitute for, fair use."[55] In 2015, Google announced it would offer legal support to a set of YouTube videos subject to DMCA take-down notices that it deemed to be obvious fair uses.[56] Google explained it was motivated to do so because the notice and take-down process and potential for litigation can be intimidating for creators and that it hoped by defending a selection of videos it will create a "demo reel" of best practice fair use examples.[57] Google stated it expected the policy to have a "positive impact on the entire YouTube ecosystem, ensuring YouTube remains a place where creativity and expression can be rewarded."[58] But it is entirely unclear how this intervention could affect the functioning of the Content ID system, which is used to manage 98 percent of copyright matters on YouTube.

Furthermore, the recourse available to users who are subject to a Content ID claim is limited by more than the intimidating nature of litigation or a lack of understanding by users. Formally, Google's policy is that a user may dispute a Content ID claim if they believe it is invalid. On receipt of a dispute, a copyright owner has thirty days to respond, either by releasing the claim, upholding the claim, or submitting a take-down request. If the complaint is upheld, the user can appeal. If a user appeals, the copyright owner may release the claim or submit a DMCA compliant take-down request via Google's web form. While there is an active dispute, monetization will continue if both the user and claimant have opted to monetize, and YouTube retains the revenue until the dispute is resolved.[59]

Yet, Google reports that less than 1 percent of copyright claims via Content ID are disputed, and, in practice, Google's private agreements with Content ID participants can negate the counter notification policy altogether.[60] For example, as documented by Rebecca Tushnet, a video analyzing "remix culture," which featured snippets from John Hughes' films, was removed from YouTube via Content ID, and the counter notification and appeal were rejected, without the claimant commencing legal proceedings in accordance with DMCA requirements.[61] When questioned on this matter, Google revealed:

> YouTube enters into agreements with certain music copyright owners to allow use of their sound recordings and musical compositions. In exchange for this, some of these music copyright owners require us to handle videos containing their sound recordings and/or musical works in ways that differ from the usual processes on YouTube . . . In some instances, this may mean the Content ID appeals and/or counter notification processes will not be available.[62]

Similarly, in a dispute between Universal Music and Megaupload—regarding a video promoting Megaupload that Universal Music had removed from YouTube on copyright grounds—it was revealed that a private agreement between Universal Music and YouTube granted Universal Music access to a content management system that allows Universal Music to remove content on YouTube "based on a number of contractually specified criteria."[63]

In practice, through private agreements with large media and entertainment companies, Google effectively removes the opportunity for YouTube users to object to claims made against them by rightsholders.[64] This renders Google's system of copyright enforcement on YouTube, as Diane Zimmerman suggests, "uninhibited by the notions of due process that a legally imposed system would need to require: which is to say, you are presumed guilty of infringement and your defenses are adjudicated by your opponent."[65]

Even when recourse is available and utilized, it can be complex and ineffective. For example, in 2012, Content ID removed a promotional video created by the Lansdowne Public Library in Pennsylvania, which parodied a Michael Jackson song, substituting the lyrics "beat it" with "read it." After negative press coverage of the incident, Sony/ATV allowed the video to be restored; however, once restored the Content ID algorithm again determined the video to be infringing, and the video's audio was muted. When the library brought the issue to Sony/ATV's attention, Sony advised the library that it did not have the capacity to override Content ID, and the video was caught in the "YouTube Vortex."[66]

On YouTube, unilateral claims of ownership are preemptively enforced, without meaningful recourse for users, and the scope of copyright in practice is expanded through an algorithmic insensitivity to exceptions to copyright, the complexities of social digital production, and tolerated uses.[67] Devised largely through negotiations between Google and a selection of powerful content industry companies, Content ID operates to enforce the values and interests of large rightsholders—often at the expense of independent or less politically and economically powerful creators. Content ID also supports private property claims at the expense of public rights to access and use content. While informed by the law, Google's system of copyright enforcement on YouTube goes beyond Google's obligations under existing laws and is symptomatic of a broader tendency for private copyright rule-making and enforcement in digital copyright governance.

## GOVERNED BY GOOGLE: PRIVATE COPYRIGHT RULE-MAKING, ALGORITHMIC ENFORCEMENT, AND THE PUBLIC INTEREST

A decade ago, Google resisted claims that it had a responsibility to enforce copyright, declaring, "Google does not want to be a gatekeeper."[68] Contrastingly, in 2016, Google stipulated,

> Google takes the challenge of online piracy seriously—we continue to invest significant resources in the development of tools to report and manage copyrighted content, and we work with other industry leaders to set the standard for how tech companies fight piracy.[69]

The range of policies and procedures for enforcing copyright on behalf of rightsholders discussed in this chapter confirm Google's rhetoric. Today, Google's gatekeeper status is irrefutable. But why has Google's position evolved? Multiple convergent reasons account for Google's enthusiasm for enforcing copyright on behalf of rightsholders.

Over the past several years, to acquire control over works in the digital environment, the content industries have increasingly sought to enforce their rights through internet services providers.[70] Asking internet intermediaries to enforce copyright became a compelling tactic when suing individual consumers proved unpopular and ineffective, legislative efforts such as SOPA/PIPA failed, and bilateral trade agreements appeared to have limited effect on internet user behavior.[71] To enforce their private property rights, the content industries turned to internet intermediaries.[72]

The content industries' change in strategy has also been accompanied by unwavering hostility toward Google. For example, in December 2014, a presentation detailing the findings of a study undertaken on behalf of Warner Brothers and Sony Pictures Entertainment was leaked and published online.[73] The study concluded that the introduction of Google Fiber would cause drastic increases in illegal downloading, costing Hollywood over USD 1 billion per year. This figure is highly contestable. As *TorrentFreak* observed at the time, the billion-dollar loss was calculated using a method promoted by Motion Picture Association of America that counts every unauthorized download or stream as a direct loss of revenue and does not offset from the total loss any increases in revenue from other sources such as subscription services and online purchases and rentals, which the same study concluded would increase with the introduction of Google Fiber.[74]

Nonetheless, several months later, in 2015, several technology-news websites reported that Google was sending copyright infringement notices to Google Fiber users, on behalf of copyright owners, including demands for payment for amounts ranging from USD 20 to USD 300 in the form of an automated settlement.[75] In a response to the media reports, Google conceded it was not obliged to forward settlement demands to users and stated that Google's position was that directly targeting users is not an effective antipiracy policy.[76] Google's deviation from its stated position suggests Google's actions may have been a response to Hollywood's examination of and disdain for Google Fiber. In other words, self-interest must also motivate Google to privately devise and enforce copyright rules; cooperation with the content industries minimizes the risk of litigation and other hostile actions.[77] As well, as Google continues to introduce its own content-streaming services such as Google Play, YouTube Red, or YouTube Remix, services that sell access to content, Google's interests are increasingly aligned with the interests of the content industry. In some circumstances, Google now benefits from controlling access to content and strong copyright enforcement online.

Perhaps the most critical driver of private copyright rule-making and enforcement, however, is the active encouragement of industry negotiations and self-regulation by lawmakers. In the copyright setting specifically, neoliberal ideology has supported a political preference for self-regulation and private agreements over public regulation. As Zimmerman has documented, there has been an "explicit official encouragement of private agreements" by Western governments, often under an "implicit threat to enact more legislation if 'voluntary' efforts do not satisfy the content owners' needs."[78]

Through a convergence of economic and political factors, Google and other private actors are now empowered to privately regulate copyright in practice. In a recent example, in 2017, the United Kingdom's Intellectual Property Office directly negotiated a private antipiracy agreement between Google, Bing, and the British Phonographic Industry, Motion Picture Association of Europe, Middle East, and Africa, and the Alliance for Intellectual Property.[79] The agreement included a Voluntary Code of Practice requiring Google and Bing to demote websites linking to infringing content in search results and to remove terms associated with piracy from auto-complete functions.[80] In line with Zimmerman's assessment, the agreement was negotiated under the threat of a legislative solution, which the UK government indicated it would implement if voluntary negotiations were unsuccessful.[81] In 2017, Google also negotiated an antipiracy agreement with France's audiovisual industry, under which rightsholders in that jurisdiction gained increased access to YouTube's rights management systems.[82] And, of course, the history of Google News in Europe is replete with private agreements between Google and rightsholders, often devised under threat of or in avoidance of government intervention.

Article 17 of the latest EU copyright directive is a perfect example of policymakers encouraging industries stakeholders to cooperatively self-regulate. After many years of deliberation over the policy by European lawmakers, rather than providing clear direction on the enforcement responsibilities of intermediaries, the latest draft of the directive calls for "best efforts" and "stakeholder dialogues to discuss best practices for the cooperation between the online content sharing service providers and rightsholders."[83]

In this ecosystem of private copyright rule-making and enforcement, Google is an apex predator. This is because Google owns and controls large portions of the internet but also because Google's approach to copyright in practice can have the effect of "norm-setting."[84] The authors of the 2016 University of California Berkeley and Columbia University study of notice and take-down systems explain:

> Google's size, its prominence in the politics of notice and takedown, and its role in litigation, combined with its early adoption of DMCA Plus measures like content filtering on YouTube, trusted sender programs, autocomplete restrictions, and search result demotion, make it a dangerous elephant in the room. It is capable of adopting practices that could move collective perceptions of what is required for good practice, or even for safe harbor protection.[85]

Google's approach to copyright in practice has far-reaching consequences. Google is a powerful decision maker in digital copyright governance, capable of setting rules, norms, and standards that determine the scope and application of copyright law across large portions of the digital environment.

Google's position in copyright governance presents multiple problems for the public interest. The private rule-making and enforcement undertaken by Google tends to lack meaningful transparency and accountability.[86] Negotiated and implemented in private, it is difficult to assess the function and impact of Google's copyright enforcement system and to hold Google accountable for it.[87] We have to inspect, probe, test, and draw conclusions from outside the system. Google's private copyright rule-making and enforcement also threatens the public interest because it tends to prioritize private interests and values over public interests and values.[88] Julia Black explains, "in democratic countries, at least, governments are elected in the expectation that they will act to resolve collective problems . . . There is an expectation that the state will perform its public responsibility as guardian of the 'public interest' (however that may be defined)."[89] In a privately ordered system, however, private actors self-regulate and negotiate agreements seeking outcomes in their interest. We see this in Google's trusted member programs for processing copyright infringement notices and Content ID on YouTube—they enforce the private property claims of rightsholders, at the expense of copyright exceptions, accountability, and due process. Powerful private actors have negotiated and devised a system of copyright enforcement that privileges their rights and values over the public rights and values.

Of course, concern for the ability of private actors to use their power to regulate in their interest is not new. In the field of copyright specifically, there is a long history of inquiry into the dynamics of private ordering, scholars articulating concern for the distribution of power, transparency, accountability, and the underlying rights and values in private regulatory modes.[90]

What is novel today, however, is the development and deployment of automated or algorithmic regulatory systems by private actors. The use of algorithmic technologies in private copyright rule-making and enforcement, such as Content ID, significantly worsen the problems of transparency, accountability, and power imbalances inherent to private regulatory systems. Advanced algorithmic systems are opaque by design—complex technical instruments knowable only to a handful of engineers—and they are opaque because of intellectual property laws, such as trade secrets.[91] Furthermore, insomuch as litigation imposes transparency and accountability, algorithmic regulatory tools diminish transparency and accountability when they automatically resolve matters that otherwise may have been litigated. For example, when the decisions of the Content ID algorithm are applied with the counter notification process removed. When privately negotiated rules are applied algorithmically, transparency and accountability suffers.

Critically, algorithms are not apolitical. They embody past and ongoing political and economic negotiations.[92] Indeed, as Ben Wagner describes, today algorithmic technologies represent a "key loci of control where power is distributed and redistributed."[93] This is because, while all technologies embody political and economic contests and negotiations to some degree, it is particularly true for digital technologies that can be continuously modified—the malleability of digital technologies make them excellent tools through which power can be iteratively exercised.[94] Certainly, the values and principles embedded in Google's Content ID algorithm reflect the political and economic negotiations between Google and powerful rightsholders.[95] So too does the demotion signal Google includes in its search algorithm for sites associated with copyright infringement.

So far, the evolution of algorithmic technologies, and their constituting power struggles, have largely played out absent a public interest advocate. In a neoliberal ideological setting, when developing and deploying advanced algorithmic systems, private companies have been free to decide how and in whose interest they should function.[96] This is why systems like Content ID can operate without meaningful due process.[97] Private actors have been permitted to develop and apply algorithmic tools according to private values, with limited regard for public interest considerations.

This explains, in part, why there has been such a strong public backlash against Article 17 of the new EU copyright directive that makes intermediaries liable for the copyright infringements of their users. Critics fear it will result in Google (along with Facebook and other platforms) implementing automated enforcement systems like Content ID to preemptively enforce unilateral rightsholder claims to all types of copyright works—videos, images, sound recordings, memes, gifs, and so on. If platforms are presumptively liable for the activities of their users, they may be motivated to scan and filter all types of content before it is made available online. The EU policy could result in widespread adoption of private copyright rule-making and algorithmic enforcement systems under which infringement is assumed, permission is mandatory, and licenses are preemptive. The flaws, biases, and inaccuracies of the Content ID system may eventually operate upon the internet at large.

Notably, however, the latest draft of the EU directive calls for any co-operation between rightsholders and intermediaries to not limit the avail-ability of noninfringing content.[98] It also includes a requirement that platforms have a redress mechanism that is subject to human review.[99] These provisos indicate that within the European Union, policymakers are to some degree aware of the potential for errors, bias, and a lack of ac-countability within algorithmic enforcement systems.

Perhaps the latest EU copyright directive represents a turning point in copyright politics, and policymakers will take up the challenge of instilling the public interests and values within privately ordered algorithmic systems of copyright enforcement. It remains to be seen. But the one thing we can be sure of is that if autonomous enforcement systems continue to advance, in the absence of a framework of public interest principles and at the discre-tion of powerful private actors, transparent and accountable public interest outcomes in digital copyright governance will drift further out of reach.

## CONCLUSION

As Google's business has evolved, so too has its relationship to copy-right law. No longer can we characterize Google as simply an adversary of the content industries. They are now business partners. Buoyed by a dominant political ideology that favors private regulatory solutions over public regulatory solutions, Google has negotiated copyright rules with large rightsholders and has implemented large-scale algorithmic enforce-ment systems. When we view Google's copyright enforcement policies and practices in the aggregate, Google's public interest credibility is sub-stantially diminished. Google appears more threat than ally—a threat to a diverse and participatory culture—and now we must confront pointed questions about the use and distribution of private regulatory power in the digital environment.

# From Access to Monopoly

*The Results and Complexities
of Google's Copyright Logic*

The future of copyright under the influence of Google appears a little bleaker than it did when we were seeking an appropriate balance between public access to information and remuneration to rightsholders fifteen years ago. From Google Books, to the issues over Google News in Europe, to private copyright rule-making and algorithmic enforcement, we have moved beyond narrow debates about access versus remuneration, even beyond Google's "innovate first, permission later" heuristic. Today, the digital copyright debate is entangled with issues of accountability, transparency, due process, and concentrated private power in a rapidly evolving digital environment. Grappling with copyright under the influence of Google requires responding to issues that are complex, unstable, and inconsistent.

## GOOGLE'S ACCESS PARADOX

There is an intrinsic contradiction within Google's copyright logic. On the one hand, Google claims that if the public is to benefit from digital technologies, exclusive rights granted to copyright owners must be limited and public access rights expanded. On the other hand, Google has its own

*Google Rules: The History and Future of Copyright Under the Influence of Google.* Joanne Elizabeth Gray, Oxford University Press (2020). © Oxford University Press.
DOI: 10.1093/oso/9780190072070.001.0001

exclusive access to large repositories of information and content derived in significant part from copyrighted works. Google has generated databases of information by copying content owned by third parties—individuals, corporations, and the public in the case of public domain works—and fair use decisions, chiefly the cases over Google Search, Google Images, and Google Books, have granted Google exclusive access to these datasets, to enormous private benefit.

When US courts struck their public interest deal, approving Google's copying of other people's content in exchange for a socially valuable search engine, perhaps they had no way of knowing just how much Google would benefit. But Google's technological superiority depends upon its exclusive access to large repositories of information. In 2011, Google's Chief Scientist Peter Norvig reportedly let slip: "we don't have better algorithms than anyone else; we just have more data."[1] Norvig was referring to the value of data to algorithmic systems, in particular, machine learning models, and their significance to Google's operations. How does autocomplete know how to accurately finish my sentences? How does Google choose a list of search results for me before I have finished typing my search terms? How does my Google Home understand what I am saying? How can Gmail predict the responses I might want to make to my emails? The answer to all of these questions is machine learning. Machines, not humans, are finding patterns in data to learn and making predictions about user behavior.

Put simply, machine learning refers to a form of artificial intelligence in which advanced algorithms or models are trained to find patterns in data. Once trained, the model can then be applied to new data to classify or make predictions about a data point or dataset.[2] The more data a model can be applied to, the more that model can learn and eventually accomplish—in large and varied datasets, there are more patterns and more insights for a machine learning model to discover.[3]

Google's indexes of websites, images, videos, and books, along with all the information Google collects about its users, are all exceptionally large datasets that Google can exclusively use to train its models, to innovate and to improve the functionality of its products and services.[4]

Indeed, each time a Google service is used, Google receives more information, more data to add to its stockpiles.[5] Google's exclusive access to this data is how Google fuels its continuous innovations in internet search and remains the leading search engine globally. Frank Pasquale explains:

> Innovation in search depends on access to a user base that "trains" algorithms to be more responsive. But the user base belongs to Google. Innovation in analysis depends on access to large quantities of data. But the data belongs to Google. And Google isn't sharing. As long as Google's search data store remains secret, outside innovation is dead in the water.[6]

Google has a strong advantage in internet search innovation because it has exclusive access to large repositories of data derived from copyrighted content and user information.

While most information regarding the size and number of Google's data servers is protected by trade secret, in 2011 it was reported that the energy used by Google's data centers globally equated with the energy used by 200,000 homes.[7] It has also been reported that the company has over one million computers running its search engine index.[8] If these estimates are even partially correct, the advent of a serious competitor to Google, at least under current technological conditions, is difficult to imagine.[9]

It is impossible to overstate the value of this data advantage to Google. It is valuable to Google because it sustains Google's position as the most impressive search engine worldwide. But it is also value for future innovations—in the context of continuous advances in machine learning technology, the potential for future innovations are unbounded, but they require large and varied datasets.[10] Consider Google Books. According to historian George Dyson, when speaking to a Google engineer about Google's book-scanning activities, the engineer stated, "we are not scanning all those books to be read by people. We are scanning them to be read by AI."[11] Google scanned millions of books held in libraries for its public library of digitized books but at the same time obtained a vast dataset of computer readable text that it could use to train algorithms and to develop new language and text related products and services. All of Google's datasets provide opportunities for future innovations, and indeed it is the potential for future innovations that makes Google's economic position so strong over the long term.

Google's data advantage contributes to reduced competition in many of the markets in which Google operates. Digital technologies like Google's search engine are expensive to develop, requiring vast financial resource to establish; however, costs do not increase substantially with additional users. In economic theory, this is expressed as high fixed costs and low variable costs. A firm that produces under these conditions typically enjoys economies-of-scale advantages, and potential competitors face high barriers to entry. Potential competitors to Google would need to match Google's financial investments and somehow accumulate a similar data resource.[12]

In addition, Google's Content ID system on YouTube imposes substantial financial and nonfinancial barriers to entry in the video hosting market. In 2018, Google reported that it had invested more than USD 100 million in developing Content ID.[13] Even if a competitor was able to match this investment, they would still face the legal and administrative challenges of negotiating agreements with rightsholders. The costs involved in developing the technology and the licensing agreements Google has in place impose financial, administrative, and legal barriers to entry for potential competitors in the video hosting market.

For most potential competitors to Google, the current scale of Google's operations—which includes exclusive access to unrivalled and self-perpetuating repositories of information—represents a prohibitively high barrier to entry, securing, for the foreseeable future at least, Google's position as a dominant technology and information provider globally.

Inevitably, this line of analysis leads to the tricky question of monopoly. Google has always refuted claims that it is a monopoly, arguing that "if you don't like the answer that Google search provides, you can switch to another engine in literally one click."[14] Google also argues that there exists substantial competition in online search, particularly for shopping services, pointing to the dominance of Amazon and eBay.[15]

While Google may not be a pure monopoly (there are indeed competing services available globally), Google's position in the search, advertising, and video markets provides Google considerable monopoly power. In the simplest of terms, monopoly power is an immunity from the forces of competition. Monopoly power is derived from market concentration; with a large market share, firms with monopoly power have the ability to influence market conditions, for example, by setting prices or acting to exclude competitors.[16] This analysis of monopoly power also aligns with the Herfindahl Index, which measures market concentration in terms of the percentage of total industry sales attributable to the largest firms within a sector. The rationale behind the Herfindahl Index is that the size of firms in an industry provides an indication of the level of competitiveness within that industry.[17] Although Google's size cannot be fully accounted for by sales, with 85 percent of the search engine market worldwide, plus a global advertising service, YouTube, Gmail, and countless other platforms and services, we can safely say that Google enjoys substantial monopoly power within the digital environment.

In this context, Google's "innovate first, permission later" framework requires qualifying. Limiting rightsholders' private property rights in the digital environment may provide legal room for socially beneficial technological innovation, but that technological innovation will now occur within the parameters of a digital environment featuring a monopolistic technology firm. Or, more accurately, if we consider the status of Facebook, Apple, and Amazon, a digital environment owned and controlled in large part by monopolistic technology firms. The consequences of this domination of our digital environment are multidimensional, with economic, cultural, and political implications.

## ECONOMIC CONSEQUENCES OF GOOGLE'S
## MONOPOLY POWER: THE CAPACITY
## FOR ANTICOMPETITIVE PRACTICES

According to microeconomic theory, in a competitive market, selling to price-sensitive consumers, competing firms will produce and sell at the lowest possible cost in an attempt to increase their market share.[18] Monopoly power, or market concentration, signals a lack of competition, allowing a firm to act in an anticompetitive manner—increasing prices or directing production in a manner not dictated by competition for consumers. These conditions can produce an inefficient allocation of resources and harm consumers.[19] Seeking to prohibit anticompetitive practices and to support competitive market conditions, competition laws deem specific business practices illegal, for example, misuse of market power, predatory pricing, price gouging, and cartels.[20]

In multiple jurisdictions, Google has faced allegations that it undertakes anticompetitive business practices, practices enabled by its market dominance. In 2014, a group of independent record labels spoke out against the terms they were offered for Google's subscription music service, Google Play Music. The group of labels complained that they were offered less favorable terms than what was offered to the major record labels. A central component of the complaint was that the contracts included a *negative* most-favored-nation clause, applying to the revenue share paid to record labels, meaning that if one participant negotiated a lower revenue sharing rate, it would apply to all participants. The independent record labels feared that with this term in place, if the major record labels negotiated a lower share of revenue in return for some other benefit (such as a nonrecoupable advance on earnings), the independent record labels would be forced to accept the lower rate without the guarantee of the same benefit given to the major labels. With a smaller market share, the independent labels feared that unlike the major labels they would not have the necessary leverage to negotiate a supplementary benefit.

In response to the independent record label's objections, Google declared all content from the independent labels that had not agreed to

Google's terms would be excluded from Google's subscription service and their content would be remove from YouTube. Independent music association, IMPALA, responded by lodging an antitrust complaint with the European Commission. IMPALA argued Google sought to use its monopoly power in the video hosting market to compel the labels to agree to its preferred terms. In 2014, Google reached an agreement with the labels; their works were not removed from YouTube, and they were included in the launch of Google Play.[21]

In the United States and in Europe, Google has also faced allegations that it acts in an anticompetitive manner when it promotes its own shopping (and other services) over competitor services in its search results. In the United States, in 2013, the Federal Trade Commission (FTC) completed an investigation of Google's practice of giving its own shopping services better placement than competitors' services in search results. The FTC concluded Google's policy was undertaken to "improve the quality of its search product and the overall user experience" rather than to inhibit competition.[22] However, subsequent to the conclusion of the investigation, the *Wall Street Journal* obtained a copy of the internal investigation report, which revealed that the FTC had in fact concluded Google did undertake anticompetitive practices and was using its monopoly power in a manner that caused harm to "consumers and to innovation in the online search and advertising markets."[23]

The *Wall Street Journal* reported that the FTC found Google had biased its search results to favor its own services, that it "illegally took content from rival websites such as Yelp, TripAdvisor Inc. and Amazon.com Inc. to improve its own websites," and that "when competitors asked Google to stop taking their content, it threatened to remove them from its search engine."[24] Reportedly, Google had also violated antitrust laws "by placing restrictions on websites that publish its search results from also working with rivals such as Microsoft's Bing and Yahoo Inc." and by "restricting advertisers' ability to use data garnered from Google ad campaigns in advertising run on rival platforms."[25] According to the *Wall Street Journal*, the report recommended that the FTC take legal action against Google, but a conflicting report from the FTC's economic bureau recommended against legal action, and the FTC commissioners ultimately voted against taking any action against Google. By the conclusion of the investigation, Google had agreed to implement changes to its policies to allow "websites to opt out of having their content included in its competing search products" and to allow advertisers to use data collected from Google advertising campaigns on competitor platforms.[26]

In Europe, Google has faced numerous antitrust complaints submitted to the European Commission over the years, including by companies such as Yelp, TripAdvisor, ODIGEO, Aptoide, Ciao, eJustice, Foundem, VfT, BDZV, VDZ, Hot-Map, Twenga, and Streetmap.[27] In 2010, the European Commission commenced formal proceedings against Google to investigate Google's search bias. In 2013, Google submitted a settlement proposal to the European Commission, in which Google agreed to make several changes to its search service, including prominently displaying in search results links from competitors websites, clearly marking in search results which links are to Google's own services, agreeing that competitor search services "will be able to have their results removed from Google's vertical search results without hurting their overall page rank for non-specialized searches" and changes to "AdSense contracts that make it easier for sites that use the advertising service to include other ads on their pages from competing alternatives."[28] The European Commission rejected Google's settlement proposal stating, "they are not proposals that can eliminate our concerns regarding competition."[29]

In 2014, the European Parliament voted for the "break-up of Google" by separating Google Search from the company's other commercial services.[30] Fortunately for Google, the European Parliament has no authority to force the break-up of Google. But in 2015, the European Commission sent Google a Statement of Objections alleging Google "abused its dominant position in the markets for general internet search services in the European Economic Area (EEA) by systematically favouring its own comparison shopping product in its general search results pages," and in 2017, Google was fined EUR 2.4 billion by the European Commission for search bias.[31]

In 2018, the European Commission fined Google again, this time for EUR 4.34 billion for breaching EU antitrust rules. The European Commission alleged that by requiring manufactures to preinstall the Google Search and Chrome apps on Android devices and by paying some manufacturers and mobile networks to exclusively preinstall the Google Search app on phones, Google had imposed illegal restrictions to secure its dominant position in online search.[32]

Google has appealed both fines and denies acting in an anticompetitive manner. Google maintains that it curates its search results with the objective of providing the most accurate and relevant information to its users.[33] Google has also argued that its search service is free and so there is no "trading relationship" necessary for a finding of abuse of dominance under EU law.[34]

By no means is this a complete account of Google's antitrust accusations—investigations have been undertaken throughout the world, from Canada to India and Taiwan. In short, Google's history is flush with complaints about its dominance in the markets in which it operates. While an assessment of each of these cases to determine if they are indeed breaches of specific competition laws is beyond the scope of this book, each incident is a reminder of the economic dimensions of Google's monopoly power. Underlying each allegation is concern for Google's capacity to manipulate market conditions and to compel other market participants to act in accordance with Google's interests.

Whether you agree or disagree that Google's activities are illegal or inappropriate, what is undeniable is that Google's monopoly power has economic consequences—to varying degrees it gives Google the *capacity* to act in an anticompetitive manner. It gives Google the capacity to function without pressure from competitors and to compel consumers and other market participants to accept conditions at Google's discretion. Regardless of which laws Google's activities may or may not fall afoul, as a globally dominant internet service provider, the economic power that Google wields is immense.

## THE CULTURAL CONSEQUENCES OF MONOPOLY
## POWER IN AN INFORMATION MARKET

As Timothy Wu reminds us, "information industries, enterprises that traffic in forms of individual expression, can never be properly understood as 'normal' industries."[35] This is because information and ideas have social and political consequences. The information and ideas that circulate in society shape our understanding of the world in which we live. Entities that produce information and content, and entities that control access to information and content, can exert influence in society by determining the quality of information and ideas that circulate within it. For this reason, cultural theorists advise we should strive for a culture comprised of a diversity of cultural representations produced by a diversity of voices—in order to avoid a centralization of power derived from the capacity to influence society through control over the information and ideas to which we have access.

In contemporary society, Google is a critical information provider. Google is a global, monopolistic platform capable of influencing our lives by curating the information and content that circulates in our culture.[36] Like governments, newspapers, radio stations, television broadcasters, Hollywood, and so on, Google distributes information, entertainment, and advertising throughout the world.[37] Critically, Google does not neutrally provide technical access to information. The information Google provides to us is curated by Google. Google curates its search results according to numerous factors and principles—in particular, taking substantial action to enforce the copyright claims of rightsholders. We are now a long way from the original PageRank system of democratically voted search results rankings. Google chooses to manipulate its search results, exercising discretionary power and acting in response to those powerful enough to persuade Google to act.[38] We know that Google acts to enforce copyright on behalf of the content industries, often at the expense of less economically powerful creators who rely on public rights to access and engage with works, such as those provided by a copyright exception. Google's search results and other services reflect and reinforce the distribution of power in the digital environment.

Operating as a private company, Google privately makes decisions to remove or preference certain types of information and content. Operating as a private company with monopoly power, Google's discretionary capacities are broad. Free from substantial competitive pressures, Google has the *capacity* to curate its provision of information in a manner that suits its interests. At times Google's interests align with the public interest, but at other times they align with the content industries, and at all times they align with the interest of the company's shareholders.

As a monopolistic search engine, Google has the capacity to determine social and cultural conditions by influencing the ideas circulating in society and by influencing conditions of access and participation in cultural life. Whether Google acts in the public interest or not, this centralization of cultural power is a real and substantial threat to democratic cultural and political conditions.

## POLITICAL CONSEQUENCES OF GOOGLE'S MONOPOLY POWER—PRIVATE REGULATORY POWER

Beyond the economic and social consequences, Google's monopoly power has a political dimension: Google's monopoly power represents a concentration of private regulatory power. It is true that Google litigates to create legal precedents in its favor and Google lobbies policymakers, spending millions of dollars every year in the United States and Europe in particular, in an attempt to secure laws suitable to its interests. But Google's regulatory influence goes beyond legal precedents, lobbying, and negotiating with politicians. Google is a powerful decision maker in the digital environment.

Google's capacity to regulate stems in significant part from the neoliberal self-regulatory model. The policies of privatization and deregulation common in Western democracies since the 1980s and the preference for engaging the private sector to own and administer the development of the digital environment have resulted in the transfer of substantial regulatory responsibilities to dominant commercial entities.[39] In this political setting, Google has become a powerful participant in the regulation of the internet. Through self-regulation, private agreements, and the decisions Google makes with regard to the functioning and structure of its platforms and algorithms, Google privately regulates large sections of the digital environment.[40]

In previous chapters, I noted specific examples of Google's voluntary and privately negotiated regulation in the copyright context, including the US Best Practices and Guidelines for Ad Networks to Address Piracy and Counterfeiting; the antipiracy agreement negotiated between Google, Bing, and the British Phonographic Industry, Motion Picture Association of Europe, Middle East, and Africa, and the Alliance for Intellectual Property; and the 2017 antipiracy agreement negotiated with France's audio-visual industry. These are examples of negotiated or self-regulation activities undertaken with government oversight.

In less transparent processes, Google also privately devises copyright rules, commonly in negotiation with large media and entertainment companies. This is evident from the history of Google News in Europe, where Google has sought and obtained private agreements with news publishers; and it is evident in Google's approach to enforcing copyright across its own platforms. From trusted member programs, to search sanitization and Content ID, Google has privately devised rules and implemented policies and programs for enforcing copyright. Google undertakes private copyright rule-making and enforcement.

This cocktail of regulatory power, along with Google's capacity for economic and social influence, places Google in an extraordinarily powerful position in contemporary life. Google is a private regulator, a monopolistic firm, and a dominant information provider. In the digital environment, a great degree of power is concentrated around a multinational corporation, with critical implications for democratic cultural and political conditions.

## DEMOCRACY AND CONCENTRATED PRIVATE POWER
## IN THE DIGITAL ENVIRONMENT

Democratic political systems are purposefully constructed to avoid a concentration of power. Typically, regulatory power is separated into multiple institutions to keep institutions and individuals accountable and to avoid abuses of power. The principal example of institutional separation in a democratic system is the separation of the legislature, judiciary, and executive branches of government. Each branch performs separate functions, and their separation is aimed at limiting the capacity for an abuse of power.[41]

Montesquieu famously provides a foundational rationale for the separation of powers doctrine:

> When legislative power is united with executive power in a single person or in a single body of the magistracy, there is no liberty, because one can fear that the same monarch or senate that makes tyrannical laws will execute them tyrannically. Nor is there liberty if the power of judging is not separate from legislative power and from executive power. If it were joined to legislative power, the power over the life and liberty of the citizens would be arbitrary, for the judge would be the legislator ... All would be lost if the same man or the same body ... exercised these three powers: that of making the law, that of executing public resolutions, and that of judging the crimes or the disputes of individuals.[42]

In the domains that Google resides over, power is concentrated rather than separated. One entity has substantial power to make the law, execute the law, and judge disputes. Google privately negotiates rules, enforces those rules through its own policies and technologies, and decides on adjudication standards and procedures—producing a system that is fundamentally at odds with democratic governance.

The concentration of private power in the digital environment also poses problems for transparency and accountability—values central to democratic systems of governance. In a representative democracy, power is accountable to voters in elections. As well, the separation of powers doctrine provides a layer of horizontal accountability, that is, the most powerful institutions are accountable to each other.[43] In a digital environment featuring powerful private actors, copyright governance has become increasingly opaque and unaccountable. Private institutions are less transparent than state institutions. Accountability requires performance information and access to performance information requires transparency; "to be accountable is to agree to subject oneself to relationships of external scrutiny which can have consequences."[44] In comparison to public institutions, Google produces limited performance information and confronts limited vertical and horizontal accountability mechanisms.

Opaque and unaccountable regulation is likely to worsen with the deployment of more and more sophisticated artificial intelligence, such as deep-learning-based systems, in which the machine's decision-making process is to some extent unknowable, even to the engineers who developed it. Will Knight elucidates:

> by its nature, deep learning is a particularly dark black box. You can't just look inside a deep neural network to see how it works. A network's reasoning is embedded in the behavior of thousands of simulated neurons, arranged into dozens or even hundreds of intricately interconnected layers.[45]

When it comes to advanced algorithmic regulatory systems, we cannot simply look at the source code to understand the decision-making process.[46] There are layers of opacity that prevent us from understanding how they function. They are privately owned and controlled, concealed by intellectual property laws. They are designed and administered by individuals and companies that possess advanced technical capacities. And the systems themselves are created to perform tasks that are often beyond the human mind's ability to perform or comprehend.[47] Advanced algorithmic regularly systems are by design difficult to understand, evaluate, and hold to account.

The future of artificial intelligence is closely connected to the issue of Google's monopoly power. Google biographer Steven Levy asserts that Google is in the process of restructuring to become a "machine learning first" company.[48] At its 2018 Google I/O conference for developers, Google described how it was employing machine learning across a range of products and services. Google is using machine learning to build adaptive batteries for Android phones that learn usage habits and efficiently distribute battery power. It is using it to develop a digital assistant that recognizes accents and dialects and can book appointments for you. In the health care sector, Google is using machine learning to diagnose cardiovascular disease. For its self-driving cars, Google is using machine learning to recognize pedestrians and predict the movement of other cars on the road. With Google's data stockpiles and deep pockets, the machine learning possibilities are endless.

Google also seeks to have its own machine learning frameworks widely utilized. Google's machine learning software library TensorFlow is open source, and Google offers free online tutorials and "boot camps" to assist people and companies to understand how to use it. Google also provides a machine learning package specifically for mobile developers—the ML Kit. Google sells to the public its Cloud AI, a machine learning service with pretrained models, and Cloud AutoML, which uses Google's image recognition Neural Architecture Search to find the most suitable neural network for a dataset, making it easier to train a deep neural network while having limited knowledge of machine learning. Google is far from asleep at the wheel: if artificial intelligence is the future, Google is doing what it can to be the dominant service provider.

By providing free and open access to TensorFlow in particular, Google ensures that a significant portion of machine learning innovations evolve on Google's terrain. Of course, there is also the potential for revenue: if businesses use Google's machine learning tools, they are then likely to use Google's cloud platform, for which they must pay.[49] But more importantly if viewed in terms of Google's broader evolution, as more applications, products, and services are developed using machine learning, by giving away TensorFlow for free, Google is setting itself up to be a dominant platform in the machine learning space. As the digital age marches on, entering a new stage led by artificial intelligence, Google is doing what it can to remain a dominant intermediary.

All empires fall, it is true. But Google's demise is not just around the corner. Google is no printing press or Polaroid camera company. Google actively engages with and drives technological trends in order to ensure they evolve on Google's terms. If we accept that Google represents a threat to democratic, accountable, and transparent governance in the digital environment, then we should also accept that without intervention, it is a problem that is here to stay.

## CONCLUSION

By directly increasing public access to information and content through its digital indexes of websites, images, books, videos, news, and so forth, and by providing technological tools for people to create and distribute expressive works, Google has assisted in the advancement of a cultural democracy. Google has increased opportunities for participation in meaning-making and has expanded the universe of information and ideas to which the public has access. Yet it has done so while also securing its own exclusive access to vast databases of information that give Google a seemingly unassailable advantage in both current and future markets.

Whether an agent for or against the public interest, Google now reigns over a new technological and economic order that features empowered private actors and rapidly changing technological conditions. How to effectively regulate these actors—in an increasingly automated technological environment and in order to achieve public interest outcomes—is a pressing challenge for lawmakers. In copyright governance, how to respond to the domination of digital spaces and information access by Google specifically is perhaps the most pressing challenge of all.

# Conclusion

*Achieving Public Interest Outcomes
in a Digital Environment Dominated
by Monopolistic Technology Firms*

Two decades ago, when Google was but a research project at Stanford University, a central question for copyright scholars concerned with the emerging digital environment was how to ensure remuneration for rightsholders while also encouraging the development of new communication and information networks. Rightsholders demanded maximum control. Others argued the digital environment should be free to flourish without burdensome regulation and in order to realize the internet's democratic potential. Bolstered by an ideological position that markets can more efficiently organize society than can governments, policymakers supported private sector investment and models of self-regulation. Over the past two decades, in this political and ideological setting, private entities such as Google have become very powerful and the scope for privately negotiating copyright in practice broad—today, powerful private actors negotiate copyright rules, determine standards for using information and content, and enforce copyright.

When large and powerful private actors govern, democracy suffers. But we are not powerless; there are multiple courses of action available to those of us concerned with the dominance of private actors in the digital

*Google Rules: The History and Future of Copyright Under the Influence of Google.* Joanne Elizabeth Gray, Oxford University Press (2020). © Oxford University Press.
DOI: 10.1093/oso/9780190072070.001.0001

environment. We can address the problem of monopoly power head on, by breaking up companies or breaking down barriers to entry in digital markets. Or we can acknowledge the current role of intermediaries in contemporary life and impose upon them public interest responsibilities. Both pathways are viable options for lawmakers and activists seeking to curtail Google's power and to secure public interest outcomes in digital copyright governance.

## DIRECTLY ADDRESSING GOOGLE'S MONOPOLY POWER

If Google is a monopoly, why not break it up? Lawmakers could force Google to sell all its businesses outside of search, just as the European Parliament ordered in 2014. Certainly, action to force Google to divest itself of large portions of its business would have a material impact on the economic status of the company. But we would still be left with a globally dominant search engine capable of regulating the information and content to which we have access. Addressing Google's monopoly power— and its multidimensional consequences—is not straightforward. If it was, perhaps the seemingly endless antitrust investigations of Google would have produced more tangible outcomes. Google has operated under the shadow of antitrust clouds for many years, and despite numerous investigations and allegations, so far, antitrust interventions have failed to significantly curb Google's monopoly power. Even the historically large European Commission fines are unlikely to impact Google's market position. Google has the capacity to pay fines and to make adjustments to its search algorithm to address the practices deemed anticompetitive, all without diminishing its overall position.

Under most regimes, antitrust has economic parameters and lawmakers look for consumer harm and anticompetitive market conditions. With these parameters, antitrust can be useful for addressing specific anticompetitive business practices and for regulating Google's behavior on an issue-by-issue basis—for example, forcing Google to change who it preferences in its search results or what it allows phone manufacturers to do with Android. But with economic parameters, generally antitrust has a limited capacity to respond to complex issues that do not involve market transactions, such as Google's collection and use of information about its users. Given that Google's monopoly power is in significant part derived from information acquired without a classical market transaction, this is a critical limitation. Furthermore, when Google prioritizes its own services in its search results or mandates that all Android phones include Google applications, that is a *use* of monopoly power by Google. By preventing Google from acting this way, regulators are addressing the consequences but not the cause of Google's monopoly power. Directly addressing the source of Google's monopoly power requires addressing the issue of Google's exclusive access to and use of data.

In 2019, Google was fined EUR 50 million for breaching the region's data laws—the European Union's General Data Protection Rules (GDPR). Google was accused of not complying with GDPR requirements for transparency regarding the use of user data and for not obtaining sufficient consent from users to use their data. While the fine itself will not have a substantial impact on Google's economic position, it is the first intervention that comes close to striking at the source of Google's monopoly power—Google's access to and use of data. Because the GDPR is a relatively new policy intervention, how disruptive its application will ultimately be remains unclear, but the policy does represent one viable point of intervention for breaking down some of the informational barriers to entry Google enjoys in the search market. If users can wrench back more control over their data, Google is at risk of losing its footing as the world's leading internet search engine.

We cannot, however, discount the enduring value of Google's existing data stockpiles—its indexes of websites, images, videos, books, and all the information it has collected about internet users over the past two decades. Breaking down the barriers to entry that these repositories of information represent would require far more radical strategies than consumer-focused data regulations currently provide. Breaking down the informational barriers to entry that Google enjoys requires that we end Google's exclusive access to its databases of information. This proposition raises a number of serious questions. Can Google be compelled to provide public access to its databases of information? Does the public have a rightful claim to access Google's data stores? And, if so, is it an appropriate intervention? Is it feasible?

Perhaps a public access claim to Google's databases could be instigated and justified as a sui generis public interest proposal. Data is an increasingly important source of power in society, and a government could mandate public access to Google's databases on the claim that they are acting in the public interest by ensuring an equitable distribution of power derived from society's key informational resources.

Working within existing legal frameworks, the essential facilities doctrine might provide an avenue for establishing a public access claim to Google's databases. Although definitions vary across jurisdictions, broadly defined, the essential facilities doctrine provides that where there is monopolistic control over a facility that is critical for entry by competitors into a market, reasonable access to that facility may be mandated.[1] A brave policymaker might make the case that Google's databases are now an essential facility in contemporary society.

A public claim to Google's databases derived from copyrighted works might also be justified through a copyright analysis. The limited duration of copyright ensures that all copyrighted works will, at some point, fall into the public domain. When Google creates its search indexes, it draws upon copyrighted works, works that will, eventually, fall into the public domain. One could argue that the public therefore has a future claim to the indexes and, for instance, policymakers could act to ensure public access to the databases after a period of exclusive access by Google, along the lines of copyright or even patent duration.

Alternatively, policymakers could require that fair use determinations involving large repositories of information derived from copyrighted works trigger a requirement to provide public access. For example, Frank Pasquale has suggested a public access requirement could be inserted into a fair use analysis, that is, universal access would be necessary for a favorable fair use determination.[2] Of course, to impact Google, this policy would need to be retroactively applied.

These provocative proposals may provide starting points for lawmakers and activists interested in directly addressing Google's monopoly power. Ultimately, however, any intervention to compel Google to provide public access to its critical private assets must confront the question of whether, on balance, this is a reasonable intervention. At the very least, it is rational to assume such a proposal would face considerable ideological, legal, political, and economic resistance, particularly within the United States.

While hostility and motivation to regulate Google remains high in Europe, in the United States, Google largely enjoys the political support that comes with being an entity that makes a substantial contribution to the US economy. When Eric Schmidt testified to the US Senate Judiciary Subcommittee on Antitrust, Competition Policy, and Consumer Rights, he opened with a statement that specified, "while others had given up on the American economy, Google is certainly doubling down. We are investing in people. In 2002 we had fewer than 1000 employees . . . now we have more than 24,000 and we are hiring."[3] That was in 2011. Today, Google has almost 100,000 employees. The day after the European Commission announced it had fined Google close to USD 5 billion, US President Donald Trump tweeted: "I told you so! The European Union just slapped a Five Billion Dollar fine on one of our great companies, Google. They truly have taken advantage of the U.S., but not for long!"[4] In the United States, in the short to medium term at least, policymakers are unlikely to take extreme measures to directly address Google's monopoly power.

Importantly, while Google's business defies national boundaries, Google purposefully operates as a US company to remain under US jurisdiction, in large part to enjoy US copyright laws (presumably along with other advantages, such as convenient antitrust laws and low corporate tax rates). Jurisdictions outside of the United States have had varying degrees of success at regulating Google. In Europe, in 2014, lawmakers successfully compelled Google to implement policies accommodating "a right to be forgotten," whereby in certain circumstances individuals can ask Google to remove personal information from its search results. In its ruling on the matter, the Court of Justice for the European Union decided that "even if the physical server of a company processing data is located outside of

Europe, EU rules apply to search engine operators if they have a branch or a subsidiary in a Member State which promotes the selling of advertising space offered by the search engine."[5] By comparison, in November 2017, a US court sided with Google and issued a preliminary injunction essentially rendering ineffective a decision by Canada's Supreme Court that Google must remove from its search results worldwide (and not simply from Google Search in Canada) content subject to a removal request in Canada.[6]

With substantial jurisdictional and political hurdles in place, it is safe to assume that any policy intervention aimed at dissolving Google's monopoly power by providing public access to its databases is likely to require but unlikely to attain legislative action within the United States.

## IMPOSING PUBLIC INTEREST RESPONSIBILITIES UPON GOOGLE

An alternative to directly addressing the source of Google's monopoly power is to acknowledge that online intermediaries like Google are powerful regulators in contemporary society and to impose upon them, through either regulation or negotiation, a duty to act in the public interest. The critical first step along this pathway is accepting that private entities that possess economic, social, and regulatory power bear some responsibility to act in the public interest.

Evidently, this is a position held by at least some lawmakers, as the following examples attest: in 2016, the European Commission negotiated a Code of Conduct on illegal online hate speech, signed by Facebook, Google, Twitter, and Microsoft;[7] in 2017, the UK government announced a proposal for a voluntary levy on internet companies to be used to "combat and raise awareness about online bullying and other web dangers" and to "help pay for the policing of online offences";[8] and in 2017, Google, Facebook, and Twitter were required to testify to the US Congress regarding the use of digital platforms by Russia to spread information in order to influence the outcome of the US 2016 presidential election.[9] In these examples, we see lawmakers cognizant of the social influence and regulatory capacities of the corporations that dominate the digital environment and at least some willingness to compel these private actors to act in the public interest.

In the copyright context, when imposing public interest obligations upon Google, in my view, policymakers should tackle the issues that pose the greatest threat to democratic governance, which will involve diluting the regulatory capacities of private actors, improving transparency, accountability, and due process in digital copyright governance, and protecting public rights and values in the digital environment.

## PUBLIC INTEREST COPYRIGHT LAW REFORMS

A high-impact copyright law reform would be to limit the scope of private copyright rule-making and enforcement, including the use of algorithmic technologies, so that private entities may only identify infringing content and any action beyond identification falls to a neutral public enforcer and arbitrator. This proposal aligns with what is sometimes called a "notice and notice" system of copyright enforcement by intermediaries, as an alternative to a "notice and take-down" system.[10] A notice and notice system would directly limit the regulatory power of Google, and other intermediaries, by separating regulatory functions among multiple institutions. It would ensure that one entity is not acting as lawmaker, enforcer, and adjudicator. It would also ensure that a public entity is undertaking copyright enforcement; a public entity that is, in principle, publicly accountable, transparent, and operating according to public rather than private objectives.

Another high-impact reform would be to change intermediary safe harbor so that it is strictly conditional upon intermediaries accounting for copyright exceptions. Under contemporary copyright regimes, copyright exceptions are essential for ensuring public access to existing information and content and for supporting cultural participation. Ensuring their continued application in the digital environment is critical for achieving the conditions of a cultural democracy and the foundational public access objective of copyright law. As systems of private copyright rule-making and algorithmic enforcement continue to advance, protecting copyright exceptions remains squarely in the public interest.[11]

Intermediary liability regimes could also be reformed to make standards for transparency, accountability, and due process conditions for intermediary safe harbor.[12] As algorithmic regulatory methods become more widespread, this policy could compel their creators to encode public interest values into their systems. A recent policy intervention within the European Union indicates that the European Commission is willing to take action to improve transparency, accountability, and due process in automated decision-making: Recital 71 of the GDPR articulates a "right to an explanation," whereby users subject to an automated decision made about them have the right to ask for an explanation of the decision.[13] The policy seeks to improve transparency in an increasingly algorithmically regulated digital environment, and an iteration of this policy could be incorporated as a condition for intermediary safe harbor.

Ultimately, any policy that alters the responsibilities of intermediaries must intersect with established intermediary safe harbor laws that have been propagated throughout the world through multilateral and bilateral agreements for decades. In my view, the issue of concentrated private power and the use of algorithmic regulatory tools in digital copyright governance merits a new comprehensive multilateral copyright treaty—digital copyright governance is a transnational phenomenon that has grown in scope and complexity since the negotiation of the Internet Treaties in the 1990s. The latest European copyright directive is the most recent attempt at such an undertaking. Unfortunately, however, this attempted reform has largely played out as a battle between two powerful industry interests—US technology companies and Europe's most powerful media companies— and the latest version of the directive has largely concluded industry cooperation is the correct path forward. Once again, what is still missing is a clear vision for the public interest. If we are to address the public interest deficit in digital copyright governance through a multilateral treaty undertaking, the public interest, as distinct from all industry interests, must take center stage.

Public lawmaking is the most important avenue for protecting the public interest in digital copyright governance. Democracy depends upon publicly accountable individuals and institutions devising, enacting, and enforcing our laws. Yet we must be realistic about its limitations. Public lawmaking in the copyright setting is often complex and protracted, one that infrequently produces tangible outcomes over short to medium time frames. Treaty and legislative lawmaking proposals must inevitably confront complex political processes, including an abiding political preference for private solutions.

As such, for the short to medium term, a strategic approach seems warranted: we may need to negotiate with the companies that dominate the digital environment, compelling and enticing them to self-regulate in the public interest. Negotiating is a tactical methodology, one that takes into account existing political and economic conditions, the continuing influence of neoliberal ideology, and the role that intermediaries play in digital copyright governance. In the following section, I outline four principles that establish some basic expectations of companies that participate in digital copyright governance, in particular, focusing upon critical problems affecting digital copyright governance that Google itself may be able to address. This is, after all, a book about Google and copyright.

## SELF-REGULATING IN THE PUBLIC INTEREST

In the copyright setting, in order to safeguard democratic cultural and political conditions, when private companies fight over their duties and obligations regarding copyright, they must be required to consider the public interest in access to information and cultural participation, as well as principles of accountability, transparency, and due process. Accordingly, I propose four practical policies that we should ask of Google and other companies that privately regulate copyright. These guidelines should be considered a baseline for lawmakers and activists willing to take up the challenge of negotiating with Google regarding its responsibility to ensure public interest outcomes in copyright governance.

*1. Private copyright enforcement mechanisms, including algorithmic technologies, should account for copyright exceptions and limitations.* This policy assumes intermediaries have a responsibility to act in the public interest by ensuring public access rights in the digital environment are not diminished by private agreements and algorithmic enforcement. It calls for intermediaries to avoid copyright enforcement practices that unfairly privilege private property claims over public access rights. It is aimed at ensuring that information gatekeepers act to support a diverse and participatory culture. This policy will not by itself solve the problem of concentrated cultural power, but it can place some limitations upon it.

*2. Intermediaries should make public the copyright rules that govern their platforms, including those negotiated by private agreement and implemented algorithmically.* This policy assumes intermediaries have a responsibility to act transparently because transparency in copyright goverance is a critical first step in achieving fair and accountable copyright goverance.[14] An advantage of this principle is that it sidessteps technical questions about the feasbility of transparency and accountability in algorithmic systems. Instead of asking Google and other intermediaries to explain and expose the inner workings of their technical systems, we ask them to explain and expose the decisions that occur prior to their engineering. In other words, rather than trying to understand the process and outcomes of opaque and unknowable automated decision-making systems, we ask for transparent decision-making by real people so that we may hold them to account against public interest criteria.

*3. When content is removed from the internet, including algorithmically, the individual or organization that posted the content should be sent a notice. The notice should include information outlining the legal recourse available to them. Recourse should include a counter-notification process that cannot be circumvented by private agreement or algorithmic processes.* This third policy assumes intermediaries have a responsibility to inform and empower their users. It is aimed at preventing intermediaries and rightsholders from negotiating away due process. All internet users subject to an automated decision that regulates their behavior and impacts their social, cultural, political, and economic lives are entitled to due process, and they should have the opportunity to participate in the regulatory or enforcement process.

*4. Intermediaries should document all copyright enforcement actions undertaken by the intermediary, including by algorithm, and make the data publicly available.* This final policy assumes intermediaries have a responsibilty to provide performance information to facilitate accountability and improve public understanding of digital copyright goverance. As automated systems advance, performance information that is made available to the public will support vital research into the impact of these evolving technological systems.

As we move deeper into the digital age and automated regulatory systems continue to advance, these four policies assert an expectation of intermediaries to act not only in the interest of rightsholders but in the interest of a broad range of stakeholders.

Opting to negotiate with Google requires that we accept that private actors are powerful participants in digital copyright governance and their cooperation may be necessary for effective reform. Google has proven itself very capable of pushing back against policies that are not in its interest, and so any copyright reforms aimed at regulating Google will surely benefit from Google's cooperation.

The development of best practice guidelines, a code of conduct, or a voluntary public interest copyright agreement negotiated directly with Google also provides an opportunity for public discourse and norm-setting in the public interest. Google's copyright enforcement practices have industry-wide influence. Google's participation in the development and implementation of public interest copyright policies has the potential to influence other intermediaries—established and emerging—regarding public interest obligations in private copyright rule-making and algorithmic enforcement.[15]

Of course, you might ask, what would motivate Google to self-regulate in the public interest? There are several reasons for optimism. First, there is an alignment of interests. Both Google and the public benefit from a regulatory environment that provides freedom to access and engage with information and content in order to innovate and create. Google continues to rely on and seeks to ensure copyright regimes include robust copyright exceptions and limitations, and these principles underpin the four proposed policies. In short, Google may be motivated to self-regulate in the public interest because key policies that are in the public interest align with Google's copyright agenda.

In fact, Google has publicly supported and in some cases already implements aspects of the four public interest policies. For example, Google has supported law reforms to ensure copyright exceptions are not disabled by private agreement. In 2012, Google submitted to the Australia government:

> Copyright laws contain a complex balance between the rights of copyright owners to protect their works and the public interest in ensuring access to knowledge and the creation of new works. This balance is sensitively and carefully constructed, which should not be able to be altered or replaced by private arrangements. Google would support an amendment to the Copyright Act that prevented the contractual override of copyright exceptions.[16]

While Google may not always adhere to its own recommendations, its strong support and reliance on copyright exceptions persists. Google is also vocal about the importance of transparency and makes publicly available the number of removal requests it receives from rightsholders through its Transparency Report.[17] It also submits the take-down requests it receives to the Lumen archive—a research project of the Berkman Klein Center for Internet and Society at Harvard University—and makes the data available for download by the public.[18] Google claims to do so in order to promote transparency: "we want to be transparent about the process so that users and researchers alike understand what kinds of materials have been removed from our search results and why."[19] Not only does Google continue to have a vested interest in copyright exceptions, but in its rhetoric and actions we see evidence that Google considers itself to have a responsibility to act transparently. Effectively, the fourth policy I put forward affirms the importance of transparency, and calls for higher standards and industry-wide adoption of reporting protocols.

Google is heavily invested in its copyright agenda—including years of litigation, lobbying, and direct investments of financial and technological resources. In the right circumstances, Google could prove a powerful private actor taking action in the public interest.

I also note that Google has publicly recognized that the recent pace of developments in automated technologies has potentially far-reaching social consequences and that technology companies bear some responsibility in this regard. In 2016, Google, Amazon, Facebook, IBM, and Microsoft founded the (rather Orwellian in name) Partnership on Artificial Intelligence to Benefit People and Society.[20] This organization states its purpose is to "study and formulate best practices on AI technologies, to advance the public's understanding of AI, and to serve as an open platform for discussion and engagement about AI."[21]

As this examination of Google's relationship to copyright law shows, when it comes to political pressures and policy debates, Google is alert, vigilant, and typically willing to negotiate. What is key is ensuring that as private actors continue to negotiate copyright rule-making and enforcement, there are public interest considerations on the negotiating table.

Because Google is embedded so deeply in contemporary society, achieving public interest outcomes in copyright governance requires a multidimensional approach. We need to understand, interrogate, and challenge the source of Google's power. We need to work within existing legal regimes to regulate the consequences of that power. We need to reform existing laws to limit Google's power and to improve levels of accountability and transparency. And we must negotiate with Google. Negotiating with Google is a pragmatic, albeit initial, step toward addressing some of the problematic dimensions of private power and algorithmic technologies in digital copyright governance.

## CONCLUSION

This book traces the rise of a powerful technology company through its legal, commercial, and political negotiations over copyright and analyzes the wider consequences of that ascendancy. Google emerged at a critical moment in the development of our digital environment, and its founders devised an eloquent way to profit from the open structure of the internet and the free flow of information online. Yet today, the internet is far less open and information flows far less freely. Private companies, Google in particular, make decisions about what we see and do online. As our societies become increasingly digital, and increasingly automated, in the presence of powerful private companies like Google, we must take action to safeguard the public interest in access to information and in a diverse and participatory culture.

In this book, I have tried to dig beneath the conventional copyright policy debates and to isolate and assert the public interest. In this chapter, I have outlined pathways for infusing public interest outcomes in digital copyright governance, now and into the future. The most direct approach to limiting Google's influence is government intervention to end Google's exclusive access to informational resources. But legal and legislative interventions for addressing the economic, social, and political consequences of Google's monopoly power are probably more feasible. So too is negotiating with Google to develop guidelines to ensure that when Google and other private actors undertake copyright rule-making and algorithmic enforcement, they respect the public interest. This final proposal is a calculated proposition—one that is accepting of the continuing influence of neoliberal ideology and of the current distribution of regulatory power in the digital environment.

We live in thrilling times. Technological innovation is sure to continue to evolve and to astound us. But in this dazzling world we inhabit, we must not be deterred by complexity, and we must not lose sight of the eternal and universal public interest in access to knowledge, the importance of cumulative creativity, and the impact that our culture can have on our experiences of freedom, power, and democracy.

**PREFACE**
1. *See* MARY DOUGLAS, HOW INSTITUTIONS THINK (1986).

**CHAPTER 1**
1. GOOGLE INC., GOOGLE ANNUAL REPORT 2014, at 2 (2014).
2. Google, FROM THE GARAGE TO THE GOOGLEPLEX GOOGLE, https://www.google.com/about/our-story/ (last visited Feb. 3, 2019).
3. Statute of Anne, 8 Ann. c. 19 § I-II (1710). The long title of the Statute of Anne is *An Act for the Encouragement of Learning, by Vesting the Copies of Printed Books in the Authors or Purchase of such Copies, during the Times therein mentioned.*
4. *Id.* at V.
5. Molly Shaffer Van Houweling, *Distributive Values in Copyright*, 83 TEX. L. REV. 1535, 1539 (2005).
6. World Intellectual Property Organization, WIPO Copyright Treaty, Dec. 20, 1996; World Intellectual Property Organization, WIPO Performances and Phonograms Treaty, Dec. 20, 1996. *See also IceTV Pty Limited v. Nine Network Australia Pty Limited*, in which the High Court of Australia discussed "the longstanding theoretical underpinnings of copyright legislation," noting:

> Copyright legislation strikes a balance of competing interests and competing policy considerations. Relevantly, it is concerned with rewarding authors of original literary works with commercial benefits having regard to the fact that literary works in turn benefit the reading public . . . The "social contract" envisaged by the Statute of Anne, and still underlying the present Act, was that an author could obtain a monopoly, limited in time, in return for making a work available to the reading public.

IceTV Pty Limited v. Nine Network Australia Pty Limited, HCA 14 1, 24–25 (2009).

In the United States, the Constitution frames copyright as a tool for promoting "the Progress of Science and useful Arts, by securing for limited Times to Authors and Inventors the exclusive Right to their respective Writings and Discoveries." U.S. Const. art. I, § 8, cl. 8. In *Feist Publications, Inc. v. Rural Telephone Service Co.*, the US Supreme Court explained:

> It may seem unfair that much of the fruit of the compiler's labor may be used by others without compensation. As Justice Brennan has correctly observed, however, this is not "some unforeseen byproduct of a statutory scheme." *Harper & Row*, 471 U.S., at 589 (dissenting opinion). It is, rather, "the essence of copyright," *ibid.*, and a constitutional requirement. The primary objective of copyright is not to reward the labor of authors, but "[t]o promote the Progress of Science and useful Arts." Art. I, § 8, cl. 8 . . . To this end, copyright assures authors the right to their original expression, but encourages others to build freely upon the ideas and information conveyed by a work.

Although not a copyright dispute, *see also Associated Press v. United States*, in which Justice Black expressed that the US First Amendment regarding religion and expression "rests on the assumption that the widest possible dissemination of information from diverse and antagonistic sources is essential to the welfare of the public." Associated Press v. United States, 326 U.S. 1, 20 (1945).

7. *See, e.g.*, Library of Congress U.S. Copyright Office 37 C.F.R. Part 201 [Docket No. 2014-07] *Exemptions to Prohibition on Circumvention of Copyright Protection Systems for Access Control Technologies*; Tobias McFadden v. Sony Music Entertainment Germany GmbH, C-484/14 170 (ECLI-EU, 2016); Lenz v. Universal Music Corp, 815 3D 1145 (2015); Joanne Gray, *Copyright According to Google, in* COPYRIGHT, PROPERTY AND THE SOCIAL CONTRACT 227, 228 (John Gilchrist & Brian Fitzgerald eds., 2018).

8. Gray, *supra* note 7, at 228.

9. *Id.*

10. WILLIAM PATRY, MORAL PANICS AND THE COPYRIGHT WARS 26 (2009).

11. Here I have paraphrased Patry, who describes:

> In the world of Internet-based companies, a completely different approach to consumers is taken . . . Open systems are not only consistent with the architecture of the Internet, but—and this is the key dividing line between the copyright industries and Internet companies—open systems are consistent with the experience users want from the Internet: the ability to access and use information when and how you want. *Id.* at 27.

12. BRUCE A. LEHMAN, INTELLECTUAL PROPERTY AND THE NATIONAL INFORMATION INFRASTRUCTURE. THE REPORT OF THE WORKING GROUP ON INTELLECTUAL PROPERTY RIGHTS (1995).

13. JESSICA LITMAN, DIGITAL COPYRIGHT 74–75 (2001).

14. *Id.* at 90. *See also* Distinguished Professor of Law and Information Management at UC Berkeley, Pamela Samuelson:

> Why would the Clinton administration want to transform the emerging informa-
> tion superhighway into a publisher-dominated toll road? The most plausible expla-
> nation is a simple one: campaign contributions. The administration wants to please
> the copyright industry, especially members of the Hollywood community, who are
> vital to the president's reelection bid. And what this copyright industry wants in
> return is more legal control than ever before over the products they distribute.

Pamela Samuelson, *The Copyright Grab*, WIRED (Jan. 1, 1996, 12:00 PM), https://
www.wired.com/1996/01/white-paper/. *See also* Gray, *supra* note 7, at 229.

15. INFORMATION INFRASTRUCTURE TASK FORCE, NATIONAL INFORMATION
    INFRASTRUCTURE: PROGRESS REPORT, SEPTEMBER 1993–1994, at 369 (1994).
16. LITMAN, *supra* note 13, at 122.
17. Pamela Samuelson, *The US Digital Agenda at WIPO*, 37 VA. J. INT'L L. 369, 373
    (1996).
18. BLAYNE HAGGART, COPYFIGHT: THE GLOBAL POLITICS OF DIGITAL COPYRIGHT
    REFORM 118 (2014).
19. Samuelson, *supra* note 17, at 435.
20. WIPO Copyright Treaty, art. 8, Dec. 20, 1996; WIPO Performances and
    Phonograms Treaty, art. 15, Dec. 20, 1996. WIPO Copyright Treaty, art. 11, Dec. 20,
    1996; WIPO Performances and Phonograms Treaty, art. 18, Dec. 20, 1996.
21. WIPO Internet Treaties, WIPO, https://www.wipo.int/copyright/en/activities/
    internet_treaties.html (last visited Feb. 1, 2019).
22. Gray, *supra* note 7, at 230.
23. The long title of the DMCA is *To Amend Title 17, United States Code, to Implement
    the World Intellectual Property Organization Copyright Treaty and Performances
    and Phonograms Treaty, and for Other Purposes*.
24. Yafit Lev-Aretz, *Copyright Lawmaking and Public Choice: From Legislative Battles
    to Private Ordering*, 27 HARV. J.L. TECH. 203, 206 (2013). *See also* LITMAN, *supra*
    note 13.
25. LITMAN, *supra* note 13, at 134–35; Gray, *supra* note 7, at 229.
26. Kimberlee Weatherall, *The New (Old) War on Copyright Infringement, and How
    Context Is Opening New Regulatory Possibilities*, 143 MEDIA INT. AUST. 110, 111
    (2012).
27. *See, e.g.*, the US Senate on the purpose of intermediary safe harbor: "Title II will
    provide certainty for copyright owners and Internet service providers with respect
    to copyright infringement liability online . . . In short, Title II ensures that the ef-
    ficiency of the Internet will continue to improve and that the variety and quality
    of services on the Internet will expand." UNITED STATES SENATE, SENATE REPORT
    105–190 THE DIGITAL MILLENNIUM COPYRIGHT ACT OF 1998, at 2 (1998). Gray,
    *supra* note 7, at 236.
28. 17 U.S.C. § 512(a)–(d) (2012).
29. LITMAN, *supra* note 13, at 145. Litman argues "copyright legislation written by
    multiparty negotiation is . . . kind to the status quo, and hostile to potential new
    competitors. It is also overwhelmingly likely to appropriate value for the benefit of
    major stakeholders at the expense of the public." At 144. *See also* Fisher describing

the 1976 US copyright law reform negotiations: "the negotiations privileged groups with interests sufficiently strong and concentrated to have formal representatives. Very rarely was the public—the consumers of intellectual property—represented in any way." William W. Fisher, *The Growth of Intellectual Property: A History of the Ownership of Ideas in the United States*, 1999, https://cyber.harvard.edu/people/tfisher/iphistory.pdf (last visited Feb. 3, 2019).

30. LITMAN, *supra* note 13, at 143.
31. Stop Online Piracy Act, H.R.3261 112th Cong. (2011) and Preventing Real Online Threats to Economic Creativity and Theft of Intellectual Property Act, S.968 112th Cong. (2011). *See generally* Mark Lemley, David S. Levine, & David G. Post, *Don't Break the Internet*, 64 STAN. L. REV. ONLINE 34 (2011); Gray, *supra* note 7, at 230.
32. Anti-Counterfeiting Trade Agreement, Oct. 1, 2011.
33. *See* Trans-Pacific Partnership Intellectual Property Rights Chapter Draft (Feb. 10, 2011), KEEP THE WEB OPEN, http://keepthewebopen.com/assets/pdfs/TPP%20IP%20Chapter%20Proposal.pdf (last visited Jan. 5, 2016). *See, e.g.*, GOOGLE, PUBLIC CONSULTATION ON THE REVIEW OF THE EU COPYRIGHT RULES (2013).
34. Gray, *supra* note 7, at 231.
35. *See generally* Patricia Loughlan, *Pirates, Parasites, Reapers, Sowers, Fruits, Foxes. The Metaphors of Intellectual Property*, 28 SYDNEY L. REV. 211 (2006); LITMAN, *supra* note 13, at 29; Patricia L. Loughlan, *"You Wouldn't Steal a Car . . .": Intellectual Property and the Language of Theft*, 29 EUR. INTELLECT. PROP. REV. 401 (2007); Gray, *supra* note 7, at 231.
36. James Boyle, *(When) Is Copyright Reform Possible?*, *in* COPYRIGHT LAW IN AN AGE OF LIMITATIONS AND EXCEPTIONS, 206–11 (Ruth Okediji ed., 2017).
37. Julie Cohen, *Between Truth and Power*, *in* FREEDOM AND PROPERTY OF INFORMATION: THE PHILOSOPHY OF LAW MEETS THE PHILOSOPHY OF TECHNOLOGY (Mireille Hildebrandt & Bibi van den Berg eds., 2014).
38. Gray, *supra* note 7, at 231.
39. DAVID HARVEY, A BRIEF HISTORY OF NEOLIBERALISM 2 (2007). I acknowledge that the concept and experience of neoliberalism is widely contested. In this book, I do not attempt a thorough critique of neoliberalism. Rather, I accept neoliberalism as a dominant political philosophy in recent decades and identify its influence on copyright theory, rhetoric, law, and policy. I follow political economy professor David Levi-Faur in his assessment that "much debate has taken place over the causes and impact of neoliberalism, but few doubt that neoliberalism has become an important part of our world." David Levi-Faur, *The Global Diffusion of Regulatory Capitalism*, 598 ANNALS AM. ACAD. POL. SOC. SCI. 12, 13 (2005).
40. Stephanie Lee Mudge, *What Is Neo-Liberalism?*, 6 SOCIO-ECON. REV. 703, 706–07 (2008).
41. David Harvey, *Neoliberalism as Creative Destruction*, 610 ANNALS AM. ACAD. POL. SOC. SCI. 22, 24 (2007); HARVEY, *supra* note 39, at 5.
42. HARVEY, *supra* note 39, at 5.
43. *Id.* at 64.
44. *Id.* at 2.

45. Maureen Ryan, *Cyberspace as Public Space: A Public Trust Paradigm for Copyright in a Digital World*, 79 OR. L. REV. 647, 657 (2000).

46. HARVEY, *supra* note 39, at 64. *See also* Julie E. Cohen, *Lochner in Cyberspace: The New Economic Orthodoxy of "Rights Management,"* 97 MICH. L. REV. 462, 481–82 (1998).

47. MILTON FRIEDMAN & ROSE FRIEDMAN, FREEDOM TO CHOOSE 58 (1980).

48. HARVEY, *supra* note 39, at 65. *See also* Damien Cahill, *"Actually Existing Neoliberalism" and the Global Economic Crisis*, 20 LABOUR IND. J. SOC. ECON. RELAT. WORK 298, 298 (2010); Benjamin Farrand, *Regulatory Capitalism, Decentered Enforcement, and Its Legal Consequences for Digital Expression: The Use of Copyright Law to Restrict Freedom of Speech Online*, 10 J. INF. TECH. POL. 404, 407 (2013).

49. HARVEY, *supra* note 39, at 65.

50. Mudge, *supra* note 40, at 704.

51. For an example from copyright law, *see, e.g.*, Joseph P. Liu, *Regulatory Copyright*, 83 N.C. L. REV. 87 (2004). Liu examines what he describes as the increasing willingness of the US Congress to "intervene in the structure of copyright markets." *Id.* at 91.

52. Farrand, *supra* note 48, at 407. Farrand argues there have been "twin effects" of neoliberal theories on copyright: "the primacy of property protection as a regulatory goal" and "the proliferation of self and intermediary-based regulation." *Id.* at 405. *See also* Levi-Faur, who posits that "at the ideological level neoliberalism promotes deregulation, at the practical level it promotes, or at least is accompanied by, regulation." Levi-Faur, *supra* note 39, at 14.

53. Farrand, *supra* note 48, at 413. *See also* Des Freedman, *The Internet of Rules: Critical Approaches to Online Regulation and Governance, in* MISUNDERSTANDING THE INTERNET (James Curran & Natalie Fenton eds., 2016).

54. *See* Lucas D. Introna & Helen Nissenbaum, *Shaping the Web: Why the Politics of Search Engines Matters*, 16 INF. SOC. 169, 170 (2000).

55. Weatherall, *supra* note 26, at 115.

56. *Id.*

57. *See, e.g.*, Robin Mansell, *New Visions, Old Practices: Policy and Regulation in the Internet Era*, 25 CONTINUUM 19, 22 (2011); Des Freedman, *Outsourcing Internet Regulation, in* MISUNDERSTANDING THE INTERNET 120 (James Curran & Natalie Fenton eds., 2016); Anupam Chander, *How Law Made Silicon Valley*, 63 EMORY L.J. 639, 648 (2013). Professor Chander submits:

> Silicon Valley's success in the Internet era has been due to key substantive reforms to American copyright and tort law that dramatically reduced the risks faced by Silicon Valley's new breed of global traders. Specifically, legal innovations in the 1990s that reduced liability concerns for Internet intermediaries, coupled with low privacy protections, created a legal ecosystem that proved fertile for the new enterprises. *Id.* at 642.

58. Chander, *supra* note 57, at 645.

59. For an examination of self-regulation models in the digital setting, *see, e.g.,* CHRISTOPHER T. MARSDEN, INTERNET CO-REGULATION: EUROPEAN LAW, REGULATORY GOVERNANCE AND LEGITIMACY IN CYBERSPACE (2011); D. TAMBINI, D. LEONARDI, & C. MARSDEN, CODIFYING CYBERSPACE: COMMUNICATIONS SELF-REGULATION IN THE AGE OF INTERNET CONVERGENCE (2007).

60. UNITED STATES SENATE, *supra* note 27, at 20.

61. There have been other multilateral intellectual property treaty undertakings since the signing of the Internet Treaties (and enactment of the DMCA); for example, World Intellectual Property Organization, *Marrakesh Treaty to Facilitate Access to Published Works for Persons Who Are Blind, Visually Impaired or Otherwise Print Disabled,* June 27, 2013.

62. Google, *supra* note 2.

63. Gray, *supra* note 7, at 231.

64. Broadly defined, an algorithm is a method or procedure for computing a function. Hartley Rogers, Jr. explains, "roughly speaking, an algorithm is a . . . procedure which can be applied to any of a certain class of symbolic *inputs* and which will eventually yield, for each such input, a corresponding symbolic *output.*" HARTLEY ROGERS JR., THEORY OF RECURSIVE FUNCTIONS AND EFFECTIVE COMPUTABILITY 1 (1987). In the context of the digital environment, broadly defined, "an algorithm is an instruction that we give to a computer in the form of some kind of program to ensure that it gives us a specific outcome." Keith Turvey, ALGORITHM SAGE KNOWLEDGE, http://sk.sagepub.com/video/algorithm (last visited Feb. 19, 2019).

65. Google announced this figure in 2016, and at time of writing there has been no further update by Google. Barry Schwartz, *Google Knows of 130 Trillion Pages on the Web—100 Trillion More in 4 Years,* SEARCH ENGINE ROUNDTABLE, Nov. 14, 2016, https://www.seroundtable.com/google-130-trillion-pages-22985.html (last visited Feb. 3, 2019); YouTube, *You know what's cool? A billion hours,* YOUTUBE OFFICIAL BLOG (Feb. 27, 2017), https://youtube.googleblog.com/2017/02/you-know-whats-cool-billion-hours.html.

66. Sergey Brin, *Playboy Interview: Google Guys, in* PROSPECTUS: GOOGLE CLASS A COMMON STOCK B-6, https://www.sec.gov/Archives/edgar/data/1288776/000119312504143377/d424b4.htm (last visited Feb. 3, 2019).

67. GOOGLE INC., GOOGLE ANNUAL REPORT 2015, at 13 (2015).

68. Google, *Ten things we know to be true Google,* https://www.google.com/about/philosophy.html (last visited Feb. 3, 2019).

69. *See* Google Algorithm Change History, MOZ, https://moz.com/google-algorithm-change (last visited Feb. 3, 2019).

70. Steven Levy, *Exclusive: How Google's Algorithm Rules the Web,* WIRED, 2010, https://www.wired.com/2010/02/ff_google_algorithm/ (last visited Feb. 3, 2019).

71. GOOGLE INC., *supra* note 1, at 23.

72. AdSense Help, GOOGLE, https://support.google.com/adsense/answer/9713?hl=en (last visited Feb. 3, 2019).

73. *Id.* Google, PRIVACY POLICY (2017), https://www.google.com/intl/en_JP/policies/privacy/archive/20170417/ (last visited Feb. 3, 2019). In 2017, Google announced it had stopped scanning emails sent through Gmail. Diane Greene, *As G Suite gains traction*

*in the enterprise, G Suite's Gmail and consumer Gmail to more closely align*, THE KEYWORD (June 23, 2017), https://blog.google/products/gmail/g-suite-gains-traction-in-the-enterprise-g-suites-gmail-and-consumer-gmail-to-more-closely-align/.

74. Google, *supra* note 73. Greene, *supra* note 73.

75. AdSense Help, *supra* note 72.

76. This figure is based on information reported in Google and Alphabet's US Annual Reports on Form 10-K; *see* Investor Relations: Numbers, ALPHABET, https://abc.xyz/investor/previous/#numbers (last visited Feb. 3, 2019).

77. GOOGLE, PROSPECTUS: GOOGLE CLASS A COMMON STOCK (2004), https://www.sec.gov/Archives/edgar/data/1288776/000119312504143377/d424b4.htm (last visited Feb. 3, 2019).

78. Statista reports Google has maintained between 80 and 90 percent market share of the global search engine market since 2010. Worldwide desktop market share of leading search engines from January 2010 to October 2018, STATISTA, https://www.statista.com/statistics/216573/worldwide-market-share-of-search-engines/ (last visited Feb. 3, 2019). Google's market share varies across jurisdictions. For example, in April 2017, Google's market share for search in China was below 2 percent. In December 2016, in the United States, Google held a 63.5 percent market share. In Europe, Google has maintained over 90 percent market share in search for several years. *See* CIW Team, *China search engine market share in Apr 2017*, CHINA INTERNET WATCH, 2017, https://www.chinainternetwatch.com/20538/search-engine-market-share-apr-2017/ (last visited Feb. 3, 2019); Greg Sterling, *Data: Google Monthly Search Volume Dwarfs Rivals Because of Mobile Advantage*, SEARCH ENGINE LAND, Feb. 9, 2017; Matt Rosoff, *Here's where Google dominates in Europe*, BUSINESS INSIDER AUSTRALIA, Apr. 21, 2016. *See also* Google Still Dominates the World Search Ad Market: The Search Giant Will Take in Nearly a Third of All Digital Ad Spending This Year, EMARKETER, July 26, 2016.

79. GOOGLE, *supra* note 77, at 73. Google also states: "we believe that our user focus is the foundation of our success to date. We also believe that this focus is critical for the creation of long-term value. We do not intend to compromise our user focus for short-term economic gain."

80. Matteo Pasquinelli, *Google's PageRank Algorithm: A Diagram of Cognitive Capitalism and the Rentier of the Common Intellect, in* DEEP SEARCH: THE POLITICS OF SEARCH ENGINES BEYOND GOOGLE 152, 161 (Konrad & Stalder Becker eds., 2009).

81. TIM WU, THE MASTER SWITCH 287 (2010).

82. *Id.* at 287.

## CHAPTER 2

1. With some exceptions, for copyright to subsist in a work, that work must be fixed in a tangible format. *See, e.g.*, 17 U.S.C. § 102(a) (2012). The digital environment has complicated copyright's fixation requirement. Professor Ira Brandriss reflects:

> say, you are "talking" on-line in real time as part of a chat group, where there may be not just one, but many, many "listeners" to what you have to say. You

may just stumble—as many of us do in conversation—into saying something brilliant. But all the words are only in RAM, seemingly but a transitory form. Copyrightable?

Ira Brandriss, *Writing in Frost on a Window Pane: E-Mail and Chatting on RAM and Copyright Fixation*, 43 J. COPYRIGHT SOC. USA 237, 238 (1996). *Cf.* Professor Jane Ginsburg, who posits, "in principle, the rights copyright confers will be the same whatever the format of the work, whether originally created in hard copy or in digital format, including . . . works created in whole or in part on digital networks." Jane C. Ginsburg, *Putting Cars on the "Information Superhighway": Authors, Exploiters, and Copyright in Cyberspace*, 95 COLUM. L. REV. 1466, 1475 (1995). For discussions on the issue of fixation and reproduction rights in the context of the digital environment, *see, e.g.*, David Nimmer, *Brains and Other Paraphernalia of the Digital Age*, 10 HARV. J.L. TECH. 1 (1996); Joseph P. Liu, *Owning Digital Copies: Copyright Law and the Incidents of Copy Ownership*, 42 WM. & MARY L. REV. 1245 (2001); Aaron Perzanowski, *Fixing Ram Copies*, 104 Nw. U. L. REV. 1067 (2010).

2. For the purpose of this description, the list of intermediaries is limited to the more conventional, predigital, model of intermediary. More recently, Google and other technology companies have emerged as additional intermediaries, providing infrastructure and services that disseminate works. As their business models do not center upon owning or controlling copyrights, these new intermediaries are substantially dissimilar to predigital intermediaries, conventionally defined. However, they do align with Professor Wu's modular copyright system analysis. Wu posits twenty-first-century copyright law comprises two regimes, authorship and communications, the latter regulating disseminators:

> The first regime is the familiar system, run by the courts, that grants exclusive rights to encourage creativity. The second is a messier regulatory regime comprised mainly of the sections of copyright that have always perplexed copyright theorists and have never fit the central theme of author-incentives. This *de facto* communications regime runs through the legislative process and the courts, and largely takes the form of industry specific liability rules, court created immunities, and special considerations.

Timothy Wu, *Copyright's Communications Policy*, 103 MICH. L. REV. 278, 279 (2004).

3. *See generally* Mark A. Lemley, *Romantic Authorship and the Rhetoric of Property*, 75 TEX. L. REV. 895 (1997).

4. Martha Woodmansee, *The Genius and the Copyright: Economic and Legal Conditions of the Emergence of the "Author,"* 17 EIGHTEENTH-CENTURY STUD. 425, 426 (1984). *See also* MARK ROSE, AUTHORS AND OWNERS: THE INVENTION OF COPYRIGHT (1993); Jessica Silbey, *The Mythical Beginnings of Intellectual Property*, 15 GEO. MASON L. REV. 319 (2008); Peter Jaszi, *Toward a Theory of Copyright: The Metamorphoses of "Authorship,"* 1991 DUKE L.J. 455 (1991).

5. Martha Woodmansee, *On the Author Effect: Recovering Collectivity*, 10 CARDOZO ARTS & ENT. L.J. 279, 280 (1992).

6. Woodmansee, *supra* note 5, at 427.

7. *Id.* at 434.

8. Martha Woodmansee, *On The Author Effect: Recovering Collectivity*, 10 CARDOZO ARTS ENTERTAIN. LAW J. 279, 280 (1992). Here Woodmansee presents writing from the 1753 *Allegemeines Oeconomisches Lexicon* by Georg Heinrich Zinck, describing the process for manufacturing a book.

9. Woodmansee, *supra* note 5, at 433.

10. *Id.* at 427.

11. William W. Fisher, *The Growth of Intellectual Property: A History of the Ownership of Ideas in the United States*, 1999, https://cyber.harvard.edu/people/tfisher/ iphistory.pdf (last visited Feb. 3, 2019); Woodmansee, *supra* note 5, at 427.

12. Woodmansee, *supra* note 5, at 430.

13. Carys J. Craig, *Reconstructing the Author-Self: Some Feminist Lessons for Copyright Law*, 15 AM. U. J. GEND. SOC. POL'Y L. 207, 212 (2006); Martha Woodmansee, *On The Author Effect: Recovering Collectivity*, 10 CARDOZO ARTS ENTERTAIN. LAW J. 279, 281 (1992).

14. Craig, *supra* note 13, at 213. Similar values were held in China, deriving from Confucian ethics. John Lehman describes, the "view of art as imitation, copying, and commentary became especially important with the Ming dynasty, where the primary role of literary creativity was to excel on the highly standardized literary section of the civil service exams." John Alan Lehman, *Intellectual Property Rights and Chinese Tradition Section: Philosophical Foundations*, 69 J. BUS. ETHICS 1, 5 (2006). Lehman further explains, "similarly, the view that art promotes socially useful knowledge or behavior (rather than expressing the artist's creativity or enter-taining people) is not a new theory which Chairman Mao inflicted on China; it is at least 2500 years old." *See also* WILLIAM P. ALFORD, TO STEAL A BOOK IS AN ELEGANT OFFENSE: INTELLECTUAL PROPERTY LAW IN CHINESE CIVILIZATION (1995).

15. Craig, *supra* note 13, at 220.

16. *See* Solee I. Shin & Lanu Kim, *Organizing K-Pop: Emergence and Market Making of Large Korean Entertainment Houses, 1980–2010*, 30 EAST ASIA INT. Q. 255 (2013).

17. PETER ACKROYD, CHAUCER: ACKROYD'S BRIEF LIVES 45 (2007). *See also* KENNETH MUIR, THE SOURCES OF SHAKESPEARE'S PLAYS (2009).

18. John Carlin, *Culture Vultures: Artistic Appropriation and Intellectual Property Law*, 13 COLUM.—VLA J.L. ARTS 103, 108 (1988). Indeed, Pablo Picasso is credited as saying, "Good artists borrow, great artists steal." Rebecca Tushnet, *Copy This Essay: How Fair Use Doctrine Harms Free Speech and How Copying Serves It*, 114 YALE L.J. 535, 552 (2004).

19. Carlin, *supra* note 18, at 106. *See also* Fisher, *supra* note 11, at 16–17.

20. *Mark Ronson at TED2014: How Sampling Transformed Music*, TED (May 9, 2014), https://www.ted.com/talks/mark_ronson_how_sampling_transformed_music/ up-next.

21. Craig, *supra* note 13, at 265; Madhavi Sunder, *IP3*, 59 STAN. L. REV. 257, 324 (2006).

22. *See* Julie E. Cohen, *Creativity and Culture in Copyright Theory (Symposium: Intellectual Property and Social Justice)*, 40 UC DAVIS L. REV. 1151, 1183 (2007). *See also* Julie C.

Van Camp, *Originality in Postmodern Appropriation Art*, 36 J. ARTS MGMT. L. SOC'Y 247–58, 255 (2007).

23. Sunder, *supra* note 21, at 324. *See also* JULIE E. COHEN, CONFIGURING THE NETWORKED SELF (2012); Cohen, *supra* note 22; Craig, *supra* note 13.

24. COHEN, *supra* note 23, at 83–84, 107.

25. *Id.* at 85.

26. *Id.* at 93–94.

27. *See* William Fisher, *Theories of Intellectual Property*, *in* NEW ESSAYS IN THE LEGAL AND POLITICAL THEORY OF PROPERTY 168, 168 (Stephen Munzer ed., 2001).

28. For example, Locke wrote: "thus this law of reason makes the deer that Indian's who hath killed it; it is allowed to be his goods, who hath bestowed his labour upon it, though before it was the common right of every one." JOHN LOCKE, TWO TREATISES ON GOVERNMENT 211–12 (1821). *See also* Fisher, *supra* note 27, at 170.

29. Justin Hughes, *The Philosophy of Intellectual Property*, 77 GEO. L.J. 287, 302 (1988).

30. *Id.* at 310. Locke's labor theory of value features a condition or "proviso." Locke stipulated that when obtaining property through labor, "no man but he can have a right to what that is once joined to, at least where there is enough, and as good, left in common for others." LOCKE, *supra* note 28 at 210. Professor Adam Moore explains, "the underlying rationale of Locke's proviso is that if no one's situation is worsened, then no one can complain about another individual appropriating part of the commons. If no one is harmed by an acquisition and one person is bettered, then the acquisition ought to be permitted." Adam D. Moore, *A Lockean Theory of Intellectual Property Revisited*, 49 SAN DIEGO L. REV. 1069, 1072 (2012).

31. Adam Mossoff, *Savings Locke from Marx: The Labor Theory of Value in Intellectual Property Theory*, 29 SOC. PHIL. POL'Y 283 (2012).

32. *Id.* at 297.

33. *Id.* at 298.

34. Stewart E. Sterk, *Rhetoric and Reality in Copyright Law*, 94 MICH. L. REV. 1197, 1236 (1996).

35. CREDIT SUISSE RESEARCH INSTITUTE, GLOBAL WEALTH REPORT 2015 4 (2015).

36. FABRICE MURTIN & MIRA D'ERCOLE, HOUSEHOLD WEALTH INEQUALITY ACROSS OECD COUNTRIES: NEW OECD EVIDENCE 1 (2015).

37. Edwin C. Hettinger, *Justifying Intellectual Property*, 18 PHIL. PUB. AFF. 31, 41 (1989). *See also* Fisher, *supra* note 27, at 188.

38. Stanley C. Brubaker, *Coming into One's Own: John Locke's Theory of Property, God, and Politics*, 74 REV. POLIT. 207 (2012). *See generally* C. B. MACPHERSON, THE POLITICAL THEORY OF POSSESSIVE INDIVIDUALISM: HOBBES TO LOCKE (1962).

39. Hughes adopts this approach: "my own view is that a labor theory of intellectual property is powerful, but incomplete. I believe we also need the support of a personality theory, such as the one proposed by Hegel, in which property is justified as an expression of the self." Hughes, *supra* note 29, at 329. *See also* Fisher, *supra* note 27, at 171.

40. BENEDICT A. C. ATKINSON & BRIAN F. FITZGERALD, A SHORT HISTORY OF COPYRIGHT: THE GENIE OF INFORMATION 35–36 (2014).

41. G. W. F. HEGEL, PHILOSOPHY OF RIGHT xlix (2008).

42. *Id.* at xlix.
43. Hughes, *supra* note 29, at 331. *See also* William W. Fisher, *The Implications for Law of User Innovation (Cyberspace and the Law: Privacy, Property, and Crime in the Virtual Frontier)*, 94 Minn. L. Rev. 1417, 1451 (2010).
44. Hughes, *supra* note 29, at 330. Personality theory underpins the doctrine of moral rights, from the European tradition of copyright. Moral rights operate on the assumption that authors have an important personal connection to their work and moral rights regimes often include, for example, the rights of attribution, integrity, disclosure, and withdrawal; providing an author the right to receive continued recognition for their work, control over modifications of their work, and control over when a work is available to the public. *See, e.g.*, Cyrill P. Rigamonti, *Deconstructing Moral Rights*, 47 Harv. Int'l L.J. 353, 355 (2006). *See also* France's intellectual property code, which provides authors *droits moraux*, including rights of attribution, integrity, disclosure, modification, or withdrawal *Code de la propriété intellectuelle* art. L121-1–L121-9 (1992). Moral rights are usually inalienable and apply only to the author, the actual creator of the work, not to any associated interests. *See, e.g.*, Berne Convention for the Protection of Literary and Artistic Works, art. 6bis(1), Dec. 5, 1887, which provides:

    > Independently of the author's economic rights, and even after the transfer of the said rights, the author shall have the right to claim authorship of the work and to object to any distortion, mutilation or other modification of, or other derogatory action in relation to, the said work, which would be prejudicial to his honor or reputation.

45. Jeanne C. Fromer, *Expressive Incentives in Intellectual Property*, 98 Va. L. Rev. 1745, 1770 (2012).
46. *Id.* at 1778.
47. *See* William W. Fisher III, *Reconstructing the Fair Use Doctrine*, Harv. L. Rev. 1659, 1700 (1988).
48. Fisher, *supra* note 27, at 169.
49. William M. Landes & Richard A. Posner, *An Economic Analysis of Copyright Law*, 18 J. Leg. Stud. 325, 325 (1989).
50. *See, e.g.*, Fisher III, *supra* note 47, at 1702.
51. Brett M. Frischmann, *Evaluating the Demsetzian Trend in Copyright Law (New Directions in Copyright Law and Economics)*, 3 Rev. L. Econ. 649, 666 (2007). *See also* Fisher III, *supra* note 47, at 1699. Frischmann, *supra* note at 658.
52. Fisher III, *supra* note 47, at 1703.
53. Yochai Benkler, *Freedom in the Commons: Towards a Political Economy of Information*, 52 Duke L.J. 1245, 1264 (2003); Maureen Ryan, *Cyberspace as Public Space: A Public Trust Paradigm for Copyright in a Digital World*, 79 Or. L. Rev. 647, 657 (2000).
54. Ryan, *supra* note 53, at 656. Ryan makes a distinction between the incentive justification as rhetoric and the neoclassical justification in practice: the incentive justification is used rhetorically to claim copyright should be crafted to incentivize

creative production, while the neoclassical approach in practice claims free markets should be used to direct copyright production. *Id.* at 649, 657.

55. Amy Kapczynski, *Intellectual Property's Leviathan*, 77 L. & Contemp. Probs. 131, 132 (2014).

56. *See* Landes & Posner, *supra* note 49, at 327.

57. Sunder, *supra* note 21, at 303. *See also* Fisher, *supra* note 43, at 1431.

58. Cohen, *supra* note 23, at 51–52.

59. *Id.*

60. Julie E. Cohen, *Lochner in Cyberspace: The New Economic Orthodoxy of "Rights Management,"* 97 Mich. L. Rev. 462. *See also* Ryan, "neoclassical economic theory equates public interest with a maximization of total social wealth, regardless of the distribution of that wealth." Ryan, *supra* note 53, at 685.

61. Martha Nussbaum, *Constitutions and Capabilities: "Perception" Against Lofty Formalism*, 121 Harv. L. Rev. 4, 19 (2007).

62. Jane C. Ginsburg, *The Role of the Author in Copyright*, in Copyright Law in an Age of Limitations and Exceptions 60, 67 (Ruth L. Okediji ed., 2017).

63. Craig, *supra* note 13, at 233.

64. Jessica Silbey, Eureka Myth Creators, Innovators, and Everyday Intellectual Property 12 (2014).

65. A cultural theory of copyright is an approach explored by legal scholars such as Professors William Fisher, Julie Cohen, Neil Natanel, Yochai Benkler, Madhavi Sunder, Oren Bracha, and Talha Syed, each with their own theoretical proposals. The works of all of these scholars and others inform this chapter, however, my framework broadly aligns with cultural democracy theory summarized by Bracha and Syed. Accordingly, I use cultural theory to describe an "eclectic yet loosely connected group of normative accounts of intellectual property" and, as Bracha contends, although the "various accounts do not form one coherent and uniform theory . . . Nevertheless these accounts do share a strong family resemblance and many common features, arguments and commitments." Oren Bracha, *Standing Copyright Law on Its Head? The Googlization of Everything and the Many Faces of Property (Symposium: Frontiers of Intellectual Property)*, 85 Tex. L. Rev. 1799, 1843 (2007). *See also* Oren Bracha & Talha Syed, *Beyond Efficiency: Consequence-Sensitive Theories of Copyright*, 29 Berkeley Tech. L.J. 229 (2014).

66. Sunder, *supra* note 21, at 257. Sunder also suggests copyright should be understood as regulating social and cultural relations. *Id.* at 274.

67. *See generally* Fisher III, *supra* note 47, at 1744–62.

68. *Id.* at 1746.

69. Barbara L. Fredrickson & Marcial F. Losada, *Positive Affect and the Complex Dynamics of Human Flourishing*, 60 Am. Psychol. 678, 678 (2005).

70. For a more detailed discussion on cultural theory and human flourishing, *see* Fisher, *supra* note 43, at 1463. An important contribution to cultural theory is the capabilities approach advanced by philosophers Amartya Sen and Martha Nussbaum. The capabilities approach is a political philosophy in which the fundamental purpose of the law and government "is to secure for all citizens the prerequisites of a life worthy of human dignity." Nussbaum, *supra* note 61. Amartya Sen, *Capability and*

*Well-Being, in* THE QUALITY OF LIFE 30 (Amartya Sen & Martha C. Nussbaum eds., 1993). These prerequisites "range from basic needs, such as the right to life and health, to more expansive freedoms of movement, creative work, and participation in social, economic, and cultural institutions." Sunder, *supra* note 21, at 313. The capabilities approach proposes all people deserve respect and critical to providing respect is the ability to make meaningful choices regarding the state of one's own existence. Nussbaum, *supra* note 61, at 10. According to Nussbaum, "People come into the world with rudimentary abilities to lead a dignified life. These abilities, however, need support from the world, especially the political world, if they are to develop and become effective." *Id.* at 11. In this way, the capabilities approach draws upon liberal ideals, but it is not limited to economic considerations.

71. Bracha & Syed, *supra* note 65, at 254.
72. *Id.* at 255.
73. *Id.* at 255.
74. Jack M. Balkin, *Digital Speech and Democratic Culture: A Theory of Freedom of Expression for the Information Society*, 79 N.Y.U. L. REV. 1, 36 (2004).
75. TIM WU, THE MASTER SWITCH 12 (2010).
76. YOCHAI BENKLER, THE WEALTH OF NETWORKS: HOW SOCIAL PRODUCTION TRANSFORMS MARKETS AND FREEDOM 141 (2006). *See also* WU, *supra* note 75, at 302.
77. BENKLER, *supra* note 76, at 129.
78. Sunder, *supra* note 21, at 267.
79. Bracha, *supra* note 65, at 1846.
80. Balkin, *supra* note 74, at 3–4.
81. Bracha & Syed, *supra* note 65, at 256.
82. Bracha, *supra* note 65, at 1846–47.
83. *Id.* at 1846.
84. *Id.* at 1845.
85. For discussions on the links between information, media and democracy, *see, e.g.*, Saima Saeed, *Negotiating Power: Community Media, Democracy, and the Public Sphere*, 19 DEV. PRAC. 466 (2009); Richard van der Wurff, *Do Audiences Receive Diverse Ideas from News Media? Exposure to a Variety of News Media and Personal Characteristics as Determinants of Diversity as Received*, 26 EUR. J. COMM. 328 (2011); James Bohman, *Political Communication and the Epistemic Value of Diversity: Deliberation and Legitimation in Media Societies*, 17 COMM. THEORY 348 (2017); Serena Carpenter, *A Study of Content Diversity in Online Citizen Journalism and Online Newspaper Articles*, 12 NEW MEDIA SOC. 1064 (2010); Antonio Ciaglia, *Pluralism of the System, Pluralism in the System*, 75 INT'L COMM. GAZ. 410 (2013); D. Raeijmaekers & P. Maeseele, *Media, Pluralism and Democracy: What's in a Name?*, 37 MEDIA CULTURE SOC'Y 1042, 1042 (2015).
86. Bracha, *supra* note 65, at 1844.
87. Sunder, *supra* note 21, at 259; Joanne Gray, *Copyright According to Google, in* COPYRIGHT, PROPERTY AND THE SOCIAL CONTRACT 227, 238 (John Gilchrist & Brian Fitzgerald eds., 2018).
88. Cohen, *supra* note 22, at 1177, 1183.

89. Sunder, *supra* note 21, at 323.

90. Bracha, *supra* note 65, at 1807.

91. Rebecca Tushnet, *Economies of Desire: Fair Use and Marketplace Assumptions (Boundaries of Intellectual Property Symposium)*, 51 WM. & MARY L. REV. 513, 539 (2009).

92. Netanel Neil Weinstock, *Asserting Copyright's Democratic Principles in the Global Arena*, 51 VAND. L. REV. 218, 227 (1998).

93. Fisher, *supra* note 27, at 192. Fisher III, *supra* note 47, at 1762–66.

94. Bracha, *supra* note 65, at 1807. Netanel relates, "while the democratic paradigm may incorporate neoclassicist insights about how copyright operates in the market, it makes clear that copyright's paramount objective is not allocative efficiency, but citizen participation in democratic self-rule." Neil Weinstock Netanel, *Copyright and a Democratic Civil Society*, YALE L.J. 283, 386 (1996). According to Netanel, copyright should "circumscribe the propertization [*sic*] of publicly disseminated expression, even as it grants a limited monopoly over the use of expression." *Id.* at 363.

95. Balkin, *supra* note 74, at 57.

96. BENKLER, *supra* note 76, at 175.

97. Niva Elkin-Koren, *Cyberlaw and Social Change: A Democratic Approach to Copyright Law in Cyberspace*, 14 CARDOZO ARTS & ENT. L.J. 215, 236 (1996).

98. *Id.* at 267.

99. Sonia K. Katyal, *The New Surveillance*, 54 CASE W. RES. L. REV. 297, 299 (2003).

100. Christian Fuchs, *Information and Communication Technologies and Society a Contribution to the Critique of the Political Economy of the Internet*, 24 EUR. J. COMM. 69, 77 (2009).

101. SHEILA JASANOFF, THE ETHICS OF INVENTION: TECHNOLOGY AND THE HUMAN FUTURE 167 (2016).

102. Balkin, *supra* note 74, at 52.

## CHAPTER 3

1. Andrew McLaughlin, *Google Goes to Washington*, GOOGLE OFFICIAL BLOG (Oct. 6, 2005), https://googleblog.blogspot.com.au/2005/10/google-goes-to-washington.html.

2. *Id.*

3. This figure was derived from the data collated by the Center for Responsive Politics. The Center for Responsible Politics compiles US lobbying data using disclosure reports filed with the Secretary of the Senate's Office of Public Records. The category selected by Google most frequently on its disclosure reports was "Copyright, Patent, Trademark." *See* Google Inc., THE CENTER FOR RESPONSIVE POLITICS, https://www.opensecrets.org/pacs/lookup2.php?strID=C00428623 (last visited Jan. 31, 2019).

4. The number of registered meetings provides an indication of lobbying activity within the European Union. The second most active company for the same period was Microsoft Corporation with 111 meetings, followed by Shell Companies with 60 meetings. *See* Statistics, LOBBY FACTS, https://lobbyfacts.eu/reports/

lobby-costs/all/0/2/2/2/21/0?sort=meetings&order=desc (last visited Jan. 31, 2019). The European Commission's Transparency Register reports Google spent between €6,000,000 and €6,249,999 on lobbying in 2017. *See* Europa Transparency Register, EUROPEAN UNION, http://ec.europa.eu/transparencyregister/public/consultation/displaylobbyist.do?id=03181945560-59 (last visited Jan. 31, 2019).

5.  Sergey Brin, *2010 Founders' Letter*, ALPHABET (2010), https://abc.xyz/investor/founders-letters/2010/. Page and Brin's involvement with the open source movement informs their belief in the democratizing power of technology. Page explains, "Sergey and I (and Google) grew up with Linux and we have all benefited greatly from that open model. We believe that it is a great way to run a healthy and vibrant high tech ecosystem." Larry Page & Sergey Brin, *2009 Founders' Letter*, ALPHABET (2009), https://abc.xyz/investor/founders-letters/2009/. Several of Google's products are open source—including Chrome, Chrome OS, Maps, and Android—and Google posits that by making these products open source they are encouraging innovation by other developers. Google's Counsel for Public Policy and Government Affairs, Matt Dawes, explains: "our open platforms and services like Android and Google Maps enable other technology developers to create new phones, web services and applications within their own products." Matt Dawes, ALRC REVIEW—COPYRIGHT AND THE DIGITAL ECONOMY TO PROFESSOR JILL MCKEOUGH 7 (2012). Of course, said technology developers are innovating and creating within the parameters of Google's platforms.

6.  Jim Lecinski, *Growing America's Businesses Online*, GOOGLE PUBLIC POLICY BLOG (July 17, 2014), https://publicpolicy.googleblog.com/2014/07/growing-americas-businesses-online.html.

7.  Larry Page & Sergey Brin, 2004 FOUNDERS' IPO LETTER ALPHABET (2004), https://abc.xyz/investor/founders-letters/2004/ipo-letter.html.

8.  Brin, *supra* note 5.

9.  *Id.*

10. KEN AULETTA, GOOGLED: THE END OF THE WORLD AS WE KNOW IT 33 (2010). Similarly, Sergey Brin lists physicist Richard P. Feynman, Apple's Steve Jobs, and billionaire Warren Buffett as "heroes." Brin, *supra* note 5.

11. *See, e.g.*, Brin, *supra* note 5.

12. Richard Barbrook & Andy Cameron, *The Californian Ideology*, 6 SCI. CULT. 44 (1996).

13. *Id.* at 49. Technological determinism refers to the belief "that technologies have a built-in momentum that shapes and drives the course of history." SHEILA JASANOFF, THE ETHICS OF INVENTION: TECHNOLOGY AND THE HUMAN FUTURE 247 (2016). For a historical account of the initial convergence of San Francisco's counterculture and Silicon Valley, *see* FRED TURNER, FROM COUNTERCULTURE TO CYBERCULTURE: STEWART BRAND, THE WHOLE EARTH NETWORK, AND THE RISE OF DIGITAL UTOPIANISM (2010).

14. Barbrook & Cameron, *supra* note 12, at 45.

15. Mihaela Kelemen & Warren Smith, *Community and Its "Virtual" Promises: A Critique of Cyberlibertarian Rhetoric*, 4 INF. COMM. SOC'Y 370, 371 (2001).

16. Brin, *supra* note 5.

17.  Barbrook & Cameron, *supra* note 12, at 56. *See also* Paulina Borsook, *Cyberselfish: Ravers, Guilders, Cypherpunks, and Other Silicon Valley Life-Forms*, 3 YALE J.L. TECH. 4 (2001). Consider too Evgeny Morozov's critique of Silicon Valley's technological solutionism, a mindset that any phenomenon can become a "problem" simply because technology can provide a solution:

> They are driven by a pervasive and dangerous ideology that I call "solutionism": an intellectual pathology that recognizes problems as problems based on just one criterion: whether they are "solvable" with a nice and clean technological solution at our disposal . . . and not because we've weighed all the philosophical pros and cons.

Evgeny Morozov, *The Perils of Perfection*, N.Y. TIMES, Mar. 2, 2013, http://www.nytimes.com/2013/03/03/opinion/sunday/the-perils-of-perfection.html.

18.  *See also* Oren Bracha & Frank Pasquale, *Federal Search Commission? Access, Fairness, and Accountability in the Law of Search*, 93 CORNELL L. REV. 1149, 1157 (2008).

19.  Google, SUBMISSION TO PRODUCTIVITY COMMISSION ISSUES PAPER "BUSINESS SETUP, TRANSFER AND CLOSURE" 5 (2015), http://www.pc.gov.au/__data/assets/pdf_file/0004/188122/sub037-business.pdf.

20.  Dawes, *supra* note 5, at 22.

21.  Google, SUBMISSION TO THE COPYRIGHT REVIEW COMMITTEE (IRELAND) 2 (2011), https://dbei.gov.ie/en/Consultations/Consultations-files/Google.pdf.

22.  Google, SUBMISSION TO ISSUES PAPER COMPETITION POLICY REVIEW (AUSTRALIA) 14 (2014), http://competitionpolicyreview.gov.au/files/2014/06/Google.pdf.

23.  *Id.*

24.  Google, *supra* note 19, at 6.

25.  John Ure, COMMENTS ON THE HONG KONG COPYRIGHT LAW—PARODY EXCEPTION TO DIVISION 3 COMMERCE INDUSTRY AND TOURISM BRANCH COMMERCE AND ECONOMIC DEVELOPMENT BUREAU OF HONG KONG 1 (2013). In 2010, Google and eBay founded the Asian Internet Coalition with the objective of promoting "the understanding and resolution of Internet policy issues in the Asia Pacific region" with current members including Yahoo, Apple, Facebook, LinkedIn, and Twitter. *About,* ASIAN INTERNET COALITION, https://www.aicasia.org/about/ (last visited Feb. 5, 2019).

26.  Google, GOOGLE CONTRIBUTION ON CREATIVE CONTENT ONLINE 7 (2008), http://ec.europa.eu/archives/information_society/avpolicy/docs/other_actions/col_2008/comp/google_en.pdf.

27.  Google, GOOGLE SUBMISSION TO ALRC DISCUSSION PAPER COPYRIGHT IN THE DIGITAL ECONOMY (ALRC DP 79) 17 (2013), http://www.alrc.gov.au/sites/default/files/subs/600._org_google.pdf.

28.  Google, GOOGLE AUSTRALIA'S SUBMISSION TO THE PRODUCTIVITY COMMISSION INTELLECTUAL PROPERTY ARRANGEMENTS ISSUES PAPER 10 (2015), https://www.pc.gov.au/__data/assets/pdf_file/0011/194861/sub102-intellectual-property.pdf. *See also* Google: "in today's digital world, properly understood, copyright must be a key plank in Australia's innovation policy." *Id.* at 1.

29. *Id.* at 1.

30. Dawes, *supra* note 5, at 6.

31. Google, SUBMISSION TO THE INDEPENDENT REVIEW OF INTELLECTUAL PROPERTY AND GROWTH (UK) 3 (2011), https://webarchive.nationalarchives.gov.uk/20140603125526/http://www.ipo.gov.uk/ipreview-c4e-sub-google.pdf.

32. Google, *supra* note 28, at 10.

33. Google, *supra* note 31, at 9.

34. *Id.* at 3.

35. *Id.* at 9.

36. *Id.* at 9.

37. Google, *supra* note 28, at 11.

38. Google, *supra* note 31, at 6.

39. Carolyn Dalton, CONSULTATION DRAFT: DIGITAL ECONOMY FUTURE DIRECTIONS PAPER TO DEPARTMENT OF BROADBAND COMMUNICATIONS AND THE DIGITAL ECONOMY (AUSTRALIA) 2 (2009).

40. Ishtar Vij, NATIONAL CULTURAL POLICY TO OFFICE FOR THE ARTS DEPARTMENT OF THE PRIME MINISTER AND CABINET (AUSTRALIA) 1 (2011).

 41. GOOGLE, PUBLIC CONSULTATION ON THE REVIEW OF THE EU COPYRIGHT RULES 14 (2013); *Id*, at 1.

42. GOOGLE, *supra* note 41, at 13.

43. Dawes, *supra* note 5, at 35. Google has also tacitly rejected the theory that economic incentive is necessary for creative practice, stating, "copyright provides an additional, economic incentive for the creation and dissemination of new works, to complement the natural human instinct to be creative." Google, *supra* note 31, at 2.

 44. GOOGLE, *supra* note 41, at 13.

45. *Id.*

46. Google, SUBMISSION TO THE COPYRIGHT REVIEW COMMITTEE (IRELAND) 8 (2012), https://dbei.gov.ie/en/Consultations/Consultations-files/Google1.pdf.

47. Google, *supra* note 27, at 3.

48. Kent Walker, *The Trans-Pacific Partnership: A step forward for the Internet*, THE KEYWORD (June 10, 2016), https://blog.google/topics/public-policy/the-trans-pacific-partnership-step/.

49. Trans-Pacific Partnership Agreement, Feb. 4, 2016. The TPP also includes a requirement for safe harbors for online intermediaries at arts 18.81–82.

50. Google New Zealand, TRANS-PACIFIC PARTNERSHIP AGREEMENT AMENDMENT BILL TO THE COMMITTEE SECRETARIAT FOREIGN AFFAIRS, DEFENCE AND TRADE SELECT COMMITTEE (NEW ZEALAND) (2016).

51. Google, *supra* note 31, at 3; *Id.* at 2.

52. *See, e.g.*, Australia's fair dealings exception Copyright Act 1968 (Cth) § 103A–103C (2018).

53. 17 U.S.C. § 107 (2012).

54. 17 U.S.C. § 107(1) (2012).

55. Campbell v. Acuff-Rose Music Inc., 510 U.S. 569, 579 (1994).

56. 17 U.S.C. § 107(2) (2012).

57. *See, e.g.*, Blanch v. Koons, 467 F. 3d 244 (2d Cir. 2006).

58. 17 U.S.C. § 107(3) (2012).

59. *See, e.g.*, Castle Rock Entertainment v. Carol Publishing Group, 159 F. 3d 132 (2d Cir. 1998).

60. 17 U.S.C. § 107(4) (2012).

61. Campbell v. Acuff-Rose Music Inc., 510 U.S. 569, 578 (1994); Kelly v. Arriba Soft Corp., 336 F. 3d 811, 818 (9th Cir. 2003); US Const. art. I § 8 cl 8.

62. Google, *supra* note 31, at 3.

63. Google, *supra* note 28, at 18.

64. *Id.* at 2, 17.

65. This assertion has been put forward, for example, by scholars contributing to the debate in Australia over the possible introduction of a flexible fair use exception to replace Australia's static fair dealings exception. *See, e.g.*, Professors June Besek, Jane Ginsburg, and Philippa Loengard, who submitted, "many in the United States—including users, legal practitioners and courts—do not regard the law of fair use as consistent and predictable, although they wish it were. The US benefits from the flexibility of the fair use exceptions, but that flexibility comes at a cost." JUNE M. BESEK, JANE C. GINSBURG, & PHILIPPA S. LOENGARD, COMMENTS ON ALRC DISCUSSION PAPER 79 COPYRIGHT AND THE DIGITAL ECONOMY 6 (2013).

66. Google, GOOGLE AUSTRALIA'S SUBMISSION TO THE PRODUCTIVITY COMMISSION'S DRAFT REPORT INTO INTELLECTUAL PROPERTY ARRANGEMENTS 4 (2016), http://www.pc.gov.au/__data/assets/pdf_file/0018/201546/subdr523-intellectual-property.pdf.

67. Google, *supra* note 28, at 31.

68. Dawes, *supra* note 5, at 1.

69. Google, *supra* note 28, at 2.

70. Google, GOOGLE'S RESPONSE TO THE GOVERNMENT CONSULTATION ON PROPOSALS TO CHANGE THE UK'S COPYRIGHT SYSTEM 1 (2012).

71. Google, *supra* note 31, at 4–5.

72. *Id.* at 4; Joanne Gray, *Copyright According to Google*, *in* COPYRIGHT, PROPERTY AND THE SOCIAL CONTRACT 227, 233 (John Gilchrist & Brian Fitzgerald eds., 2018).

73. Google, *supra* note 31, at 8.

74. Google, *supra* note 27, at 1.

75. Google, *supra* note 31, at 4.

76. Google, *supra* note 66, at 4.

77. Google, *supra* note 31, at 6.

78. *Id.* at 4.

79. Google, *supra* note 28, at 29.

80. Dawes, *supra* note 5, at 14.

81. *Id.* at 14.

82. Google, *supra* note 31, at 4.

83. Google, *supra* note 46, at 42.

84. *Id.* at 45.

85. Gray, *supra* note 72, at 235.

86. Google, *supra* note 31, at 5.

87.  17 U.S.C. § 512(a)–(d) (2012).

88.  17 U.S.C. § 512(k)(1)(B) (2012).

89.  *See* 17 U.S.C. § 512(i)(1)(A) (2012), 17 U.S.C. § 512(i)(1)(B) (2012) and 512(i)(2) (2012).

90.  Google, Testimony of Katherine Oyama, Sr. Copyright Policy Counsel, Google Inc. House Judiciary Subcommittee on Courts, Intellectual Property, and the Internet. Hearing on "Section 512 of Title 17" 3 (2014), https://docs.house.gov/meetings/JU/JU03/20140313/101837/HHRG-113-JU03-Wstate-OyamaK-20140313.pdf.

91.  *Id.*

92.  *See* 17 U.S.C. § 512(c)–(d) (2012).

93.  Google, Re: Section 512 Study: Notice and Request for Public Comment Docket No. 2015-7 (December 31, 2015) to The Honorable Maria A. Pallante Register of Copyrights U.S. Copyright Office 7 (2016).

94.  *Id.*

95.  *Id.*

96.  *Id.* at 1.

97.  Google, *supra* note 31, at 5.

98.  Google, *supra* note 93, at 3.

99.  *Id.* at 5–6.

100. Asian Internet Coalition, AIC's Response to the Proposal to "Strengthen Copyright Protection in the Digital Environment", email to The Secretary for Commerce and Economic Development, Hong Kong 4 (2010).

101. John Ure, Comments on the Proposed Amendments to Thailand's Copyright Act B.E. 2537 to Nitwattumrong Boonsongpaisan Deputy Prime Minister and Minister of Commerce Ministry of Commerce Thailand 2 (2013).

102. Ishtar Vij, Revising the Scope of the Copyright Safe Harbour Scheme to Attorney-General's Department 2 (2011)

103. *Id.*; Gray, *supra* note 72, at 236.

104. European Commission, Copyright—Commission Launches Public Consultation (2013), http://europa.eu/rapid/press-release_IP-13-1213_en.htm?locale=en.

105. Google, *supra* note 41, at 9.

106. *Id.* at 10.

107. *Id.* at 16; Gray, *supra* note 72, at 232.

108. *Id.* at 7.

109. *Id.* at 8.

110. Google, *supra* note 105.

111. *Id.* at 10.

112. Google, *supra* note 93, at 10.

113. Google, *supra* note 105.

114. *Id.*

115. *See* Article 13, The European Parliament and the Council of the European Union, Proposal for a Directive of the European Parliament and of

THE COUNCIL ON COPYRIGHT IN THE DIGITAL SINGLE MARKET (2019), http://
www.europarl.europa.eu/meetdocs/2014_2019/plmrep/COMMITTEES/JURI/
DV/2019/02-26/Copyright-AnnextoCOREPERletter_EN.pdf.

116.   YouTube, SAVE YOUR INTERNET, https://www.youtube.com/saveyourinternet/
       (last visited Nov. 14, 2018).

117.   Susan Wojcicki, *A Final Update on Our Priorities for 2018*, YOUTUBE CREATOR
       BLOG (Oct. 22, 2018), https://youtube-creators.googleblog.com/2018/10/a-final-
       update-on-our-priorities-for.html.

118.   Iarla Flynn, DEREGULATION: INITIATIVES IN THE COMMUNICATIONS SECTOR TO
       THE HON MALCOM TURNBULL MP MINISTER FOR COMMUNICATIONS 5 (2013);
       Gray, *supra* note 72, at 232.

119.   Asian Internet Coalition, AIC's RESPONSE TO THE HONG KONG COPYRIGHT
       (AMENDMENT) BILL 2011 (2011).

120.   Google, *supra* note 93, at 2.

121.   Flynn, *supra* note 118, at 5; Vij, *supra* note 40, at 10.

122.   Google, *supra* note 93, at 4.

123.   *Id.* at 4.

124.   Google, *supra* note 28, at 5.

125.   Google, *supra* note 93, at 3.

126.   GOOGLE, *supra* note 105, at 12.

127.   *Id.* at 12–24.

128.   *Id.* at 24.

129.   Pablo L. Chavez, COMMENTS: DEPARTMENT OF COMMERCE GREEN PAPER,
       COPYRIGHT POLICY, CREATIVITY AND INNOVATION IN THE DIGITAL ECONOMY
       TO THE HONORABLE TERESA STANEK REA DEPUTY UNDER SECRETARY OF
       COMMERCE FOR INTELLECTUAL PROPERTY AND DEPUTY DIRECTOR OF THE
       UNITED STATES PATENT AND TRADEMARK OFFICE AND THE HONORABLE
       LAWRENCE E. STRICKLING ASSISTANT SECRETARY OF COMMERCE FOR
       COMMUNICATIONS AND INFORMATION UNITED STATES DEPARTMENT OF
       COMMERCE (2013).

130.   *Id.*

131.   Google, *supra* note 26, at 9.

132.   *Id.*

133.   Google, ONLINE COPYRIGHT INFRINGEMENT DISCUSSION PAPER (AUSTRALIA)
       3–4 (2014).

134.   *Id.* at 7.

135.   Gray, *supra* note 72, at 238.

CHAPTER 4

1.   *See* Google, GOOGLEBOT SEARCH CONSOLE HELP, https://support.google.com/
     webmasters/answer/182072?hl=en.

2.   Google, BLOCK URLS WITH ROBOTS.TXT SEARCH CONSOLE HELP, https://
     support.google.com/webmasters/answer/6062608?hl=en.

3.   Field v. Google Inc., 412 F. Supp. 2d 1106, 1110 (D. Nev. 2006).

4.   *Id.* at 1113.

5.  *Id.* at 1109

6.  Miquel Peguera, *When the Cached Link Is the Weakest Link: Search Engine Caches Under the Digital Millennium Copyright Act*, 56 J. COPYRIGHT SOC'Y USA 589, 592 (2009). Peguera also notes, "*Field v. Google* is also the first decision that applies the DMCA system caching safe harbor." Peguera, *supra* note.

7.  *Google Inc.*, 412 F. Supp. at 1115.

8.  *Id.*

9.  17 U.S.C. § 512(b) (2012).

10. Peguera, *supra* note 6, at 601, 610.

11. The District Court also held Field was estopped from asserting his copyright claim because he knew of Google's allegedly infringing conduct before it took place, he intended for Google to rely upon his decision not to include the robots.txt code in his website design, Google was not aware that Field did not want cached links to his works included in Google Search results, and Google relied on Field's silence. *Google Inc.*, 412 F. Supp. at 1116.

12. *Id.*

13. *See* Monika Isia Jasiewicz, *Copyright Protection in an Opt-Out World: Implied License Doctrine and News Aggregators*, 122 YALE L.J. 837, 845 (2012); Matthew Sag, *Copyright and Copy-Reliant Technology*, 103 Nw. U. L. REV. 1607, 1609 (2009).

14. Kelly v. Arriba Soft Corp., 336 F. 3d 811 (9th Cir. 2003).

15. *Id.* at 818.

16. *Google Inc.*, 412 F. Supp. at 1112.

17. *Id.* at 1120. The District Court found the second factor, the nature of the copyrighted work, to fall only slightly in Field's favor. The court reasoned that although Field's poems were creative in nature, they were published and available for free on his website. The District Court determined the third factor, the amount and substantiality of the use, to neither support nor weigh against a fair use finding, as Google used "no more of the works than is necessary in allowing access to them through 'Cached' links." The District Court found the fourth factor, the impact on potential markets, to weigh strongly in favor of a fair use determination, because Field presented no evidence of any market for his poems. Finally, the District Court considered the fact that Google acted in good faith—by applying standard industry practices and removing cached links to Field's website upon notice of his complaint—to also weighed in favor of a fair use finding. *Id.* at 1120–22.

18. GORDON PARKER, 29 REASONS NOT TO BE A NICE GUY (2000); Parker v. Google Inc., 422 F. Supp. 2d 492, 495 (ED Pa. 2006).

19. *Google Inc.*, 422 F. Supp. at 496.

20. *Id.* at 495.

21. *Id.* at 497.

22. *Id.*

23. *Id.* at 498. The District Court also dismissed Parker's second claim that Google was liable for contributory copyright infringement because Google permits users to view infringing content. The District Court found Parker had failed to show infringement of a specific copyrighted work (Parker referred only to general claims of "infringed content" and "USENET postings") or that Google had knowledge of

the infringing activity. Similarly, the District Court dismissed Parker's third claim of vicarious copyright infringement on the grounds that Parker failed to show a specific infringement or to establish any direct financial interest on the part of Google. *Id.* at 498–500.

24.  *Id.* at 498.

25.  In 2013, Google updated the design and function of Google Images to include larger higher resolution copies of images. Google claimed the change was made in order to "provide a better search experience." Hongyi Li, *A faster image search*, WEBMASTER CENTRAL BLOG (Jan. 23, 2013), https://webmasters.googleblog.com/2013/01/faster-image-search.html. In 2016, Getty Images cited the change to Google Images as a central reason for an antitrust complaint against Google submitted to the European Commission. Getty Images claims Google's image search is anticompetitive because it creates "captivating galleries of high-resolution, copyrighted content," which permits Google "to reinforce its role as the internet's dominant search engine, maintaining monopoly over site traffic, engagement data and advertising spend." *See* Getty Images to file competition law complaint against Google, GETTYIMAGES (2016), http://press.gettyimages.com/getty-images-files-competition-law-complaint-against-google/ (last visited Feb. 11, 2019). In February 2018, Getty Images announced it had agreed to a multiyear global licensing deal with Google. Shortly after the announcement Google also removed the "View Image" button from Google Images. The View Image button in-line linked to the source images, often resulting in a user having the ability to view and copy a higher resolution version of an image without visiting the source website. Now, users must visit the web page hosting the site to view the larger image by clicking on the "Visit Website" button in Google Images. Getty Images and Google announce a new partnership, GETTYIMAGES (2018), http://press.gettyimages.com/getty-images-files-competition-law-complaint-against-google/ (last visited Nov. 10, 2018).

26.  Perfect 10 Inc. v. Amazon.com Inc., 508 F. 3d 1146, 1155 (9th Cir. 2007).

27.  *See, e.g.,* Lee Burgunder & Barry Floyd, *The Future of Inline Web Designing After Perfect* 10, 17 TEX. INTELL. PROP. L.J. 1 (2008).

28.  *Amazon.com Inc.,* 508 F. at 1156.

29.  Perfect 10 v. Google Inc., 416 F. Supp. 2d 828, 832 (CD Cal. 2006).

30.  Perfect 10 Inc. v. Amazon.com Inc., 508 F. 3d 1146 (9th Cir. 2007).

31.  *Id.* at 1159. Perfect 10 also claimed Google was liable under the theories of contributory and vicarious copyright infringement, when Google users download Perfect 10's photos and when third-party websites reproduce, display, and distribute Perfect 10's photos without permission. *Google Inc.,* 416 F. Supp. at 852.

32.  *Amazon.com Inc.,* 508 F. at 1146.

33.  *Google Inc.,* 416 F. Supp. at 839; *Amazon.com Inc.,* 508 F. at 1160.

34.  *Amazon.com Inc.,* 508 F. at 1159.

35.  *Id.* at 1161. Although the Ninth Circuit rejected the claim of direct infringement, it suggested Google may be liable for secondary liability (involving the direct infringement by third-party websites that reproduce, display, and distribute Perfect 10's images) and remanded the issue back to the District Court. The District Court was instructed to resolve factual disputes over the nature of Perfect 10's notifications to

Google and Google's immunity under the DMCA safe harbor provisions. In 2010, the District Court found Google's caching and Blogger functions qualified for safe harbor, but denied safe harbor for a limited number of Web and Image Search infringements. In 2011, the Ninth Circuit affirmed the District Court's decision, and in 2012 the case was dismissed without option for appeal. In the 2011 decision, the Ninth Circuit also considered a claim by Perfect 10 that when Google forwarded take-down notices to chillingeffects.org Google infringed Perfect 10's copyright. The Ninth Circuit rejected this claim. Perfect 10 Inc. v. Google Inc., 653 F. 3d 976 (9th Cir. 2011).

36. *Amazon.com Inc.*, 508 F. at 1162. The Ninth Circuit applied similar reasoning to the issue of Google's caching of websites hosting infringing copies of Perfect 10's photos. The Ninth Circuit held Google had not infringed Perfect 10's copyrights because "it is the website publisher's computer, rather than Google's computer, that stores and displays the infringing image." *Id.* at 1162.

37. Robert A. McFarlane, *The Ninth Circuit Lands a "Perfect 10" Applying Copyright Law to the Internet*, 38 GOLDEN GATE U. L. REV. 381, 404 (2008).

38. *Amazon.com Inc.*, 508 F. at 1146.

39. *Id.*

40. *Id.*

41. *Id.* at 1163.

42. *Id.* at 1165.

43. *Id.*

44. *Id.*; Kelly v. Arriba Soft Corp., 336 F. 3d 811, 818–19 (9th Cir. 2003).

45. *Amazon.com Inc.*, 508 F. at 1165.

46. *Id.* at 1166; Campbell v. Acuff-Rose Music Inc., 510 U.S. 569, 579 (1994).

47. Perfect 10 v. Google Inc., 416 F. Supp. 2d 828, 851 (CD Cal. 2006).

48. Perfect 10 Inc. v. Amazon.com Inc., 508 F. 3d 1146, 1166 (9th Cir. 2007).

49. *Id.* Similarly, in its analysis of the fourth factor, the effect on potential markets, the Ninth Circuit held "Google's use of thumbnails for search engine purposes is highly transformative, and so market harm cannot be presumed." *Amazon.com Inc.*, 508 F. at 1168.

50. *Id.* at 1167. The Ninth Circuit found the second fair use factor, the nature of the copyrighted work, to weigh slightly against fair use. The court reasoned that although the photos were creative in nature, they had been published, and once Perfect 10 had published its photos on its website, the company had exploited the "commercially valuable right of first publication" and was "no longer entitled to the enhanced protection available for an unpublished work." The third factor, the amount and substantiality of the portion used, was deemed neutral, mirroring the decision in *Kelly*, where the Ninth Circuit held an exact copy was an appropriate amount for the purpose of a search engine. *Id.* at 1168. *See also* Kelly v. Arriba Soft Corp., 336 F. 3d 811 (9th Cir. 2003).

51. *Id.* at 1166–1168.

52. As Professor Samuelson remarked, without the decisions in *Field, Parker,* and *Perfect 10,* Google might not have forged ahead with its plan to make digital copies of millions of books. Pamela Samuelson, *The Google Book Settlement as Copyright Reform*, 480 WIS. L. REV. 477, 492 (2011).

53. Google, GOOGLE BOOKS HISTORY, http://www.google.com.au/googlebooks/about/history.html (last visited Feb. 11, 2019).

54. *Id.*

55. *Id.* For an examination of the initial participating libraries, *see* MATTHEW RIMMER, DIGITAL COPYRIGHT AND THE CONSUMER REVOLUTION: HANDS OFF MY iPOD 229–32 (2007).

56. Authors Guild Inc. v. Google Inc., 954 F. Supp. 2d 282, 285 (SD NY 2013). *See also* Google, PROMOTE YOUR BOOKS ON GOOGLE—FOR FREE, https://www.google.com/googlebooks/partners/tour.html (last visited Feb. 11, 2019).

57. *Id.*

58. Google, GOOGLE BOOKS LIBRARY PROJECT—AN ENHANCED CARD CATALOG OF THE WORLD'S BOOKS, https://www.google.com/googlebooks/library/ (last visited Feb. 11, 2019).

59. *Google Inc.*, 954 F. Supp. at 286.

60. *Id.* at 285.

61. *Id.* at 286.

62. Complaint, Authors Guild Inc. v. Google Inc., No. 05-CV-8136, 2 (SD NY 2005).

63. *Id.* The same year, a suit was also filed against Google by members of the Association of American Publishers. In 2012, the publishers and Google announced a settlement agreement providing Google access to the publishers' works for the Google Library Project. *See* Google, *Publishers and Google Reach Agreement*, NEWS FROM GOOGLE (Oct. 4, 2012), http://googlepress.blogspot.com/2012/10/publishers-and-google-reach-agreement.html.

64. *Google Inc.*, No. 05-CV-8136 at 2–3.

65. *Id.*

66. Susan Wajcicki, *Google Print and the Authors Guild*, GOOGLE OFFICIAL BLOG (Sept. 20, 2005), https://googleblog.blogspot.com.au/2005/09/google-print-and-authors-guild.html.

67. Eric Schmidt, *Books of Revelation*, WALL ST. J., Oct. 18, 2005. Eric Schmidt is currently a technical advisor to Alphabet, Inc. He stepped down as CEO of Google in 2011 and as executive chairman of Alphabet, Inc. in 2017. Eric Schmidt to Become Technical Advisor to Alphabet, ALPHABET (2017), https://abc.xyz/investor/news/releases/2017/1221.html (last visited Feb. 11, 2019).

68. Authors Guild v. Google Inc., 804 F. 3d 202, 206 (2d Cir. 2015).

69. Google, *Authors, Publishers, and Google Reach Landmark Settlement*, NEWS FROM GOOGLE (Oct. 28, 2008), http://googlepress.blogspot.com.au/2008/10/authors-publishers-and-google-reach_28.html. *See* Google, INCREASING ACCESS TO BOOKS: THE GOOGLE BOOKS SETTLEMENT, https://sites.google.com/a/pressatgoogle.com/googlebookssettlement/home (last visited Feb. 11, 2019). A revised settlement was submitted to the US District Court for the Southern District of New York in 2009. Dan Clancy, *Modifications to the Google Books Settlement*, GOOGLE PUBLIC POLICY BLOG (Nov. 13, 2009), https://publicpolicy.googleblog.com/2009/11/modifications-to-google-books.html.

70. Dan Clancy, *supra* note 69.

71. Authors Guild v. Google Inc., 770 F. Supp. 2d 666, 671 (SD 2011).

72. *Id.*

73. *Id.* at 672.

74. *Id.* at 686. Pamela Samuelson contends the Google Books Settlement (GBS) was effectively an attempt at copyright law reform: "an intriguing way to view the GBS settlement is as a mechanism through which to achieve copyright reform that Congress has not yet been and may never be willing to do." Samuelson, *supra* note 52, at 482.

75. *Google Inc.*, 770 F. Supp. at 680–81.

76. *Id.* at 677.

77. Authors Guild, Inc. v. Google Inc., 721 F. 3d 132, 134–35 (2d Cir. 2013).

78. Authors Guild, Inc. v. Google Inc., 954 F. Supp. 2d 282, 289–93 (SD NY 2013).

79. *Id.* at 293.

80. Authors Guild v. Google Inc., 804 F. 3d 202, 208 (2d Cir., 2015). The portion of the book available for view depends upon the copyright status of the book or, in the case of the Google Books Partner Program, Google's agreement with the rightsholders.

81. *Google Inc.*, 954 F. Supp. at 287.

82. *Id.*

83. *Id. at* 291.

84. Bill Graham Archives v. Dorling Kindersley, 448 F. 3d 605 (2d Cir. 2006).

85. *Google Inc.*, 954 F. Supp. at 291.

86. *Id.* at 292.

87. *Id.* The second factor, the nature of the works, was also found to weigh in favor of fair use, on the grounds that all the books copied were published works and a majority of the books copied were nonfiction. In 2013, over 90 percent of the books in Google's database were nonfiction and a majority were no longer in print. *Id.* at 285.

88. *Id.* at 293.

89. *Id.* at 292.

90. *Id.* at 293.

91. Authors Guild Inc. v. HathiTrust, 755 F. 3d 87, 90 (2d Cir. 2014). *See also* Our Digital Library, HATHITRUST DIGITAL LIBRARY, https://www.hathitrust.org/digital_library (last visited Feb. 12, 2019). The Second Circuit also cited the decision in *Perfect 10*. *See* Authors Guild v. Google Inc., 804 F. 3d 202, 217–27 (2d Cir. 2015); Authors Guild Inc. v. HathiTrust, 902 F. Supp. 2d 445, 448 (SD NY 2012). In its agreement with the libraries, Google agreed to indemnify the libraries against copyright infringement claims, for example, the agreement between Google and the University of California provides, in clause 10.1 that "Google shall defend, indemnify, and hold harmless University from and against any and all liabilities, damages, charges, fees, including reasonable attorneys' fees, costs, and expenses arising out of or in any way related to a third party claim, lawsuit, and/or any other legal, quasi-legal, or administrative proceeding alleging . . . copyright infringement." Google & University of California, COOPERATIVE AGREEMENT, http://www.cdlib.org/services/collections/massdig/docs/uc_google_agreement.pdf (last visited Feb. 12, 2019).

92.  *HathiTrust*, 755 F. at 91. The HDL also provides access to books in full for persons
     with a print disability, and it provides a book preservation function for members,
     issuing replacement copies of books previously owned by a member library that
     are lost, stolen, or damaged and are otherwise "unobtainable at a fair price." At 92.

93.  *HathiTrust*, 902 F. Supp. at 449.

94.  *HathiTrust*, 755 F. at 97.

95.  *Google Inc.*, 804 F. at 207.

96.  *Id.* The Authors Guild made two further claims: they claimed Google's book da-
     tabase was vulnerable to hackers, who might release their books online for free,
     diminishing the value of their copyrights, and they claimed providing digital
     copies of books to libraries was not a fair use and represented another poten-
     tial risk to the value of their copyright. The Second Circuit found there was not
     sufficient evidence to show hacking posed an unreasonable risk, and, regarding
     the provision of copies to libraries, the court maintained that given the purpose
     of the digital copy was noninfringing digital searches and that "the possibility
     that libraries may misuse their digital copies is sheer speculation" there was "no
     basis . . . to impose liability on Google." *Id.* at 229.

97.  *Id.* at 207.

98.  *Id.*

99.  *Id.* at 212.

100. *Id.* at 215.

101. *Id.* at 217.

102. *Id.* at 217.

103. *Id.* at 218.

104. *Id.* at 207.

105. *Id.* at 214.

106. *Id.* at 219. The Second Circuit cited *Cariou v. Prince*, 714 F. 3d 694 (2d Cir. 2013);
     *Campbell v. Acuff-Rose Music Inc.*, 510 U.S. 569 (1994); *Castle Rock Entertainment
     v. Carol Publishing Group*, 150 F. 3d 132 (2d Cir. 1998).

107. *Id.* at 222–23.

108. *Id.* at 224.

109. *Id.* at 225.

110. *Id.*

111. *Id.* at 225–26.

112. *Petition For A Writ of Certiorari* No. 15-849 (In the Supreme Court of the United
     States, Dec. 31, 2015). The Authors Guild's petition was denied in April 2016.
     *Order List: 578 US*, Orders in Pending Cases, 2 (Supreme Court Apr. 18, 2016).

113. Kenneth A. Plevan, *The Second Circuit and the Development of Intellectual
     Property Law: The First 125 Years*, 85 Fordham L. Rev. 143, 157 (2016); Kelvin
     Hiu Fai Kwok, *Google Book Search, Transformative Use, and Commercial
     Intermediation: An Economic Perspective*, 17 Yale J.L. Tech. 283 (2015); Caile
     Morris, *Transforming Transformative Use: The Growing Misinterpretation of the
     Fair Use Doctrine*, LF 5 Pace Intell. Prop. Sports Ent. 10 (2015).

114. Harper & Row, Publishers, Inc. v. Nation Enterprises, 471 U.S. 539, 566 (1985).

115. Stewart v. Abend, 495 U.S. 207, 238A (1990).

116.  Campbell v. Acuff-Rose Music Inc., 510 U.S. 569, 579 (1994). Notably, the 2015 Second Circuit decision in *Authors Guild* was written by Judge Pierre N. Leval, author of the 1990 article "Towards a Fair Use Standard," in which Leval argues the critical factor in a fair use analysis is whether a work is transformative, the approach adopted by the US Supreme Court in *Campbell. See* Pierre N. Leval, *Toward a Fair Use Standard*, 103 HARV. L. REV. 1105 (1990).

As noted in this chapter, the District Court in *Field* held Google's for-profit status did not weigh against a fair use finding because "the transformative purpose of Google's use is considerably more important." Field v. Google Inc., 412 F. Supp. 2d 1106, 1120 (D. Nev. 2006). In *Perfect 10*, the Ninth Circuit concluded, "the transformative nature of Google's use is more significant than any incidental superseding use of the minor commercial aspects of Google's search engine and website." Perfect 10 Inc. v. Amazon.com Inc., 508 F. 3d 1146, 1166 (9th Cir. 2007). As well, regarding the market impact, in *Perfect 10*, the Ninth Circuit concluded, "Google's use of thumbnails for search engine purposes is highly transformative, and so market harm cannot be presumed." At 1168. In *Authors Guild*, the Second Circuit stated: "the more the appropriator is using the copied material for new, transformative purposes, the more it serves copyright's goal of enriching public knowledge and less likely it is that the appropriation will serve as a substitute for the original or its plausible derivatives, shrinking the protected market opportunities." Authors Guild v. Google Inc., 804 F. 3d 202, 214 (2d Cir. 2015).

117.  *See, e.g.*, Andrew Ross Sorkin, *Dot-Com Boom Echoed in Deal to Buy YouTube*, N.Y. TIMES, Oct. 10, 2006; and Google to Acquire YouTube, ALPHABET (2006), https://investor.google.com/releases/2006/1009.html (last visited Jan. 10, 2017).

118.  Viacom International Inc. v. YouTube Inc., 718 F. Supp. 2d 514 (SD NY 2010). Viacom and YouTube had attempted to negotiate an advertising revenue sharing agreement, but negotiations broke down, prompting Viacom to send YouTube take-down notices seeking the removal of more than 100,000 YouTube videos. Amir Hassanabadi, *Viacom v. YouTube—All Eyes Blind: The Limits of the DMCA in a Web 2.0 World*, 26 BERKELEY TECH. L.J. 405, 421 (2011).

119.  Viacom International Inc. v. YouTube Inc., 676 F. 3d 19, 26 (2d Cir. 2012).

120.  *See* 17 U.S.C. § 512(c)(1)(A)–(C) (2012).

121.  *YouTube Inc.*, 718 F. Supp. at 516.

122.  *Id.* at 518.

123.  Memorandum of Law in Support of Viacom's Motion for Parial Summary Judgment on Liability and Inapplicability of the Digital Millennium Copyright Act Safe Harbor Defence, Case No 1:07-cv-02103, 1 (SD NY 2010).

124.  *YouTube Inc.*, 676 F. at 34.

125.  *Id.*

126.  Memorandum of Law in Support of Viacom's Motion for Parial Summary Judgment on Liability and Inapplicability of the Digital Millennium Copyright Act Safe Harbor Defence, Case No 1:07-cv-02103, 31 (SD NY 2010).

127.  *Id.* at 32.

128.  *Id.* at 34.

129.  *Id.* at 33.

130.	*Id.* at 34. Viacom asserted YouTube's use of the videos also went beyond storage at the direction of the user, as required under Section 512(c). Viacom pointed to the automated software functions that are activated when a video is uploaded to YouTube. In a process known as transcoding, when a video is uploaded to YouTube, the video is copied into various formats to enable access across multiple platforms. YouTube also had in place agreements with third-party device suppliers (for example, Apple, Sony, and Panasonic), allowing users of those devices to access videos directly from YouTube. In addition, YouTube makes videos available to view on a "watch" page and "related videos" features. Viacom argued all of these uses were not for reason of user storage. *See* Viacom International Inc. v. YouTube Inc., 718 F. Supp. 2d 514, 516 (SD NY 2010); Viacom International Inc. v. YouTube Inc., 676 F. 3d 19, 28–39 (2d Cir. 2012); Viacom International Inc. v. YouTube Inc., 940 F. Supp. 2d 110, 122 (SD NY 2013).

131.	Memorandum of Law in Support of Viacom's Motion for Parial Summary Judgment on Liability and Inapplicability of the Digital Millennium Copyright Act Safe Harbor Defence, Case No 1:07-cv-02103, 31 (SD NY 2010).

132.	*Id.*

133.	*Id.* at 20, 39.

134.	*Id.* at 46.

135.	*Id.* at 58.

136.	*Id.* at 59.

137.	*Id.* at 58.

138.	Viacom International Inc. v. YouTube Inc., 718 F. Supp. 2d 514 (SD NY 2010). In addition to Viacom, the Football Association Premier League Limited et al. were named as plaintiffs in the case. In 2007, the Football Association Premier League (Football Association), along with other rightsholders including the French Tennis Federation, the National Music Publishers Association, and several music publishers, sued YouTube for copyright infringement for the appearance of their works on YouTube. In 2009, the US District Court for the Southern District of New York dismissed the claims for punitive damages and statutory damages for works not registered in the United States, with the exception of statutory damages for works that qualified for the live broadcast exemption. The Football Association Premier League v. YouTube Inc., 633 F. Supp. 2d 159 (SD NY 2009). Under Section 412 of the US Copyright Act, to be eligible for statutory damages a work must be registered either before the act of infringement or within three months of first publication. 17 U.S.C. § 412 (2012). The Football Association argued this requirement did not apply to foreign works, but the District Court held the Copyright Act included no express exemption for foreign works and the legislative history showed no congressional intention for such an exemption. At 162–63. The court rejected the Football Association's argument that requiring registration would violate the United States' obligations under the Berne Convention and the Agreement on Trade-Related Aspects of Intellectual Property Rights (TRIPs). The Court held the Berne Convention's requirement that copyright protection is provided without formalities was not incompatible with the requirement for registration for statutory damages under 17

U.S.C. § 412 (2012). At 164. Moreover, the District Court held that if there was an inconsistency with TRIPs, Congress had mandated that in such cases of conflict, US domestic law should prevail. *Id.* The District Court found the Football Association did qualify for statutory damages for any live broadcasts, which are exempt from the requirements for registration under 17 U.S.C. § 411(c) (2012) but dismissed the Football Association's claim for punitive damages, stating, "such damages are, as a matter of law, not obtainable under the Act." At 167. In 2010, YouTube filed a motion for summary judgment against both Viacom and The Football Association, claiming safe harbor under the DMCA. In 2013, YouTube and the Football Association agreed to a voluntary dismissal. *See* Owen Gibson, *Premier League Drops Copyright Infringement Case Against YouTube*, The Guardian, Nov. 11, 2013, https://www.theguardian.com/football/2013/nov/11/premier-league-copyright-case-youtube.

139.  Viacom International Inc. v. YouTube Inc., 718 F. Supp. 2d 514, 519 (SD NY 2010).

140.  *Id.* at 523.

141.  *Id.* at 524–25.

142.  *Id.* at 525.

143.  *Id.* at 519. The District Court also rejected Viacom's claim that YouTube had the right and ability to control the infringing activity, stating, "the 'right and ability to control' the activity requires knowledge of it, which must be item-specific." *Id.* at 527.

144.  Viacom International Inc. v. YouTube Inc., 676 F. 3d 19, 30 (2d Cir. 2012).

145.  *Id.* at 31.

146.  *Id.* at 26.

147.  *Id.* at 34. The Second Circuit also asked the District Court to determine whether YouTube was willfully blind to the infringing activities of its users. At 36. The Second Circuit held "the willful blindness doctrine may be applied, in appropriate circumstances, to demonstrate knowledge or awareness of specific instances of infringement under the DMCA." At 35. However, on remand, the District Court held Viacom had failed to show "knowledge or awareness of any specific infringements of clips-in-suit" and so held Viacom had not successfully established YouTube willfully blinded itself to specific infringements. Viacom International Inc. v. YouTube Inc., 940 F. Supp. 2d 110, 115–16 (SD NY 2013).

The Second Circuit also remanded for consideration by the District Court the question of whether YouTube had the right and ability to control the infringing activity and whether YouTube had received direct financial benefit from the activity. The Second Circuit rejected the District Court's conclusion that item specific knowledge was necessary in order to have the right and ability to control, instead, the Second Circuit reasoned, the right and ability to control required "something more" than the ability to remove or block access to infringing material. The Second Circuit suggested "something more" would "involve a service provider exerting substantial influence on the activities of users, without necessarily—or even frequently—acquiring knowledge of specific infringing activity." *YouTube Inc*, 676 F. at 36–38. The Second Circuit also considered whether YouTube's activities went beyond storage at the direction of a user. The Second

Circuit held the structure of the DMCA and relevant case law make certain the statute covers software functions facilitating access to user-stored material, and, therefore, YouTube's transcoding and the "watch" and "related video" features on fell within the scope of Section 512(c). At 39. The Second Circuit remanded the third-party syndication issue back to the District Court for fact finding, in order to establish whether YouTube had syndicated any of the clips in suit. At 40. On remand, the District Court found the clips in suit were not syndicated and stated that the syndication agreements fell within the scope of the provision as they were "steps by a service provided taken to make user-stored videos more readily accessible." *YouTube Inc.*, 940 F. Supp. at 123.

148.   *YouTube Inc.*, 940 F. Supp. at 115. This was not disputed by Viacom, which submitted to the court "it has now become clear that neither side possesses the kind of evidence that would allow a clip-by-clip assessment of actual knowledge." At 113. The District Court also held YouTube did not have the right and ability to control infringing activity under Section 512(c). The District Court stated, "a service provider, even without knowledge of specific infringing activity, may so influence or participate in that activity, while gaining a financial benefit from it, as to lose the safe harbor." Yet, the District Court asserted, "the governing principle must remain clear: knowledge of the prevalence of infringing activity, and welcoming it, does not itself forfeit the safe harbor. To forfeit that, the provider must influence or participate in the infringement." The District Court recognized that YouTube did exercise some influence over its users, for example:

exercising its right not to monitor its service for infringements, by enforcing basic rules regarding content (such as limitations on violent, sexual or hate material), by facilitating access to all userstored material regardless (and without actual or constructive knowledge) of whether it was infringing, and by monitoring its site for some infringing material and assisting some content owners in their efforts to do the same.

However, the court found there was no evidence that YouTube

induced its users to submit infringing videos, provided users with detailed instructions about what content to upload or edited their content, prescreened submissions for quality, steered users to infringing videos, or otherwise interacted with infringing users to a point where it might be said to have participated in their infringing activity

Accordingly, the District Court concluded YouTube did not influence or participate in the infringing activity in such a manner that provided YouTube the right and ability to control the infringing activities of its users, and so was not disqualified from safe harbor. *YouTube Inc.*, 940 F. Supp. at 118–22.

149.   Viacom and Google Resolve Copyright Lawsuit, Viacom (2014), https://ir.viacom.com/news-releases/news-release-details/viacom-and-google-resolve-copyright-lawsuit?ReleaseID=833547 (last visited Feb. 12, 2019).

150. Google, Re: Section 512 Study: Notice and Request for Public Comment Docket No. 2015-7 (December 31, 2015) to The Honorable Maria A. Pallante Register of Copyrights U.S. Copyright Office 13–14 (2016).

151. About, Java, https://www.java.com/en/about/ (last visited Jan. 10, 2016).

152. *Id. See also* Christopher Jon Sprigman, *Oracle v. Google: A High-Stakes Legal Fight for the Software Industry*, 58 Comm. ACM, 28 (2015).

153. Oracle America Inc. v. Google Inc., 872 F. Supp. 2d 974, 978 (ND Cal. 2012); Google I/O Keynote (Google I/O '17), YouTube, https://www.youtube.com/watch?v=Y2VF8tmLFHw (last visited Feb. 12, 2019).

154. *Id.* at 977.

155. *Id.*

156. *Id.*

157. Sprigman, *supra* note 152, at 28.

158. *Google Inc.*, 872 F. Supp. at 978.

159. *Id.* at 977.

160. *Id.* at 978.

161. Peter S. Menell, *API Copyrightability Bleak House: Unraveling and Repairing the Oracle v. Google Jurisdictional Mess*, 31 Berkeley Tech. L.J. 1515 (2016).

162. *Google Inc.*, 872 F. Supp. at 978.

163. *Id.*

164. *Id.* at 999–1000.

165. *Id.* at 998.

166. 17 U.S.C. § 102(b) (2012).

167. 17 U.S.C. § 102(b) (2012).

168. *Google Inc.*, 872 F. Supp. at 998.

169. *Id.* at 999–1000.

170. *Id.* at 985. The District Court cited the US Supreme Court decision in *Baker v. Selden*, 101 U.S. 99 (1880).

171. The District Court cited US Copyright Office regulation 37 C.F.R. 202.1(a) on material not subject to copyright—which includes "words and short phrases such as names, titles, and slogans; familiar symbols or designs; mere variations of typographic ornamentation, lettering or coloring; mere listing of ingredients or contents"—and noted the regulation was followed in *Sega Enterprises Ltd. v. Accolade Inc.*, 977 F. 2d 1510 (9th Cir. 1992). The District Court further warned, "we should not yield to the temptation to find copyrightability merely to reward an investment made in a body of intellectual property." *Google Inc.*, 872 F. Supp. at 983–84.

172. *Google Inc.*, 872 F. Supp. at 1002.

173. Oracle America Inc. v. Google Inc., 750 F. 3d 1339 (Fed. Cir. 2014). 17 U.S.C. § 102(b) (2012).

174. *See generally* Clark D. Asay, *Copyright's Technological Interdependencies*, Stan. Tech. L. Rev. 189, 230 (2014).

175. *Google Inc.*, 750 F. at 1339.

176. *Id.* at 1367.

177. *Id.*

178. *Id.*
179. Computer Associates International Inc. v. Altai Inc., 982 F. 2d 693 (2d Cir. 1992).
180. *Google Inc.*, 750 F. at 1357.
181. *Id.* at 1357–58
182. *Id.* at 1363.
183. *Id.* at 1361.
184. *Id.* The Federal Circuit also held the *scènes à faire* doctrine did not render the declaring code uncopyrightable, as the *scènes à faire* doctrine "is a component of the infringement analysis" and does not exclude a work from protection, rather, "certain copying is forgiven as a necessary incident of *any* expression of the underlying idea." *Id.* at 1364.
185. *Id.* at 1355–57.
186. *Id.*
187. *Id.* at 1365–68.
188. *Id.* at 1372.
189. *Id.* at 1377.
190. Google Inc., Petitioner v. Oracle America No. 14-410, UNITED STATES COURT OF APPEALS FOR THE FEDERAL CIRCUIT (2014), https://www.supremecourt. gov/Search.aspx?FileName=/docketfiles/14-410.htm. However, note that in *SAS Institute v. World Programming*, the District Court for the Northern District of California did not follow *Oracle*. SAS alleged World Programming had infringed SAS software copyrights when World Programming used SAS "language functions and by copying the resulting output formats that are produced when a user runs those language functions through the SAS System"—SAS argued the SAS Language elements were analogous to the Java declaring code copied by Google. The District Court for the Northern District of California rejected this claim. *See* SAS Institute v. World Programming, 125 F. Supp. 3d 579 (ND Cal. 2015). In another factually similar case, *Cisco Systems v. Arista Networks* of the District Court of the Northern District of California, a jury found Arista's copying of Cisco's command-line interface was not copyright infringement, accepting "a *scenes a faire* defense in which Arista argued that its actions in copying Cisco was legally permissible because of Arista's need for hardware technical compatibility with Cisco's industry standard commands." Steve Brachmann, *Cisco v. Arista Patent and Copyright Infringement Cases See Conflicting Rulings at ITC, N.D. Cal.*, IPWATCHDOG, Jan. 12, 2017, http://www.ipwatchdog.com/2017/01/12/cisco-v-arista-patent-copyright-infringement-conflicting-rulings/id=76615/. *See Cisco Systems Inc. v. Arista Networks, Inc.*, Case No. 14-cv-05344-BLF (ND Cal., 2016).
191. Nicholas A. Holton, *Google, Inc. v. Oracle America, Inc.: Supreme Court Declines to Review Reversal of Landmark API Copyright Decision*, 62 LOYOLA L. REV. 189, 235 (2016).
192. Menell, *supra* note 161, at 40–41; Oracle America Inc. v. Google Inc., Special Verdict Form No. C 10-03561 WHA (ND Cal. 2016).
193. Oracle America Inc. v. Google Inc., Order Denying Rule 50 Motions No. C10-03561 WHA, 14 (ND Cal. 2016); Pamela Samuelson, *Fair Use Prevails in Oracle v. Google*, 59 COMM. ACM 24, 25 (2016).

194. *Id.* at 10.
195. Oracle America, Inc v. Google LLC, 886 F.3d 1179 (2018).
196. *Id.* at 1199.
197. *Id.* at 1198, 1210.
198. Menell, *supra* note 161, at 50.
199. This is a simplification of a complex history, but, as I have documented in this book, it is broadly true. Professor James Grimmelman has observed a normative progression regarding copyright and digital technologies evident in Google's litigation history. For example, of the Google Books fair use decision, Grimmelman remarked: "what seemed insanely ambitious and this huge effort that seemed very dangerous in 2004 now seems ordinary." Claire Miller & Julie Bosman, *Siding with Google, Judge Says Book Search Does Not Infringe Copyright*, N.Y. Times, Nov. 14, 2019, http://www.nytimes.com/2013/11/15/business/media/judge-sides-with-google-on-book-scanning-suit.html?_r=1&.
200. Professor Frank Pasquale notes "landmark cases like Sony v Universal have set a precedent for taking such broad public interests into account in the course of copyright litigation." Frank A. Pasquale, *Internet Nondiscrimination Principles: Commercial Ethics for Carriers and Search Engines*, Seton Hall Public Law Research Paper 1, 29 (2008). Through Google's case law, this precedent has been extended.

## CHAPTER 5

1. Carlo D'Asaro Biondo, *Let's work together to support quality journalism*, Google Europe Blog (Apr. 28, 2015), https://europe.googleblog.com/2015/04/lets-work-together-to-support-quality.html.
2. Mercedes Bunz, *Rupert Murdoch: "There's No Such Thing as a Free News Story*,*"* The Guardian, Dec. 1, 2009, https://www.theguardian.com/media/2009/dec/01/rupert-murdoch-no-free-news.
3. *See* Chrysanthos Dellarocas et al., *Attention Allocation in Information-Rich Environments: The Case of News Aggregators*, 62 Mgmt. Sci. 2543 (2016); M. Calin & C. Dellarocas, *Attention allocation in information-rich environments: the case of news aggregators*, No. 2013-4 B.U. Sch. Mgmt. Research Paper (2013).
4. NERA Economic Consulting, Impacto del Nuevo Artículo 32.2 de la Ley de Propiedad Intelectual (2015), http://www.aeepp.com/pdf/InformeNera.pdf. Hostility toward news aggregation may also be provoked by the more abstract confrontation it represents to the traditional news media industry. News aggregation effectively "upends the traditional model of information gatekeeping . . . by inverting the normal pattern of information retrieval." Hsiang Iris Chyi, Seth C. Lewis, & Nan Zheng, *Parasite or Partner? Coverage of Google News in an Era of News Aggregation*, 93 J. Mass Comm. Q. 789, 792 (2016). Rather than reading content curated by one authoritative publication, news aggregation provides content from multiple sources, and readers choose a publication to visit, based on their interest in a particular news item. This model challenges both the traditional structure and function of new distribution, as well as the ideology of journalism as a profession. As Lewis explains, journalists perceive their role to

serve a social purpose; the role of a journalist is to "fulfill the functions of watch-dog publishing, truth-telling, independence, timeliness, and ethical adherence in the context of news and public affairs." Seth C. Lewis, *The Tension Between Professional Control and Open Participation: Journalism and its Boundaries*, 15 INFO. COMM. SOC'Y 836, 845 (2012). Furthermore, journalists "derive much of their sense of purpose and prestige through their control of information in their normative roles." *Id.* at 845. In this way, news aggregation is "more than a challenge to an industry model built on scarcity. It also strikes at the heart of a model that was built on an implicit bargain between journalists and the public—an assumption about how society should handle the collection, filtering, and distribution of news information." *Id.* at 838.

5. *See* GARETH PRICE, OPPORTUNITIES AND CHALLENGES FOR JOURNALISM IN THE DIGITAL AGE: ASIA AND EUROPEAN PERSPECTIVES 3 (2015), https://www.chathamhouse.org/sites/files/chathamhouse/field/field_document/20150826Jour nalismDigitalAgePrice.pdf. *See also* Amy Mitchell & Jesse Holcomb, STATE OF THE NEWS MEDIA 2016 PEW RESEARCH CENTRE JOURNALISM & MEDIA (2016), http://www.journalism.org/2016/06/15/state-of-the-news-media-2016/2012/ (last visited Feb. 14, 2019).

6. Michael Barthel, DESPITE SUBSCRIPTION SURGES FOR LARGEST U.S. NEWSPAPERS, CIRCULATION AND REVENUE FALL FOR INDUSTRY OVERALL PEW RESEARCH CENTER JOURNALISM & MEDIA (2017), http://www.pewresearch.org/fact-tank/2017/06/01/circulation-and-revenue-fall-for-newspaper-industry/ (last visited Feb. 14, 2019).

7. Lewis, *supra* note 4, at 838.

8. Neil Weinstock Netanel, *New Media in Old Bottles? Barron's Contextual First Amendment and Copyright in the Digital Age*, 76 GEO. WASH. L. REV. 952, 978 (2008).

9. NIC NEWMAN ET AL., REUTERS INSTITUTE DIGITAL NEWS REPORT 2016 7 (2016).

10. Netanel, *supra* note 8, at 953–78.

11. Chyi, Lewis, & Zheng, *supra* note 4, at 790.

12. Complaint for Preliminary and Permanent Injunction and Copyright Infringement, Agence France-Presse v. Google Inc., No. 1:05 Civ. 00546, 3 (D. DC 2005).

13. *Id.* at 1, 17.

14. *Google's Motion and Memorandum for Partial Summary Judgment Dismissing Count II for Lack of Protectable Subject Matter, Agence France-Presse v. Google Inc.*, No. 1:05 Civ. 00546 (D. DC 2005). Google also argued it had an implied license to use AFP's articles because AFP failed to implement the robots.txt exclusion protocol. Google Inc Answer and Counterclaims, Agence France Presse v. Google Inc., No. 1:05-cv-00546, 19, 29 (D. DC 2005).

15. *Google Inc.*, No 1:05 Civ. 00546 at 3. Google cited C.F.R. 37 § 202.1(a).

16. *Google Inc.*, No 1:05 Civ. 00546 at 4.

17. Eric Auchard, *AFP, Google News Settle Lawsuit over Google News*, REUTERS, Apr. 8, 2007, https://www.reuters.com/article/us-google-afp-idUSN0728115420070407; *Agency France Press v. Google Inc. Stipulation of Dismissal*, Civial Action No., 1:05CV00546 (GK) (D. DC 2007).

18. Josh Cohen, *Original stories, from the source*, GOOGLE NEWS BLOG (Aug. 31, 2007), https://news.googleblog.com/2007/08/original-stories-from-source.html.

19. *Id.*

20. KEN AULETTA, GOOGLED: THE END OF THE WORLD AS WE KNOW IT 164–65 (2010).

21. *Id.* at 165.

22. Two additional collection societies were parties to the claim against Google: *Société de droit d'Auteur des Journalistes*, which represents journalists, and *Assucopie*, which represents scientific and educational authors. Google Inc. v. Copiepresse, JBC No. 2176, 6 (The Court of Appeal of Brussels, 9th Chamber, 2011).

23. *Copiepresse*, JBC No. 2176 at 26. Notably, Google had argued American law was applicable "on the grounds that it is in the United States that it inserted, on its servers, the pages published on the Belgian websites of the Belgian newspaper editors." *Id.* at 13. The court disagreed and held that under the Berne Convention, protection in the country of origin is governed by that country's domestic law, and the country of origin is the country of first publication. The court decided that as the articles were published first in Belgium and it was in Belgium where protection was sought, Belgian law, not American law, governed. *See* Berne Convention for the Protection of Literary and Artistic Works, arts. 5(3) and 5(4)(a), Dec. 5, 1887.

24. *Id.* at 25.

25. *Id.* at 36.

26. *Id.*

27. *Id.* at 37.

28. *Id.* at 36. The court also found Google's caching was outside of the scope of Directive 2001/19, which excludes from liability copies "which are transient or incidental and an integral and essential part of a technological process." Directive 2001/29/EC of the European Parliament and of the Council of 22 May 2001 on the harmonisation of certain aspects of copyright and related rights in the information society, art. 5(1). The court held Google's caching was not functionally necessary to its service, it was not for the purpose of improving processing speeds, and it was not a temporary, transient reproduction. *Id.* at 21–23. *Cf.* the decision in Field v. Google Inc., 412 F. Supp. 2d 1106 (D. Nev. 2006).

29. Directive 2001/29/EC of the European Parliament and of the Council of 22 May 2001 on the harmonisation of certain aspects of copyright and related rights in the information society, art. 5(1).

30. *Copiepresse*, Vol. JBC No. 2176 at 48–49.

31. Chloe Albanesius, *Google to Reindex Belgian Newspapers Amidst "Boycott" Complaints*, PC MAG, 2011, http://www.pcmag.com/article2/0,2817,2388635,00. asp. In a statement reported by *PC Mag*, Google stipulated:

> We are delighted that Copiepresse has given us assurances that we can re-include their sites in our Google search index without court-ordered penalties . . . We never wanted to take their sites out of our index, but we needed to respect a court

order until Copiepresse acted. We remain open to working in collaboration with Copiepresse members in the future.

32.  *See* Francois Le Hodey, *Google's Brutal Attitude*, La Libre, 2011, http://www.lalibre. be/economie/digital/attitude-brutale-de-google-51b8d6e6e4b0de6db9c25135.

33.  Thierry Geerts, *Partnering with Belgian news publishers*, Google Europe Blog (Dec. 12, 2012), https://europe.googleblog.com/2012/12/partnering-with-belgian-news-publishers.html.

34.  *Id.*

35.  *Id.*

36.  *Id.* Google also agreed to pay for Copiepresse's legal fees and although not confirmed by Google or Copiepresse, it was reported that the advertising revenue amounted to USD 6 million. *See, e.g.*, Jeff Roberts, *Did Google pay Belgian newspapers a $6M copyright fee? Sure looks like it*, Gigaom, 2012, https://gigaom.com/2012/12/13/did-google-pay-belgian-newspapers-a-6m-copyright-fee-sure-looks-like-it/.

37.  Geerts, *supra* note 33.

38.  Interventions 2009, Autorità Garante della Concorrenza e del Mercato, http://www.agcm.it/168-notizie/nascosta/5602-interventi-effettuati-2009.html.

39.  Uta Kohl, *Google: The Rise and Rise of Online Intermediaries in the Governance of the Internet and Beyond (Part 2)*, Int'l J.L. Info. Tech. 187, 226 (2013); Eric Pfanner, *A Google Worry Recedes, for Now, as Italy Ends Investigation into News Service*, N.Y. Times, Jan. 17, 2011, http://www.nytimes.com/2011/01/18/technology/18iht-google18.html.

40.  Federazione Italiana Editori Giornale, Fieg E Google Annunciano Un Accordo Per La Crescita Del Settore Editoriale Nel Digitale (2016), http://www.fieg.it/salastampa_item.asp?sta_id=979.

41.  Silvia Scalzini, *Is There Free-Riding? A Comparative Analysis of the Problem of Protecting Publishing Materials Online in Europe*, 10 J. Intell. Prop. L. Pract. 454, 461 (2015).

42.  *Id. See also* Eleonora Rosati, *Neighbouring Rights for Publishers: Are National and (Possible) EU Initiatives Lawful?*, 47 IIC 569, 573 (2016).

43.  Rosati, *supra* note 42, at 573.

44.  Gerrit Rabenstein, *Google News bleibt offene Plattform für alle deutschen Verlage*, Der offizielle Google Produkt-Blog (June 21, 2013), https://germany.googleblog.com/2013/06/google-news-bleibt-offene-plattform-fuer-verlage.html.

45.  Greg Sterling, *German Publishers to Google: We Want Our Snippets Back*, Search Engine Land, 2014, http://searchengineland.com/german-publishers-google-want-snippets-back-206520.

46.  Rosati, *supra* note 42, at 573; Philipp Justus, *News zu News bei Google*, Der offizielle Google Produkt-Blog (Oct. 1, 2014), https://germany.googleblog.com/2014/10/news-zu-news-bei-google.html.

47.  Philipp Justus, *supra* note 46.

48.  D. B. Hebbard, *German Publishers "Bow to Pressure," Will Allow Google to Display Search Result Snippets*, Talking New Media, Oct. 23, 2014, http://

www.talkingnewmedia.com/2014/10/23/german-publishers-bow-to-pressure-will-allow-google-to-display-search-result-snippets/; Harro Ten Wolde & Eric Auchard, *Germany's top publisher bows to Google in news licensing row*, REUTERS, Nov. 5, 2014, https://www.reuters.com/article/us-google-axel-sprngr/germanys-top-publisher-bows-to-google-in-news-licensing-row-idUSKBN0IP1YT20141105. In January 2016, VG Media announced it had filed a civil complaint against Google seeking to "enforce the ancillary copyright for press publishers" in order to receive payment from Google for the inclusion of VG Media works in Google News. Michelle Martin, *German publishers have filed complaint against Google: VG Media*, Jan. 6, 2016, https://www.reuters.com/article/us-google-media-germany-idUSKBN0UJ1KF20160105. In May 2017, the Berlin Regional Court suspended VG Media's case and requested a preliminary ruling from the of Justice of the European Union on whether Germany had properly notified the European Commission of the introduction of the *Leistungsschutzrecht für Presseverleger.* Under "Directive (EU) 2015/1535 Member States must inform the Commission of any draft technical regulation prior to its adoption." The Notification Procedure in Brief, EUROPEAN COMMISSION (2015), http://ec.europa.eu/growth/tools-databases/tris/en/about-the-20151535/the-notification-procedure-in-brief1/. *See also* VG Media, BERLIN REGIONAL COURT DECLARES PRESS PUBLISHERS' SUIT AGAINST GOOGLE INC. TO BE JUSTIFIED IN PART, SUBMITS TO ECJ THE QUESTION OF WHETHER NOTIFICATION REQUIREMENT APPLIES TO ANCILLARY COPYRIGHT FOR PRESS PUBLISHERS (2017), https://www.vg-media.de/images/en/downloads/press/170509_PM_LG-Berlin_VG-Media_EN.pdf.

49.   Rosati, *supra* note 42, at 572.

50.   *Id.* at 572.

51.   Olivier Esper, *The facts about our position on French copyright proposals*, GOOGLE EUROPE BLOG (Oct. 18, 2012), https://europe.googleblog.com/2012/10/the-facts-about-our-position-on-french.html.

52.   Eric Schmidt, *Google creates €60m Digital Publishing Innovation Fund to support transformative French digital publishing initiatives*, THE KEYWORD (Feb. 1, 2013), https://blog.google/topics/journalism-news/google-creates-60m-digital-publishing.

53.   Rosati, *supra* note 42, at 572.

54.   Schmidt, *supra* note 52.

55.   *See* Scalzini, *supra* note 41, at 462.

56.   *Id.* at 462.

57.   *Id.* at 462.

58.   Richard Gingras, *An update on Google News in Spain*, GOOGLE EUROPE BLOG (Dec. 11, 2014), https://europe.googleblog.com/2014/12/an-update-on-google-news-in-spain.html.

59.   *Id.*

60.   David Drummond, *Supporting high quality journalism*, GOOGLE EUROPE BLOG (June 19, 2015), https://europe.googleblog.com/2015/06/supporting-high-quality-journalism.html.

61.   NERA Economic Consulting, *supra* note 4, at xv–xvi.

62. Sílvia Majó-Vázquez, Ana S. Cardenal, & Sandra González-Bailón, *Digital News Consumption and Copyright Intervention: Evidence from Spain Before and After the 2015 "Link Tax,"* 22 J. Computer-Mediated Comm. 284, 297 (2017).

63. Biondo, *supra* note 1.

64. The DNI Launched with 11 Founding Partners and over 1000 Organisations From Across Europe Have Since Expressed Interest in One or Several of Our Programmes, Digital News Initiative (2017), https://www.digitalnewsinitiative. com/participants/. *See also* Ludovic Blecher, *Digital News Initiative: first funding brings €27m to projects in 23 countries,* The Keyword (Feb. 24, 2016), https:// blog.google/around-the-globe/google-europe/digital-news-initiative-first-funding_24/.

65. The DNI Innovation Fund, Digital News Initiative, https://digitalnewsinitiative. com/dni-fund/#faq_faq-1 (last visited Jan. 5, 2017).

66. Drummond, *supra* note 585. *See also* Biondo:

> Google recognises and admires high quality journalism. As a strong advocate for the free flow of information we know the crucial role it plays in democratic societies. We recognise that technology companies and news organisations are part of the same information ecosystem. We want to play our part in the common fight to find more sustainable models for news. I firmly believe that Google has always wanted to be a friend and partner to the news industry, but I also accept we've made some mistakes along the way. Biondo, *supra* note 1.

67. Blecher, *supra* note 64.

68. *See* Ben McOwen Wilson: "today, through a unique partnership between YouTube and a number of leading European news publishers, we're launching a new video solution specifically tailored to the needs of news industry; with a goal of reducing complexity and increasing reach and revenue potential." Ben McOwen Wilson, *Digital News Initiative: Introducing the YouTube Player for Publishers,* The Keyword (Sept. 14, 2016), https://blog.google/topics/journalism-news/ digital-news-initiative-introducing.

> *See* David Besbris:

> Today, after discussions with our DNI partners in Europe and publishers and technology companies around the world, we're announcing a new open source initiative called Accelerated Mobile Pages, which aims to dramatically improve the - performance of the mobile web. We want webpages with rich content like video, animations and graphics to work alongside smart ads and to load instantaneously. We also want the same code to work across multiple platforms and devices so that content can appear everywhere in an instant—no matter what type of phone, tablet or mobile device you are using.

> David Besbris, *Introducing the Accelerated Mobile Pages Project, for a faster, open mobile web,* Google Europe Blog (Oct. 7, 2015), https://europe.googleblog.com/ 2015/10/introducing-accelerated-mobile-pages.html.

69. Besbris, *supra* note 68.

70. *Id.*
71. European Commission, Proposal for a Directive of the European Parliament and of the Council on copyright in the Digital Single Market (2016). The proposed directive states at Article 11(1): "Member States shall provide publishers of press publications with the rights provided for in Article 2 and Article 3(2) of Directive 2001/29/EC for the digital use of their press publications." (Note, Article 2 of Directive 2001/29/EC provides the reproduction right and Article 3(2) the making available right in European Union law.)
72. *Id.* at 19.
73. Caroline Atkinson, *European copyright: there's a better way*, Google Blog (Sept. 14, 2016), https://blog.google/topics/public-policy/european-copyright-theres-better-way/. In 2017, a similar policy was proposed in Canada. *See* Dean Beeby, *Squeeze Cash from Facebook, Google, Say Canadian News Media Leaders*, CBC News, Jan. 11, 2017, http://www.cbc.ca/beta/news/politics/newspapers-news-media-digital-public-policy-forum-google-facebook-tax-1.3929356.
74. *Id.*
75. Anand Paka, *Redesigning Google News for Everyone*, Google Blog (June 27, 2017), https://www.blog.google/outreach-initiatives/google-news-initiative/redesigning-google-news-everyone/.
76. *Id.*
77. Richard Gingras, *Driving the future of digital subscriptions*, The Keyword (Oct. 2, 2017), https://www.blog.google/outreach-initiatives/google-news-initiative/driving-future-digital-subscriptions/.
78. *Id.*
79. *Id. The Financial Times* also reported Google's initiatives include a plan to share revenue with publishers:

> Google plans to share revenues with publishers which benefit from the company's new digital subscription tools, in a scheme comparable to its successful advertising revenue model. The search giant will use its trove of personal user data, combined with machine learning algorithms, to help news publishers identify potential new subscribers and target their current subscribers for renewals.

Madhumita Murgia, *Google Plans to Share Revenues with News Publishers*, Financial Times, Oct. 23, 2017.
80. EU Parliament, Amendments adopted by the European Parliament on 12 September 2018 on the proposal for a directive of the European Parliament and of the Council on copyright in the Digital Single Market COM(2016)059-C8-0383/2016-2016/0280(COD) 54 (2018).
81. Article 13, The European Parliament and the Council of the European Union, Proposal for a Directive of the European Parliament and of the Council on copyright in the Digital Single Market (2019), http://www.europarl.europa.eu/meetdocs/2014_2019/plmrep/COMMITTEES/JURI/DV/2019/02-26/Copyright-AnnextoCOREPERletter_EN.pdf.

## CHAPTER 6

1. Google, How GOOGLE FIGHTS PIRACY (2016), https://drive.google.com/file/d/0BwxyRPFduTN2TmpGajJ6TnRLaDA/view.
2. Daniel Kiat Boon Seng, *The State of the Discordant Union: An Empirical Analysis of DMCA Takedown Notices*, 18 VA. J.L. TECH. 369, 444 (2014).
3. Of the 558 million, Google removed 98 percent. Google, *supra* note 1, at 19.
4. GOOGLE, TRANSPARENCY REPORT: REQUESTS TO REMOVE CONTENT DUE TO COPYRIGHT, https://www.google.com/transparencyreport/removals/copyright/#glance.
5. Jennifer M. Urban, Joe Karaganis, & Brianna L. Schofield, NOTICE AND TAKEDOWN IN EVERYDAY PRACTICE (2017), https://papers.ssrn.com/sol3/papers.cfm?abstract_id=2755628. Seng notes the drastic increase in take-down requests received by Google commencing from 2012 correlates with the protests against the introduction of the Stop Online Piracy Act and the PROTECT IP Act, protests in which Google was a high-profile participant. Seng, *supra* note 2, at 390.
6. Urban, Karaganis, & Schofield, *supra* note 5, at 33.
7. *Id.* at 71.
8. *Id.* at 54.
9. Google, RE: SECTION 512 STUDY: NOTICE AND REQUEST FOR PUBLIC COMMENT DOCKET NO. 2015–7 (DECEMBER 31, 2015) TO THE HONORABLE MARIA A. PALLANTE REGISTER OF COPYRIGHTS U.S. COPYRIGHT OFFICE 4 (2016).
10. Google, *supra* note 1.
11. Google, *supra* note 9, at 4.
12. Urban, Karaganis, & Schofield, *supra* note 5, at 82. Google has also stated that its TCRP participants "together submit the vast majority of notices every year." Google, *supra* note 1 at 40. *Id.* at 16.
13. Urban, Karaganis, & Schofield, *supra* note 5, at 3. The qualitative component of the study involved confidential interviews and surveys with online service providers and rightsholders. The quantitative component of the study referred to here examined "a random sample of takedown notices, taken from a set of over 108 million requests submitted to the Lumen database over a six-month period (most of which relate to Google Web Search)."
14. *Id.* at 88.
15. Urban, Karaganis, & Schofield, *supra* note 5.
16. *Id.* at 35.
17. The study concludes the rates of counternotices are "extremely infrequent." *Id.* at 44.
18. *Id.* at 74.
19. Fred von Lohmann, *Transparency for Copyright Removals in Search*, GOOGLE OFFICIAL BLOG (May 24, 2012), https://googleblog.blogspot.com/2012/05/transparency-for-copyright-removals-in.html.
20. Google, *supra* note 1, at 7.
21. Google's current search algorithm includes over two hundred variables used to assess the relevance of a website to a search query. Google, *Ten things we know to be true Google*, https://www.google.com/about/philosophy.html (last visited Feb. 3, 2019).

22. Google, *supra* note 1, at 34.

23. *Id.* at 43.

24. *Id.* at 59.

25. *See generally* Google, How GOOGLE FIGHTS PIRACY (2013), https://docs.google.com/file/d/0BwxyRPFduTN2dVFqYml5UENUeUE/edit.

26. Google, *supra* note 1, at 9.

27. Victoria Espinel, *Coming Together to Combat Online Piracy and Counterfeiting*, THE WHITE HOUSE BLOG (July 15, 2013), https://www.whitehouse.gov/blog/2013/07/15/coming-together-combat-online-piracy-and-counterfeiting.

28. Cohen suggests that Google's search manipulation "mimics the results that could have been achieved under SOPA/PIPA regime" effectively accomplishing "via private and wholly nontransparent measures what the combined lobbying might of the content industries could not." Julie Cohen, *Between Truth and Power, in* FREEDOM AND PROPERTY OF INFORMATION: THE PHILOSOPHY OF LAW MEETS THE PHILOSOPHY OF TECHNOLOGY 5 (Mireille Hildebrandt & Bibi van den Berg eds., 2014).

29. *See* Kevin Delaney, *YouTube to Test Software to Ease Licensing Fights*, WALL ST. J., June 13, 2007, http://www.wsj.com/articles/SB118161295626932114; Kenneth Li & Eric Auchard, *YouTube to Test Video ID with Time Warner, Disney*, REUTERS, June 12, 2007, http://www.reuters.com/article/us-google-youtube-idUSWEN871820070612; Stefanie Olsen, *YouTube, EMI Sign Breakthrough Licensing Pact*, CNET, May 31, 2007, https://www.cnet.com/news/youtube-emi-sign-breakthrough-licensing-pact.

30. How Content ID works, YOUTUBE HELP, https://support.google.com/youtube/answer/2797370 (last visited Feb. 15, 2019). Google does not disclose exact revenue sharing arrangements.

31. Pablo L. Chavez, COMMENTS: DEPARTMENT OF COMMERCE GREEN PAPER, COPYRIGHT POLICY, CREATIVITY AND INNOVATION IN THE DIGITAL ECONOMY TO THE HONORABLE TERESA STANEK REA DEPUTY UNDER SECRETARY OF COMMERCE FOR INTELLECTUAL PROPERTY AND DEPUTY DIRECTOR OF THE UNITED STATES PATENT AND TRADEMARK OFFICE AND THE HONORABLE LAWRENCE E. STRICKLING ASSISTANT SECRETARY OF COMMERCE FOR COMMUNICATIONS AND INFORMATION UNITED STATES DEPARTMENT OF COMMERCE 3 (2013); YouTube for Press, YOUTUBE, https://www.youtube.com/intl/en-GB/yt/about/press/ (last visited Feb. 15, 2019); Google, *supra* note 1, at 6, 26.

32. Google, *supra* note 1, at 26. In 2018, Google announced an additional automated tool to help YouTube users enforce their copyright on the platform. The tool is available to YouTube channels with more than 100,000 subscribers, and it is aimed at capturing full-length re-uploads of videos. Using technology similar to Content ID, the tool scans videos when they are uploaded to YouTube, and if a match is found, it alerts the original uploader. The original uploader can elect to take no action, contact the unauthorized uploader, or submit a take-down request. Fabio Magagna, *Helping creators protect their content*, YOUTUBE CREATOR BLOG (July 11, 2018), https://youtube-creators.googleblog.com/2018/07/helping-creators-protect-their-content.html.

33. Google, *supra* note 1, at 26.

34. *Id.* at 6.

35. Google, How GOOGLE FIGHTS PIRACY (2018), https://blog.google/documents/25/ GO806_Google_FightsPiracy_eReader_final.pdf.

36. Google, *supra* note 25, at 10. The US television industry has been particularly receptive to Content ID. In 2013, YouTube received an Emmy Award in appreciation of the enforcement technology. *See* Todd Spangler, *Despite YouTube's Emmy, Google Still Has a Long Way to Go*, VARIETY, 2013, http://variety.com/2013/biz/ news/despite-youtubes-emmy-google-still-has-a-long-way-to-go-1200756170/.

37. Benjamin Boroughf, *The Next Great YouTube: Improving Content ID to Foster Creativity, Cooperation and Fair Compensation*, 25 ALB. L.J. SCI. TECH. 95, 106 (2015).

38. Nicholas Thomas DeLisa, *You(Tube), Me, and Content ID: Paving the Way for Compulsory Synchronization Licensing on User-Generated Content Platforms*, 81 BROOK. L. REV. 1275, 1291 (2016).

39. Lev-Aretz Yafit, *Second Level Agreements*, 45 AKRON L. REV. 137 (2012); Abigail R. Simon, *Contracting in the Dark: Casting Light on the Shadows of Second Level Agreements (YouTube Content ID Copyright License)*, 5 WM. & MARY BUS. L. REV. 305 (2014). *See also id.* at 316–17.

40. Lessig ultimately sued Liberation Music claiming fair use. Steve Collins, *YouTube and Limitations of Fair Use in Remix Videos*, 15 J. MEDIA PRACT. 92, 103 (2014). In 2014, the parties settled. Liberation Music agreed to compensate Professor Lessig for harm caused and to amend its DMCA compliance policies to "respect fair use." Corynne McSherry, LAWRENCE LESSIG SETTLES FAIR USE LAWSUIT OVER PHOENIX MUSIC SNIPPETS (2014), https://www.eff.org/press/releases/ lawrencelessig-settles-fair-use-lawsuit-over-phoenix-music-snippets.

41. Ernesto Van der Sar, *YouTube Copyright Complaint Kills Harvard Professor's Copyright Lecture*, TORRENTFREAK, Feb. 17, 2016, https://torrentfreak.com/ youtube-copyright-complaint-kills-harvard-professors-copyright-lecture-160217.

42. Complaint for Unjust Enrichment, Violations of US Copyright Law, and for Injunctive Relief and Declartory Relief, Benjamin Ligeri v. Google et al., 1:15-cv-00188-M-LDA 4 (DC RI 2015).

43. *Id.* at 5.

44. Tim Wu, *Tolerated Use*, 31 COLUM. J.L. ARTS 617, 619 (2008).

45. Boroughf, *supra* note 37, at 97.

46. *Id.* at 98.

47. *Id.* at 111.

48. Michael Soha & Zachary J. McDowell, *Monetizing a Meme: YouTube, Content ID, and the Harlem Shake*, 2 SOC. MEDIA SOC'Y 1 (2016).

49. *Id.*

50. *Id.* at 1.

51. *Id.*

52. *Id.* at 5.

53. *Id.* at 6.

54. GOOGLE, PUBLIC CONSULTATION ON THE REVIEW OF THE EU COPYRIGHT RULES 12, 24 (2013).

55. Pablo L. Chavez, COMMENTS: DEPARTMENT OF COMMERCE GREEN PAPER, COPYRIGHT POLICY, CREATIVITY AND INNOVATION IN THE DIGITAL ECONOMY TO THE HONORABLE TERESA STANEK REA DEPUTY UNDER SECRETARY OF COMMERCE FOR INTELLECTUAL PROPERTY AND DEPUTY DIRECTOR OF THE UNITED STATES PATENT AND TRADEMARK OFFICE AND THE HONORABLE LAWRENCE E. STRICKLING ASSISTANT SECRETARY OF COMMERCE FOR COMMUNICATIONS AND INFORMATION UNITED STATES DEPARTMENT OF COMMERCE 4 (2013).

56. Fred von Lohmann, *A Step Toward Protecting Fair Use on YouTube*, GOOGLE PUBLIC POLICY BLOG (Nov. 19, 2015), http://googlepublicpolicy.blogspot.com.au/2015/11/a-step-toward-protecting-fair-use-on.html?m=1.

57. *Id.*

58. *Id.*

59. As Simon documents, the process for disputing a Content ID claim was amended in 2012. Previously, copyright owners could unilaterally confirm a claim, now they can choose between releasing the claim or filing an official DMCA notification to override it. Simon, *supra* note 39, at 325.

60. Google, *supra* note 1, at 28.

61. Rebecca Tushnet, *All of This Has Happened Before and All of This Will Happen Again: Innovation in Copyright Licensing*, 29 BERKELEY TECH. L.J. 1447, 1461 (2014).

62. Videos Removed or Blocked Due to YouTube's Contractual Obligations, YOUTUBE HELP, https://support.google.com/youtube/answer/3045545. The extent to which Google licenses content for YouTube is unclear, but, as this comment reveals, Google does have in place agreements with rightsholders providing Google permission to use their works. Google also licenses works for its subscription music service Google Play. *See* Paul Resnikoff, *F\*&K It: Here's the Entire YouTube Contract for Indies* . . . , DIGITAL MUSIC NEWS, June 23, 2014, https://www.digitalmusicnews.com/2014/06/23/fk-heres-entire-youtube-contract-indies.

63. Yafit Lev-Aretz, *Copyright Lawmaking and Public Choice: From Legislative Battles to Private Ordering*, 27 HARV. J.L. TECH. 203, 254 (2013); Eriq Gardner, *Universal Music May Have Inadvertently Exposed a Flaw in the YouTube Takedown Process*, THE HOLLYWOOD REPORTER, Jan. 27, 2012, http://www.hollywoodreporter.com/thr-esq/megaupload-youtube-lawsuit-universal-music-285298. The full terms of the agreement are not made public.

64. Tushnet, *supra* note 61, at 1461.

65. Diane Leenheer Zimmerman, *Copyright and Social Media: A Tale of Legislative Abdication*, 35 PACE L. REV. 260, 273 (2014).

66. *See* Mike Zajko, *The Copyright Surveillance Industry*, 3 MEDIA COMM. 42, 46–47 (2015); Teens Make Parody Video, but Sony Tells Them to Beat It . . . Just Beat It! New Media Rights, NEW MEDIA RIGHTS, http://www.newmediarights.org/teens_make_parody_video_sony_tells_them_beat_it%E2%80%A6_just_beat_it (last visited Feb. 15, 2019).

67. Niva Elkin-Koren, *Copyrights in Cyberspace—Rights Without Laws?*, 73 CHI.-KENT L. REV. 1155, 1180 (1998).

68. Rachel Whestone, *Free expression and controversial content on the web*, Google Official Blog (Nov. 14, 2007), https://googleblog.blogspot.com/2007/11/free-expression-and-controversial.html.

69. Google, *supra* note 1, at 34.

70. Annemarie Bridy, *Graduated Response and the Turn to Private Ordering in Online Copyright Enforcement*, 89 Or. L. Rev. 81, 83 (2010). *See also* Zimmerman, *supra* note 65.

71. Stop Online Piracy Act, H.R.3261 112th Cong. (2011) and Preventing Real Online Threats to Economic Creativity and Theft of Intellectual Property Act, S.968 112th Cong. (2011); Anti-Counterfeiting Trade Agreement, signed 1 October 2011 (not yet in force). *Also see, e.g.*, Zimmerman, *supra* note 65.

72. Bridy, *supra* note 70, at 84.

73. Ernesto Van der Sar, *Movie Studios Fear a Google Fiber Piracy Surge*, TorrentFreak, Dec. 29, 2014, https://torrentfreak.com/movie-studios-fear-piracy-surge-due-google-fiber-141229.

74. Multiple studies have cast doubt on the direct impact of illegal downloading on sales. For example, a 2007 empirical study of the effect of file sharing on record sales found the effect to be statistically indistinguishable from zero. Felix Oberholzer Gee & Koleman Strumpf, *The Effect of File Sharing on Record Sales: An Empirical Analysis*, 115 J. Polit. Econ. 1 (2007). *See also* the 2012 study by Colombia University's American Assembly that found 18- to 29-year-olds, the age group with the largest music file collections, owned both the largest amount of purchased music and music downloaded illegally, when compared to any other age group. Where Do Music Collections Come From, The Piracy Years (2012), http://piracy.americanassembly.org/where-do-music-collections-come-from/ (last visited Feb. 19, 2019).

75. Ernesto Van der Sar, *Google Fiber Sends Automated Piracy "Fines" to Subscribers*, TorrentFreak, May 20, 2015, https://torrentfreak.com/google-fiber-sends-automated-piracy-fines-to-subscribers-150520/; Charlie Osborne, *Google Fiber pushes automatic piracy fines to subscribers*, ZD Net, May 21, 2015, http://www.zdnet.com/article/google-fiber-pushes-automatic-piracy-fines-to-subscribers; Anu Passary, *Got Google Fiber and Downloaded Illegal Content? You Might Be Receiving Notice for Piracy Fines*, Tech Times, May 21, 2015, http://www.techtimes.com/articles/54512/20150521/got-google-fiber-and-downloaded-illegal-content-you-might-be-receiving-notice-for-piracy-fines.htm. The notices also provided a "warning that repeated violations may result in a permanent disconnection." Van der Sar, *supra* note. As reported, Google's willingness to send contracts of adhesion to its users, including settlement demands, was out of step with other major US internet service providers, like Comcast, AT&T, and Verizon, who had refused to do the same (at the time of the dispute).

76. Google specified it did so in the interest of transparency. According to Google, it is in the best interest of users that they know the full extent of claims made against them by rightsholders. Ernesto Van der Sar, *Google: Targeting Downloaders Not the Best Solution to Fight Piracy*, TorrentFreak, May 22, 2015, https://torrentfreak.com/google-targeting-downloaders-not-the-best-solution-to-fight-piracy-150522/.

77. Uta Kohl, *Google: The Rise and Rise of Online Intermediaries in the Governance of the Internet and Beyond (Part 2)*, Int'l J.L. Info. Tech. 187, 220 (2013).

78. Zimmerman, *supra* note 65, at 269. Zimmerman documents explicit encouragement of self-regulation throughout US congressional hearings, copyright policy documents, and legislation such as ACTA. *Id.* at 269–70.

79. Intellectual Property Office, Search Engines and Creative Industries Sign Anti-Piracy Agreement (2017), https://www.gov.uk/government/news/search-engines-and-creative-industries-sign-anti-piracy-agreement.

80. *Id.*

81. Ernesto Van der Sar, Search Engines and Rightsholders Sign Landmark Anti-Piracy Deal (2017), https://torrentfreak.com/search-engines-and-rightsholders-sign-landmark-anti-piracy-deal-170220/.

82. Marc Rees, *Piratage: ce que dit l'accord signé entre Google et l'ALPA sous l'égide du CNC*, Next Inpact, Sept. 20, 2017, https://www.nextinpact.com/news/105211-piratage-ce-que-dit-laccord-signe-entre-google-et-lalpa-sous-legide-cnc.htm.

83. Article 13, The European Parliament and the Council of the European Union, Proposal for a Directive of the European Parliament and of the Council on copyright in the Digital Single Market (2019), http://www.europarl.europa.eu/meetdocs/2014_2019/plmrep/COMMITTEES/JURI/DV/2019/02-26/Copyright-AnnextoCOREPERletter_EN.pdf.

84. Urban, Karaganis, & Schofield, *supra* note 5, at 71.

85. *Id.*

86. Lev-Aretz, *supra* note 63, at 248. Elkin-Koren argues that even if algorithms were to include "case-by-case applications of legal standards" accountability remains a problem "when algorithms execute discretion-based decisions whose processing is a 'black box.'" P. Maayan & N. Elkin-Koren, *Accountability in Algorithmic Copyright Enforcement*, 19 Stan. Tech. L. Rev. 473, 488 (2016).

87. Lev-Aretz, *supra* note 63, at 248.

88. As Lessig posits, when private law displaces public law public values are also displaced. Lawrence Lessig, *The Law of the Horse: What Cyberlaw Might Teach*, Harv. L. Rev. 501, 528 (1999).

89. Julia Black, *Decentring Regulation: Understanding the Role of Regulation and Self-Regulation in a "Post-Regulatory" World*, 54 Curr. Leg. Probs. 103, 145 (2001).

90. *See, e.g.*, Bridy, *supra* note 70; Yochai Benkler, *An Unhurried View of Private Ordering in Information Transactions*, 53 Vand. L. Rev. 2063 (2000); Jennifer Rothman, *Copyright's Private Ordering and the Next Great Copyright Act*, 29 Berkeley Tech. L.J. 1595 (2014); Aaron Perzanowski & Jason M. Schultz, The End of Ownership: Personal Property in the Digital Economy (2016).

91. *See, e.g.*, Frank Pasquale, The Black Box Society: The Secret Algorithms that Control Money and Information (2015); Maayan Perel & Niva Elkin-Koren, *Black Box Tinkering: Beyond Transparency in Algorithmic Enforcement*, Fla. L. Rev. (2017); J. A. Kroll et al., *Accountable Algorithms*, 165 U. Pa. L. Rev. 633 (2017); C. Barabas et al., *An Open Letter to the Members of the Massachusetts Legislature Regarding the Adoption of Actuarial Risk Assessment Tools in the Criminal Justice System*, Berkman Klein Cent. Internet Soc'y (2017); Natalie

Ram, *Innovating Criminal Justice*, Research Paper No. 2018-12 Forthcoming Nw. U. L. Rev. (2017), https://papers.ssrn.com/sol3/papers.cfm?abstract_id=3012162. Laura DeNardis, The Global War for Internet Governance (2014).

92. Ben Wagner, *Algorithmic Regulation and the Global Default: Shifting Norms in Internet Technology*, 10 Etikk Praksis—Nord. J. Appl. Ethics 5, 10 (2016).

93. *Id.* at 10.

94. *Id.* at 9.

95. Essentially, Google encodes "copyright values in its automated processes." Kohl, *supra* note 77, at 220.

96. Ben Wagner, Study on the Human Rights Dimensions of Algorithms 3 (2017).

97. More Accountability for Big-Data Algorithms, 537 Nature News (2016), at 449.

98. The European Parliament and the Council of the European Union, *supra* note 83.

99. *Id.*

## CHAPTER 7

1. Scott Cleland, *Google's "Infringenovation" Secrets*, Forbes, Oct. 3, 2011, https://www.forbes.com/sites/scottcleland/2011/10/03/googles-infringenovation-secrets/#2be856ae30a6. *See also* Frank Pasquale, *Paradoxes of Digital Antitrust: Why the FTC Failed to Explain Its Inaction on Search Bias*, Harv. J.L. Tech. Occas. Pap. Ser. 1, 7 (2013).

2. Ben Buchanan & Taylor Miller, Machine Learning for Policymakers What It Is and Why It Matters 5 (2017).

3. *See, e.g.*, A. Halevy, P. Norvig, & F. Pereira, *The Unreasonable Effectiveness of Data*, 24 IEEE Intell. Syst. 8 (2009); Chen Sun et al., Revisiting Unreasonable Effectiveness of Data in Deep Learning Era (2017); More Accountability for Big-Data Algorithms, 537 Nature News (2016), at 449.

4. *See generally* Maurice Stucke & Allen Grunes, Big Data and Competition Policy (2016).

5. Oren Bracha & Frank Pasquale, *Federal Search Commission? Access, Fairness, and Accountability in the Law of Search*, 93 Cornell L. Rev. 1149, 1181 (2008). *See also* Nathan Newman, *Search, Antitrust, and the Economics of the Control of User Data*, 31 Yale J. on Regul. 401, 404 (2014).

6. Frank Pasquale, The Black Box Society: The Secret Algorithms that Control Money and Information 82 (2015).

7. Jarad Newman, *6 Things You'd Never Guess About Google's Energy Use*, Time, Sept. 9, 2011, http://techland.time.com/2011/09/09/6-things-youd-never-guess-about-googles-energy-use. *See also* James Glanz, *Google Details, and Defends, Its Use of Electricity*, N.Y. Times, Sept. 8, 2011, http://www.nytimes.com/2011/09/09/technology/google-details-and-defends-its-use-of-electricity.html.

8. Pasquale, *supra* note 6, at 82.

9. Pasquale, *supra* note 6, at 82. *See also* Siva Vaidhyanathan, The Googlization of Everything: And Why We Should Worry 19 (2012); Bracha & Pasquale, *supra* note 5, at 1181.

10.   Mark Burdon & Mark Andrejevic, *Big Data in the Sensor Society*, *in* BIG DATA IS NOT A MONOLITH, 74 (2016).

11.   GEORGE DYSON, TURING'S CATHEDRAL: THE ORIGINS OF THE DIGITAL UNIVERSE 312 (2012).

12.   *See* Bracha & Pasquale, *supra* note 5, at 1181.

13.   Google, How GOOGLE FIGHTS PIRACY (2018), https://blog.google/documents/25/GO806_Google_FightsPiracy_eReader_final.pdf.

14.   C-SPAN, TESTIMONY OF ERIC SCHMIDT TO THE UNITED STATES SENATE JUDICIARY SUBCOMMITTEE (2011), https://www.c-span.org/video/?301681-1/oversight-google.

15.   Mark Scott, *Google Rebuts Europe on Antitrust Charges*, N.Y. TIMES, Aug. 27, 2015, https://www.nytimes.com/2015/08/28/technology/google-eu-competition.html.

16.   *See* Keith Dowding, *Monopoly Power*, *in* ENCYCLOPEDIA OF POWER 424, 424–25 (Keith Dowding ed., 2011).

17.   Rogene A. Buchholz, *Herfindahl Index*, *in* ENCYCLOPEDIA OF BUSINESS ETHICS AND SOCIETY 1066, 1066 (Robert W. Kolb ed., 2008).

18.   *See, e.g.*, JOHN BURGESS & PAUL KNIEST, INTRODUCTION TO MICROECONOMICS (2000).

19.   Dowding, *supra* note 16, at 425.

20.   *See, e.g.*, Sherman Antitrust Act of 1890 15 U.S.C.

21.   *See* Steve Knopper, *YouTube's New Subscription Service: Indie Labels Speak Out*, ROLLING STONE, 2014, http://www.rollingstone.com/music/news/youtubes-new-subscription-service-indie-labels-speak-out-20140701; Ed Christman, *Inside YouTube's Controversial Contract with Indies*, BILLBOARD, 2014, http://www.billboard.com/biz/articles/news/digital-and-mobile/6128540/analysis-youtube-indie-labels-contract-subscription-service; Paul Resnikoff, *F\*&K It: Here's the Entire YouTube Contract for Indies ...*, DIGITAL MUSIC NEWS, June 23, 2014, https://www.digitalmusicnews.com/2014/06/23/fk-heres-entire-youtube-contract-indies; Dispute Between YouTube and Independent Music Companies—Formal Process Starts in Brussels, IMPALA (2014), http://www.impalamusic.org/content/dispute-between-youtube-and-independent-music-companies-%E2%80%93-formal-process-starts-brussels; Stuart Dredge & Dominic Rushe, *YouTube to block indie labels who don't sign up to new music service*, THE GUARDIAN, June 17, 2014, https://www.theguardian.com/technology/2014/jun/17/youtube-indie-labels-music-subscription; Steve Knopper, *YouTube's New Paid Streaming Music Service Rankles Some Indie Labels*, ROLLING STONE, 2014, http://www.rollingstone.com/music/news/youtubes-new-paid-streaming-music-service-rankles-some-indie-labels-20140617; Robert Cookson, *YouTube Signs with Indie Labels for Music Streaming Service*, FINANCIAL TIMES, Nov. 12, 2014, https://www.ft.com/content/ff6bf816-699a-11e4-8f4f-00144feabdc0.

22.   Federal Trade Commission, STATEMENT OF THE FEDERAL TRADE COMMISSION REGARDING GOOGLE'S SEARCH PRACTICES, IN THE MATTER OF GOOGLE INC. (2013), https://www.ftc.gov/system/files/documents/public_statements/295971/130103googlesearchstmtofcomm.pdf.

23. Brody Mullins, Rolfe Winkler, & Brent Kendall, *Inside the U.S. Antitrust Probe of Google*, WALL ST. J., Mar. 19, 2015, https://www.wsj.com/articles/inside-the-u-s-antitrust-probe-of-google-1426793274.

24. *Id.*

25. *Id.*

26. *Id.*

27. FAIR SEARCH EUROPE, CHRONOLOGY THE EUROPEAN COMMISSION GOOGLE CASE (2015), http://www.fairsearch.org/media/fse-chronology.pdf.

28. Jeff Blagdon, *EU reportedly accepts Google antitrust settlement, requiring prominent links to competitors*, THE VERGE, 2013, https://www.theverge.com/2013/4/14/4225164/eu-reportedly-accepts-google-antitrust-settlement-requires-prominent-linking.

29. Aaron Souppouris, *Google's antitrust settlement proposal "not acceptable" to European Commission*, THE VERGE, 2013, https://www.theverge.com/2013/12/20/5229760/googles-antitrust-settlement-proposal-unacceptable-to-european-commission.

30. Henry Mance, Alex Barker, & Murad Ahmed, *Google Break-Up Plan Emerges From Brussels*, FINANCIAL TIMES, Nov. 22, 2014, https://www.ft.com/content/617568ea-71a1-11e4-9048-00144feabdc0?mhq5j=e7; Samuel Gibbs, *European parliament votes yes on "Google breakup" motion*, THE GUARDIAN, Nov. 28, 2014, https://www.theguardian.com/technology/2014/nov/27/european-parliament-votes-yes-google-breakup-motion.

31. European Commission, ANTITRUST: COMMISSION SENDS STATEMENT OF OBJECTIONS TO GOOGLE ON COMPARISON SHOPPING SERVICE; OPENS SEPARATE FORMAL INVESTIGATION ON ANDROID (2015), http://europa.eu/rapid/press-release_IP-15-4780_en.htm; European Commission, ANTITRUST: COMMISSION FINES GOOGLE €2.42 BILLION FOR ABUSING DOMINANCE AS SEARCH ENGINE BY GIVING ILLEGAL ADVANTAGE TO OWN COMPARISON SHOPPING SERVICE (2017), http://europa.eu/rapid/press-release_IP-17-1784_en.htm.

32. European Commission, ANTITRUST: COMMISSION FINES GOOGLE €4.34 BILLION FOR ILLEGAL PRACTICES REGARDING ANDROID MOBILE DEVICES TO STRENGTHEN DOMINANCE OF GOOGLE'S SEARCH ENGINE (2018), http://europa.eu/rapid/press-release_IP-18-4581_en.htm.

33. Zoya Sheftalovich & Nicholas Hirst, *Google's European mea culpa*, POLITICO, 2015, https://www.politico.eu/article/googles-european-mea-culpa/. GROW WITH GOOGLE, GOOGLE AND SHOPPING (2015), https://www.youtube.com/watch?v=HCtcNBcmPZc&feature=youtu.be.

34. Foo Yun Chee, *Google says an EU antitrust fine would be "inappropriate,"* REUTERS, Nov. 4, 2015, http://www.reuters.com/article/us-eu-google-antitrust-alphabet/google-says-an-eu-antitrust-fine-would-be-inappropriate-idUSKCN0SS25W20151103?utm_campaign=trueAnthem:+Trending+Content&utm_content=56393e1b04d3015337c8f2dd&utm_medium=trueAnthem&utm_source=twitter.

35. TIM WU, THE MASTER SWITCH 80 (2010).

36. J. C. Plantin et al., *Infrastructure Studies Meet Platform Studies in the Age of Google and Facebook*, 20 NEW MEDIA & SOC'Y 293 (2016).

37. Bracha & Pasquale, *supra* note 5, at 1150. *See also* SHEILA JASANOFF, THE ETHICS OF INVENTION: TECHNOLOGY AND THE HUMAN FUTURE 167 (2016).

38. Bracha & Pasquale, *supra* note 5, at 1173.

39. Benjamin Farrand, *Regulatory Capitalism, Decentered Enforcement, and Its Legal Consequences for Digital Expression: The Use of Copyright Law to Restrict Freedom of Speech Online*, 10 J. INF. TECH. POL. 404, 407 (2013); Niva Elkin-Koren, *Copyrights in Cyberspace—Rights Without Laws?*, 73 CHI.-KENT L. REV. 1155, 1185 (1998).

40. Professor Lawrence Lessig famously described how regulation, understood broadly as constraint on behavior, occurs through four modalities: law, norms, the market, and architecture (physical or technological conditions). Lessig explains: "these four modalities regulate together. The 'net regulation' of any particular policy is the sum of the regulatory effects of the four modalities together." Lawrence Lessig, *The Law of the Horse: What Cyberlaw Might Teach*, HARV. L. REV. 501, 508 (1999). *See also* Christine Parker, *The Pluralization of Regulation*, 9 THEORETICAL INQUIRIES L. 2 (2008).

41. Louis Fisher, *Separation of Powers, in* INTERNATIONAL ENCYCLOPEDIA OF POLITICAL SCIENCE 2403, 2403 (Bertrand Badie, Dirk Berg-Schlosser, & Leonardo Morlino eds., 2011). *See also* Wu, who states, "separations are an effort to prevent any single element of society from gaining dominance over the whole, and by such dominance becoming tyrannical." WU, *supra* note 35, at 300.

42. ANNE M. COHLER, BASIA C. MILLER, & HAROLD S. STONE, CAMBRIDGE TEXTS IN THE HISTORY OF POLITICAL THOUGHT MONTESQUIEU: THE SPIRIT OF THE LAWS 157 (1989).

43. Professor Richard Mulgan explains, "horizontal accountability has become equated with the rule of law and constitutional government, seen as prerequisites for successful representative democracy." Richard Mulgan, *Accountability, in* INTERNATIONAL ENCYCLOPEDIA OF POLITICAL SCIENCE (Bertrand Badie, Dirk Berg-Schlosser, & Leonardo Morlino eds., 2011).

44. *Id.* at 150. Professor Barbara Romzek describes, "accountability without performance information is a hollow concept." Barbara Romzek, *Living Accountability: Hot Rhetoric, Cool Theory, and Uneven Practice*, 48 POLIT. SCI. POLIT. 27, 28 (2015).

45. Will Knight, *The Dark Secret at the Heart of AI*, MIT TECH. REV., Apr. 11, 2017, https://www.technologyreview.com/s/604087/the-dark-secret-at-the-heart-of-ai/.

46. ALGORITHMIC ACCOUNTABILITY POLICY TOOLKIT 5 (2018), https://ainowinstitute.org/aap-toolkit.pdf (last visited Nov. 18, 2018).

47. Jenna Burrell, *How the machine "thinks": Understanding opacity in machine learning algorithms*, 3 BIG DATA & SOC'Y 1, 1–2 (2016).

48. *See* Steven Levy, *How Google Is Remaking Itself as a "Machine Learning First" Company*, WIRED, 2016, https://www.wired.com/2016/06/how-google-is-remaking-itself-as-a-machine-learning-first-company/.

49. Mark Bergen, *Google Wants to Train Other Companies to Use Its AI Tools*, BLOOMBERG, Oct. 19, 2017, https://www.bloomberg.com/news/articles/2017-10-19/google-wants-to-train-other-companies-to-use-its-ai-tools.

## CHAPTER 8

1. Abbott B. Lipsky & J. Gregory Sidak, *Essential Facilities*, 51 Stan. L. Rev. 1187, 1190–91 (1999). *See* Sherman Antitrust Act of 1890 15 U.S.C. § 2.

2. Frank A. Pasquale, *Internet Nondiscrimination Principles: Commercial Ethics for Carriers and Search Engines*, Seton Hall Public Law Research Paper 1, 29–30 (2008). Pasquale contends that had the *Authors Guild* decision required Google to provide the Library of Congress a digital copy of each scanned book, "the problematic possibility of a Google monopoly here would be much less troubling." Frank Pasquale, *Dominant Search Engines: An Essential Cultural & Political Facility*, *in* In the Next Digital Decade: Essays on the Future of the Internet 401, 416 (Berin Szoka & Adam Marcus eds., 2011).

3. C-SPAN, Testimony of Eric Schmidt to the United States Senate Judiciary Subcommittee (2011), https://www.c-span.org/video/?301681-1/oversight-google.

4. @realDonaldTrump, Twitter (2018), https://twitter.com/realDonaldTrump/status/1019932691339399168.

5. *See* European Commission, Factsheet on the "Right to be Forgotten" ruling (C-131/12), https://www.inforights.im/media/1186/cl_eu_commission_factsheet_right_to_be-forgotten.pdf.

6. *See* Equustek Solutions Inc. v. Google Inc., 265 (BCCA, 2015); Google L.L.C. v. Equustek Solutions Inc., No. 5 17-cv-04207 (ND Cal. 2017).

7. European Commission, Code of Conduct on countering illegal online hate speech 2nd monitoring (2017), http://europa.eu/rapid/press-release_MEMO-17-1472_en.htm.

8. Owen Bowcott & Samuel Gibbs, *UK considers internet ombudsman to deal with abuse complaints*, The Guardian, Aug. 22, 2017, https://www.theguardian.com/technology/2017/aug/22/uk-considers-internet-ombudsman-to-deal-with-abuse-complaints. Peter Walker, *Google and Facebook to be asked to pay to help UK tackle cyberbullying*, The Guardian, Oct. 11, 2017, https://www.theguardian.com/technology/2017/oct/11/google-and-facebook-to-be-asked-to-pay-to-help-tackle-cyberbullying.

9. Tony Romm, *Watch: Facebook, Google and Twitter Testify to Congress About Russia and the 2016 Election*, Recode, Oct. 31, 2017, https://www.recode.net/2017/10/31/16570988/watch-live-stream-facebook-google-twitter-russia-trump-2016-presidential-election-senate.

10. Michael S. Sawyer, *Filters, Fair Use & Feedback: User-Generated Content Principles and the DMCA*, 24 Berkeley Tech. L.J. 363, 400 (2009). *See, e.g.*, Michael Geist, The Effectiveness of Notice and Notice Michael Geist (2007), http://www.michaelgeist.ca/2007/02/notice-and-notice-in-canada (last visited Feb. 18, 2019).

11. Jennifer Rothman argues the US Congress should add a fair use zone to the US Copyright Act preventing contracts, technical prevention measures, and content identification systems from restricting fair uses of copyrighted works. Jennifer Rothman, *Copyright's Private Ordering and the Next Great Copyright Act*, 29 Berkeley Tech. L.J. 1595, 1640 (2014). Similarly, Laura Zapata-Kim proposes that for service providers using automated enforcement systems, the safe harbor provisions of the DMCA should be conditional upon consideration for fair use.

Laura Zapata-Kim, *Should YouTube's Content ID Be Liable for Misrepresentation Under the Digital Millennium Copyright Act?*, 57 B.C. L. REV. 1847 (2016).

12. Frank Pasquale, *Platform Neutrality: Enhancing Freedom of Expression in Spheres of Private Power*, 17 THEORETICAL INQUIRIES L. 487, 501–02 (2016).

13. Bryce Goodman & Seth Flaxman, EUROPEAN UNION REGULATIONS ON ALGORITHMIC DECISION-MAKING AND A "RIGHT TO EXPLANATION" (2016), https://arxiv.org/pdf/1606.08813.pdf.

14. Lucas Introna & Helen Nissenbaum, *Sustaining the Public Good Vision of the Internet: The Politics of Search Engines*, 9 CENT. ARTS CULT. POLICY STUD. WORK. PAP., 34 (1999).

15. Jennifer M. Urban, Joe Karaganis, & Brianna L. Schofield, NOTICE AND TAKEDOWN IN EVERYDAY PRACTICE 71 (2017), https://papers.ssrn.com/sol3/papers.cfm?abstract_id=2755628.

16. Matt Dawes, ALRC REVIEW—COPYRIGHT AND THE DIGITAL ECONOMY TO PROFESSOR JILL MCKEOUGH 52 (2012).

17. GOOGLE, TRANSPARENCY REPORT: REQUESTS TO REMOVE CONTENT DUE TO COPYRIGHT, https://www.google.com/transparencyreport/removals/copyright/#glance.

18. Fred von Lohmann, *Transparency for Copyright Removals in Search*, GOOGLE OFFICIAL BLOG (May 24, 2012), https://googleblog.blogspot.com/2012/05/transparency-for-copyright-removals-in.html.

19. *Id.*

20. PARTNERSHIP ON AI, https://www.partnershiponai.org (last visited Feb. 18, 2019).

21. *Id.* Yet, a 2014 UNESCO study concluded intermediary transparency reports tend to be limited to requests made through legally required processes and do not typically include self-regulatory activities:

> For those intermediaries that publish "transparency reports," disclosure has been largely limited to government or other demands made through legal processes, and the companies' handling of such demands. Few efforts have been made thus far by intermediaries to be more transparent about extra-legal content restrictions, as well as content removal and account deactivation and other actions taken to enforce intermediaries' own self-regulatory terms of service. Corporate transparency around collective self-regulatory efforts was also found to lag behind transparency related to direct government requests.

REBECCA MACKINNON ET AL., FOSTERING FREEDOM ONLINE: THE ROLE OF INTERNET INTERMEDIARIES 10 (2014), http://unesdoc.unesco.org/images/0023/002311/231162e.pdf.

For the benefit of digital users, indexed terms that span two pages (e.g., 52–53) may, on occasion, appear on only one of those pages.

*A Brief History of Neoliberalism*
(Harvey), 168n39
Accelerate Mobile Pages (AMP)
project, 110
access paradox, Google's, 135–39
AdSense, 15
copyright infringements ban, 120–21
Europe, 142
*Perfect 10* decision, 73–74
advertising services, 15–16. See also
*specific types*
AdWords, 15, 105, 120–21
Agency France Presse (AFP) - United
States, 102–3, 198n14
algorithm, defined, 170n64
algorithmic copyright enforcement, 127–33,
207–9n78, 209n86, 209n88
Content ID, YouTube, 61, 117, 121–27,
205n32, 206n40, 207n59, 207n62
due process, 132
political and economic interests, 132
tools, 117
YouTube, 117
Alphabet, xiv–xv
Alsup, Judge William, 94
*Amazon.com Inc.*, 187n36
Android, xiv

Java and, 88–94 (see also *Oracle v.
Google*)
anticircumvention protections, 8–9
anticompetitive practices, monopoly
power, 140–43
Anti-Counterfeiting Trade Agreement
(ACTA), 9
antitrust complaints, Europe,
142–43, 152–53
application program interface (API), 89.
See also *Oracle v. Google*
Article 32, Ley de Propiedad Intelectual
- Spain, 108–9
artificial intelligence (AI), 117, 137–38,
148–49, 163
artistic styles, 23
Asian Internet Coalition, 56–57, 180n25
Association of American Publishers
lawsuit, 188n63
Auletta, Ken, 43, 103
*Googled: The End of the World as We
Know It*, 179n10
Australia, *IceTV Pty Limited v. Nine
Network Australia Pty Limited*, 165n6
authors and authorship
*vs.* creativity, social and cultural, 25
definitions, copyright law, 3, 20–21

authors and authorship (*Cont.*)
  definitions, Germany, 19th c., 21–22
  genius, original, 22–23, 49
  politically constructed concepts, 21–22
  reputational benefits, 28–29
  as stakeholder, 20–21
Authors Guild, 75
*Authors Guild Inc. v. Google Inc.*,
    189n80, 190n96
  outcome, 83
  settlement proposal (2008), 76
*Authors Guild Inc. v. HathiTrust*, 79,
    189n91, 190n92
authors' rights, 25–28
  labor theory, 25–26, 38–39
  personality theory, 25–26, 28
automated piracy fines, 128–29, 208n75

Baauer, Harlem Shake, 124
balanced copyright
  for digital age, 49–50
  flexible fair use exception, 50–54
  policy implications, 49–50
  safe harbors for online intermediaries,
    49–50, 54–60
Balkin, Jack, 35–36
Barbrook, Richard, 43–44
Belgium, Copiepress, 103–5, 199n22,
    199n23, 199n28, 199n31, 200n36
Berne Convention and Agreement on
    Trade-Related Aspects of Intellectual
    Property Rights (TRIPS), 192–93n138
Berne Convention for the Protection
    of Literary and Artistic Works,
    175n44, 199n23
Besbris, David, 202n68
best practice guidelines, 161
Best Practices and Guidelines for Ad
    Networks to Address Piracy and
    Counterfeiting, 60–61, 121
*Bill Graham Archives v. Dorling
    Kindersley*, 78
Biondo, Carlo D'Asaro, 202n66
Black, Julia, 130–31
Book Rights Registry, 76

Bracha, Oren, 176n65
Brandriss, Ira, 171n1
Brin, Sergey, 2, 13
  on Google's social value, 42–43
  open source movement, 179n5
  on virtues of technological
    innovation, 44
business model, 2

Californian ideology, 43–44
Cameron, Andy, 43–44
*Campbell v. Acuff-Rose Music*, 73, 81–82,
    191n116
capabilities approach, 176–77n70
Chander, Anupam, 12–13
  *How Law Made Silicon Valley*, 169n57
citizen participation, 178n94
classical liberalism, 27–28
Clinton administration white paper,
    6–7, 9–10
Cloud AI, 149
Cloud AutoML, 149
code of conduct, 161
Cohen, Julie, 24, 205n28
commodification, 33
concentrated private power. See also
    monopoly power
  democracy and, 147–50, 213n44
concentrated wealth holders, 27
Confucian ethics, 173n14
Content ID, YouTube
  algorithmic enforcement, 61, 117, 121–27,
    205n32, 206n40, 207n59, 207n62
  barriers, financial and nonfinancial, 138
  disputed claims, 125–26
  due process, 132
  problems, 131–32
content industries. See also *specific content
    providers*
  creative community and, 47–48
  definition, 5–6
  internet intermediary enforcement, 128
  lobbying, on copyright, 19–20
content removal, formal notification, 160–61
content-streaming services, Google's, 128–29

Content Verification Program (CVP), YouTube, 118
contextual targeting, 15
Copiepress - Belgium, 103–5, 199n22, 199n23, 199n28, 199n31, 200n36
copying internet, legality and litigation, 2, 17, 66–67
copyright. See also *specific topics*
  balanced (*see* balanced copyright)
  creativity and, 47–49
  exceptions and limitations, 60
  Google's agenda, xiv
  governing platforms, public access, 160
  infringement, 3
  policy agenda, Google's, 41–63 (*see also* copyright policy agenda)
  tradition, Google *vs.*, 65–96 (*see also* copyright litigation, Google)
copyright-as-economic policy, 5–6
copyright directive, European Commission, 9–10, 110–13, 203n79
  Article 17, 130, 132–33
  latest, 133, 158–59
  noninfringing content, 133
  Statement of Objections and fine, 142–43
copyright enforcement. *See also* private copyright rule-making and algorithmic enforcement, Google's; *specific topics*
  algorithmic (*see* algorithmic copyright enforcement)
  documentation, 161
  enforcement, 160
  exceptions and limitations, 160
  intermediaries, online (internet), 9–10, 128, 130
  self-regulation, 121
copyright law
  logic behind, 4
  reforms, EU (2019) and Google's response, 9–10, 59
  reforms, public interest, 157–59, 214–15n11
copyright law, digital, 2. See also *specific topics*

Google entrance, 13–17
laissez-faire evolution, 10–13
objectives, foundational, 5–6
politics of control, 6–10
tension, public *vs.* private interests, 3–4
copyright law, value and function, 19–40
  authorship and creativity, politically constructed concepts, 21–22
  authors' rights, 25–28
  creativity: social, cumulative, and appropriated, 22–25
  cultural theory, 33–38, 176n65 (*see also* cultural theory, copyright)
  economic incentive theory, 29–33
  economic model, 30
  private property right, 19–21
  public interest issues, 20
copyright litigation, Google, 65–96. See also *specific cases*
  copying internet, 66–67
  fair use and intermediary safe harbor defense, 65
  *Field v. Google,* 67–69, 83, 185n11, 185n17, 191n116
  Google Books, 74–81
  innovate first approach, 65
  *Oracle v. Google,* 88–94, 197n199, 197n200
  *Parker v. Google,* 69–70, 185–86n23
  *Perfect 10 v. Google,* 70–72, 83, 186–87n35, 187n36, 187n49, 187n50
  public interest, 74
  *Viacom v. YouTube,* 83–87, 191n118
copyright logic, Google's, results and complexities, 135–50
  access paradox, 135–39
  democracy and concentrated private power, 147–50, 213n44
  monopoly power, 138–39
  monopoly power, anticompetitive practices, 140–43
  monopoly power, cultural consequences, 144–45
  monopoly power, political consequences, 145–46, 213n40

copyright policy agenda, 41–63
  balanced copyright for digital
      age, 49–50
  copyright as economic policy, 45–47
  creativity and copyright, 47–49
  flexible fair use exception, 50–54
  innovation idealism, 42–44
  lobbying, 19–20, 41–42
  "piracy" plan, 60–62
  policy issue, 41
  political agenda, 41
  safe harbors, for online
      intermediaries, 54–60
cost-per-click advertising, 15
creative practice, 40
  appropriated and cumulative, 25
  cultural theory, 36, 37, 176n65
  economic incentive approach, 29,
      31–33, 181n43
  external factors, 22–23
  user-generated content and
      creativity, 47–48
creativity
  authorship, politically constructed
      concepts, 21–22 (see also authors and
      authorship)
  copyright, 47–49
  copyright, cultural theory, 37, 176n65
  cumulative process, 24–25
  politically constructed concepts, 21–22
  social, cumulative, and
      appropriated, 22–25
  social and cultural, 25
cultural democracy, 35–36
cultural theory, 33–38, 176n65
cultural theory, copyright, 33–38, 176n65
  creativity and copyright, 37
  human flourishing, social human, and
      cultural democracy, 34
  as right approach, 38
culture, monopoly power on, 144–45
curation, information, 144–45

data
  access, advantage, 135–39

in algorithm systems, 136
  stockpiles, enduring value, 153–54
deadweight loss, 30–31
deep–learning-based systems, 148
democracy
  concentrated private power, digital
      environment, 147–50, 213n44
  cultural, 35–36
  human flourishing, social human and,
      34, 176
  democratic participation, 35–36,
      37, 39, 40
  governance, 36
deregulation, 11–12, 145–46, 169n52
Digital Millennium Copyright Act
      (DMCA), 8–10, 167n23
  anticircumvention protections, 8–9
  safe harbors, 8–9, 12–13, 54–55, 56–57
Digital News Initiative (DNI) -
      European Union, 109–10, 202n64,
      202n66, 202n68
diversity, 35–36, 39–40
DoubleClick, copyright infringements
      ban, 120–21
downloads, illegal, 128, 207n59, 208n76
Dyson, George, 137–38

economic incentive theory, 29–30
  creative practice, 29, 31–33, 181n43
economic liberalism, with technological
      determinism, 43–44
economic model, 30
  neoliberalism, 31
economics
  algorithmic copyright
      enforcement, 132
  competitive advantage, 138–39
  monopoly power, anticompetitive
      practices and, 140–43
  policy, copyright as, 45–47
economies-of-scale advantages, 138
Elkin-Koren, Niva, 209n86
EMI, Google partnership, 121–22
enforcement, copyright. See copyright
      enforcement

Europe. See also *specific countries
     and topics*
  antitrust complaints, 142–43, 152–53
  hostility and regulatory support, 155
  right to be forgotten, 155–56
European Commission Code of Conduct,
     online hate speech, 156–57
European Commission copyright directive
     (2019), 9–10, 110–13, 203n79
  Article 17, 130, 132–33
  latest, 133, 158–59
  noninfringing content, 133
  Statement of Objections and
     fine, 142–43
European Union
  copyright reforms (2019) and Google's
     response, 9–10, 59
  Digital News Initiative, 109–10, 202n64,
     202n66, 202n68
  Google News, 97–115 (*see also* Google
     News, Europe)
  intermediary responsibilities, 57
  lobbying, by Google, 1, 41, 45–46, 48–49,
     178–79n4
European Union's General Data Protection
     Rules (GDPR), Google fine, 152,
     153, 155
exceptions, to copyright, 3, 60
  flexible fair use, 50–54
  private enforcement, 160
  static fairness, 50–52, 182n65
excludable, 30

fair use determinations, 50–51
  as Google defense, 65
  public access, 154, 214–15n11
Farrand, Benjamin, 169n52
Federazione Italiana Editori Giornali
     (FIEG) - Italy, 105–6
Field, Blake, 67–69, 83
*Field v. Google*, 67–69, 83, 185n11, 185n17,
     191n116
filtering, 61–62
fines
  automated piracy, 128–29, 208n75

Copiepress lawsuit, 104–5
European Commission copyright
     directive (2019), 142–43
European Union's General Data
     Protection Rules (GDPR), 152,
     153, 155
Fisher, William, 34
flexible fair use exception, 50–54
flourishing, human, 33–34, 35–37, 39, 40
Football Association Premier League
     Limited et al., 192–93n138
foundational objectives, digital age, 5–6
Framework for Global Electronic
     Commerce, 12
framing, 70–71
France
  Agency France Presse - United States,
     102–3, 198n14
  antipiracy agreement, 129
  Digital Publishing Innovation
     Fund, 107–8
  intellectual property code, 175n44
free markets, 10–13, 44, 60, 63, 97–98,
     175–76n54
Friedman, Milton and Rose, 11
Fromer, Jeanne, 28–29
fundamental good, 10–11

gatekeeper status, 127
genius, original, 22–23, 49
Germany, Leistungsschutzrecht Für
     Presseverleger, 106–7, 200–1n48
Getty Images, 186n25
Ginsburg, Jane, 32
Ginsburg, Jane, *Putting Cars on the
     Information Superhighway,* 171n1
good, fundamental, 10–11
goods, public, 30
Google Ads, 15
Google Books, 74–81
  Authors Guild settlement proposal
     (2008), 76
  book scanning, for algorithm
     training, 137–38
  *Campbell* approach, 73, 81–82, 191n116

Google Books (*Cont.*)
 database, 13–14
 decision significance, 81
 District Court decision (2013), 77
 Google Books Partner Program, 75
 Google scan, 75
 HathiTrust Digital Library decision, 79,
  189n91, 190n92
 Second Circuit decision (2015), 79
 social value, 42–44
Google Books Libraries Project, 75
Google Books Partner Program, 75
Google Books Settlement, 189n74
Google bot, 66–67
*Googled: The End of the World as We Know
 It* (Auletta), 179n10
Google Fiber, 128–29, 208n74
Google Images, 70, 186n25
Google News, Europe, 97–115
 Agency France Presse - United States,
  102–3, 198n14
 aggregating news articles, 98–99,
  197–98n4
 Article 32, Ley de Propiedad Intelectual
  - Spain, 108–9
 Copiepress - Belgium, 103–5, 199n22,
  199n23, 199n28, 199n31, 200n36
 Digital News Initiative - European
  Union, 109–10, 202n64,
  202n66, 202n68
 Digital Publishing Innovation Fund
  - France, 107–8
 European Commission copyright
  directive (2019), 9–10, 110–13, 203n79
 Federazione Italiana Editori Giornali
  - Italy, 105–6
 Leistungsschutzrecht Für Presseverleger
  - Germany, 106–7, 200–1n48
 news media problems, in digital age,
  100–2, 198n5
Google Play, 128–29
Google Play Music, anticompetitive
 practices, 140–41
Google scan, 75
 for algorithm training, 137–38

Google Search
 auto-complete function, 14–15
 curation, 14–15
 PageRank algorithm, 14–15
 Trusted Copyright Removal Program,
  118, 204n12
 user intent, 14–15
 web pages included, 13–14
government regulation, Google's
 disdain, 44
Grimmelman, James, 197n199

Harlem Shake, 124
*Harper & Row v. Nation
 Enterprises,* 81–82
Harvey, David, *A Brief History of
 Neoliberalism,* 168n39
hate speech online, 156–57
HathiTrust Digital Library (HDL)
 decision, 79, 189n91, 190n92
Hegel, Georg Wilhelm, 28
history, digital copyright and Google, 1–17.
  *See also* copyright law, digital
history, Google, 1–2
 ascendancy, 1
 founders, 2
 founding and regulatory environment, 1
 as index of entire web, 2
*How Law Made Silicon Valley*
 (Chander), 169n57
Hughes, Justin, 26, 174n39, 175n44
human flourishing, 33–34, 35–37, 39, 40

*IceTV Pty Limited v. Nine Network
 Australia Pty Limited,* 165n6
illegal downloads, 128, 207n59, 208n76
IMPALA, 140–41
incentive justification, 175–76n54
in-line linking, 70–71
innovate first, permission later, 47, 65
 litigating, 65–96 (*see also* copyright
  litigation, Google)
 qualifications, 139
innovation
 innovate first culture, 47, 65, 139

over tradition, 47–49
   policy, copyright in, 45–47
   technological, Brin on virtues of, 44
innovation idealism, 42–44
interest-based targeting, 15
intermediaries, online (internet), 172n2
   copyright enforcement obligations, 9–10,
     128, 130
   copyright infringement liability, Article
     17, 132–33
   current role, acknowledging, 151–52
   liability, legal innovations on, 169n57
   negotiations, 159
   public interest, copyright law
     reforms, 157–59
   public interest, duty to act, 156
   public interest, self-regulation, 160–61
   regulation propagated, 169n52
   safe harbors, 8–9
   safe harbors, balanced copyright,
     49–50, 54–60
   TensorFlow for Google
     dominance, 149–50
   Trans-Pacific Partnership
     Agreement, 181n49
   transparency reports, 215n21
intermediary safe harbor, 8–9
   algorithmic notice and take-down,
     large-scale, 118–19, 204n5,
     204n12, 204n13
   balanced copyright, 49–50, 54–60
   copyright rules governing platforms,
     public access, 160
   as Google defense, 65
   notice and stay-down model, 58–59
   notice and take-down model, 55–56
   purposes, U.S. Senate on, 167n27
   reforms, 157–59
   rightsholder benefits, 56
internet filtering, 61–62
Internet Treaties, 7, 158–59
   Digital Millennium Copyright Act, 8–9,
     12–13, 54–55, 167n23
Italy, Federazione Italiana Editori Giornali
   (FIEG), 105–6

Javaplatform, Android and, 88–94. See
   also *Oracle v. Google*

Kant, Immanuel, 28
Karaganis, Joe, 204n13
Katyal, Sonia, 39–40
*Kelly v. Arriba Soft Corp*, 68, 73, 78
Knight, Will, 148

labor theory
   authors' rights, 25–26, 38–39
   intellectual property, Hughes, 174n39
   Locke's, 25–26, 38–39, 174n30
laissez-faire evolution, digital
   environment, 10–13
large-scale algorithmic notice and take-
   down, 118–19, 204n5, 204n12, 204n13
lawmaking, public, 159
Lehman, John, 173n14
Leistungsschutzrecht Für Presseverleger
   - Germany, 106–7, 200–1n48
Lessig, Lawrence, 206n40, 209n88, 213n40
Levy, Stephen, 148–49
Lewis, Seth, 100
Ley de Propiedad Intelectual, Article 32
   - Spain, 108–9
litigation, copyright. *See* copyright
   litigation, Google
Litman, Jessica, 8–9, 167–68n29
Liu, Joseph P., *Regulatory Copyright*, 83
   N.C. L. Rev 87, 169n49
lobbying
   by content industries, 19–20
   by Google, effort and
     expenditures, 41–42
   by Google, European Union, 1, 41, 45–46,
     48–49, 178–79n4
Locke, John, 26, 174n28
   labor theory, 25–26, 38–39, 174n30
   natural law ethical theory, 26–27
   value theory of labor, 26
Luman archive, 162–63

machine learning, 136–37
   Google priority, 148–49

machine learning (*Cont.*)
  TensorFlow, as control
    mechanism, 149–50
markets
  concentration (*see* monopoly power)
  free, 10–13, 44, 60, 63, 97–98, 175–76n54
  as superior to governments, 11
  transactions, private property
    for, 32–33
McDowell, Zachary, 124
Megaupload, 126
Menell, Peter, 94–95
ML Kit, 149
modular copyright system analysis, 172n2
monopoly power, Google's
  anticompetitive practices, 140–43
  cultural consequences, 144–45
  democracy and, digital environment,
    147–50, 213n44
  directly addressing, 152–56, 214n2
  market share, 171n78
  origins, definition, and scope, 138–39
  political consequences, 145–46, 213n40
*Moral Panics and the Copyright Wars*
  (Patry), 166n11
moral rights, personality theory
  and, 175n44
Morozov, Evgeny, 180n17
Mossoff, Adam, 26–27
Mulgan, Richard, 213n43
Murdoch, Rupert, 99
music sampling, 23–24

natural law ethical theory, 26–27
negotiations. See also *specific cases and
  companies*
  *vs.* algorithms, 132
  Digital Millennium Copyright Act,
    8–9, 13
  Google Books settlement, Authors
    Guild, 76
  Google News, Europe, 98
  Google–powerful content providers,
    127, 129, 132
  political, 164
  private, 17

public interest, 161
  US, WIPO treaties, 7
neoclassical justification, 175–76n54
neoliberalism, 10–13
  deregulation, 11–12, 145–46, 169n52
  economic model, 31
  self-regulation, 12, 145–46
  twin effects, 169n52
News Corporation, on news
  aggregation, 99
news media, in digital age. See *also* Google
  News, Europe
  articles, aggregating, 98–99
  problems, 100–2, 198n5
nonexcludable, 30
nonrivalrous, 30–31
Norvig, Peter, 136
notice and notice system, 157
notice and stay-down model, 58–59
notice and take-down model, 55–56
  alternatives, 157
Nussbaum, Martha, 32, 176–77n70

online conversation, 171n1
online hate speech, 156–57
open source movement, 31, 179n5
*Oracle v. Google*, 88–94, 197n199, 197n200
  District Court Decision (2012) - no
    copyright protection for Java API, 90,
    195n171
  Federal Circuit Decision (2018), jury
    was wrong, 94
  Federal Court Decision (2014) - API
    protected by copyright, 91, 196n184
  Java platform and Google's Android, 88
  jury decision (2016), Google's copying
    fair use, 93, 196n190
  what Google copied, 89
originality, *vs.* social and cultural in
  creativity, 25

Page, Larry, 2, 13
  Google Books, origins, 74
  open source movement, 179n5
  scientific and personal ambition, 43
PageRank algorithm, Google, 14–15

Parker, Gordon, 69–70
*Parker v. Google,* 69–70, 185–86n23
participation, democratic, 33, 35–36,
    37, 39, 40
Partnership on Artificial Intelligence
    to Benefit People and Society,
    163, 215n21
Pasquale, Frank, 136–37, 154,
    197n200, 214n2
Patry, William, *Moral Panics and the
    Copyright Wars,* 166n11
*Perfect 10 v. Google,* 70–72, 83, 186–87n35,
    187n36, 187n49, 187n50
    in-line linking, 71
    thumbnail copies, 72, 191n116
personality theory
    authors' rights, 28
    moral rights, 175n44
Picasso, Pablo, 173n18
PIPA, 9–10, 128
policy issues, Google's. See also
    *specific issues*
    copyright agenda, 41–63 (*see also*
        copyright policy agenda)
    key, 41
politics
    algorithmic copyright enforcement, 132
    concept construction, authorship and
        creativity, 21–22
    digital copyright law, 6–10
    Google's mission, 41
    monopoly power, 145–46, 213n40
    private property right, 38–39
power
    concentrated private, democracy
        and, 147–50, 213n44 (*see also*
        monopoly power)
    monopoly (*see* monopoly power)
    private regulatory, 145–46, 213n40
    separation of powers, 147–48
Preventing Real Online Threats to
    Economic Creativity and Theft of
    Intellectual Property Act (PIPA),
    9–10, 128
private copyright rule-making and
    algorithmic enforcement,

Google's, 117–33. *See also* copyright
    enforcement
    Content ID, YouTube, 117, 121–27,
        205n32, 206n40, 207n59, 207n62
    large-scale algorithmic notice and take-
        down, 118–19, 204n5, 204n12, 204n13
    private copyright rule-making,
        algorithmic enforcement, and
        public interest, 127–33, 207–9n78,
        209n86, 209n88
    sanitizing search, 119–21,
        204n21, 205n28
private property
    economic model, 30
    liberating nature, 26
    for market transactions, 29–33
    for self-actualization, 28
private property rights, 10–11, 20–21
    copyright, 19–21
    labor theory, 25–26, 38–39, 174n30
    Locke, natural law ethical theory, 26–27
    Locke, value theory of labor, 26
    personality theory, 25–26, 28
    political choices, 38–39
    *vs.* public rights, 49–50
private regulatory power, 145–46, 213n40
privatization, defined, 11–12
property
    Hegel on, 28
    Kant on, 28
    Locke on, 26
    rights, private (*see* private property
        rights)
public access claim, Google databases, 154
public domain, 3, 26, 61, 75, 92, 135–36, 154
public goods, 30
public interest, xiv
    copyright infringement *vs.,* 74
    copyright law, 20
    copyright litigation, 74
    objective, 3
    obscured, 19
    private copyright rule-making,
        algorithmic enforcement and, 127–33,
        207–9n78, 209n86, 209n88
    *vs.* private interest, 3–4

public interest outcomes, with monopoly-
    dominated technology firms, 151–64
    copyright law reforms, 157–59, 214–15n11
    courses of action, 151–52
    directly addressing monopoly power,
        152–56, 214n2
    history, early, 151
    public interest responsibilities,
        imposing, 156–57
    self-regulation, 159–63, 215n21
public lawmaking, 159
*Putting Cars on the Information
    Superhighway* (Ginsburg), 171n1

regulation, copyright
    deregulation, 11–12, 145–46, 169n52
    Europe, 155
    government, Google's disdain, 44
    intermediaries, 160–61, 169n52
    private, 129
    private regulatory power,
        145–46, 213n40
    self-regulation (*see* self-regulation)
    separation of powers, 147–48
reputational benefits, 28–29
rightsholders. *See also* authors and
    authorship; *specific lawsuits and types*
    control, 5–6
    definition, 3
    Google clash, 16–17
    intermediary safe harbors benefits, 56
right to be forgotten, 155–56
rivalrous, 30
robots.txt code, 66–67
Rogers, Hartley, Jr., *Theory of
    Recursive Functions and Effective
    Computability*, 170n64
Romzek, Barbara, 213n44
Ronson, Mark, 23–24
Rothman, Jennifer, 214n2
rule-making and algorithmic enforcement,
    Google's private copyright, 117–33. *See
    also* private copyright rule-making and
    algorithmic enforcement, Google's
Ryan, Maureen, 175–76n54

safe harbor, intermediary, 8–9
    algorithmic notice and take-down,
        large-scale, 118–19, 204n5,
        204n12, 204n13
    balanced copyright, 49–50, 54–60
    Digital Millennium Copyright Act, 8–9,
        12–13, 54–55, 56–57
    as Google defense, 65
    notice and stay-down model, 58–59
    notice and take-down model, 55–56
    rightsholder benefits, 56
Samuelson, Pamela, 166–67n15, 189n74
sanitizing search, 119–21, 204n21, 205n28
Scalzini, Silvia, 108
*scènes à faire* doctrine, 196n184, 196n190
Schmidt, Eric, 75–76, 107–8, 155, 188n67
Schofield, Brianna L., 204n13
search, Google, xiv. *See also* Google
    Search; *specific topics and cases*
    identification and conceptualization, 14
    market share, 16
    sanitizing, 119–21, 204n21, 205n28
Second Circuit decision (2015), Google
    Books, 79
self-regulation, 129, 130–31
    copyright enforcement, 121
    intermediaries and public
        interest, 160–61
    neoliberalism, 12, 145–46
    public interest outcomes, with
        monopolies, 159–63, 215n21
    safe harbors, 12–13
semiotic shaping, 35–36
Sen, Amartya, 176–77n70
Seng, Daniel Kiat Boon, 204n5
separation of powers, 147–48
servers, quantity and energy use, 137
server test, 71
service provider, Digital Millennium
    Copyright Act on, 54–55
shopping recommendations, 141–42
Silbey, Jessica, 32–33
Simon, Abigail R., 207n59
site-blocking, 62
social human, 35

social justice, 43
socially conscious
    entrepreneurialism, 43–44
social value, 42–44
social welfare, 30–31
Soha, Michael, 124
solutionism, technological, 180n17
Spain, Article 32, Ley de Propiedad
    Intelectual, 108–9
stakeholders, copyright, xiv, 20–21. See
    also *specific types*
    cultural context, 33
    industry, xiv
    range, 19–20
static fairness exception, 50–52, 182n65
Statute of Anne, 4
Sterk, Stewart, 26–27
*Steward v. Abend,* 81–82
Stop Online Piracy Act (SOPA), 9–10, 128
Sunder, Madhavi, 37
Syed, Talha, 176n65

take-down
    algorithmic notice and, large-scale,
        118–19, 204n5, 204n12, 204n13
    notice and, 55–56
targeted advertising, 15–16
technological determinism
    definition, 179n13
    with economic liberalism, 43–44
technological solutionism, 180n17
technology. See also *specific types
    and topics*
    positive force, 42
TensorFlow, 149–50
terminology, xiv
*Theory of Recursive Functions and Effective
    Computability* (Rogers), 170n64
thumbnail copies, 72
    *Perfect 10 v. Google,* 72, 191n116
Time Warner Inc., Google
    partnership, 121–22
Trans-Pacific Partnership Agreement
    (TPP), 49–50, 181n49
transparency, 147–48, 215n21

treaties. *See also* Internet Treaties
    undertakings, 170n61
Trusted Copyright Removal Program
    (TCRP), for Google Search,
    118, 204n12
Tushnet, Rebecca, 37

United Kingdom, Voluntary Code of
    Practice, 129
Urban, Jennifer M., 204n13
user-centric approach, 16
user focus, 16, 171n79
utilitarianism, 32

value theory of labor, 25–26, 38–39
VG Media, 106–7
Viacom International, 83
*Viacom v. YouTube,* 83–87
    District Court Decision (2010): no duty
        to monitor, 86, 192–93n138
    intermediary safe harbor entitlement, 83
    Second Court Decision (2012):
        knowledge of infringement?, 87,
        193–95n150
    settlement (2016), 87
    user infringement, knowledge of, 84,
        192n130
    user infringement, obligation to
        monitor/investigate, 85
Voluntary Code of Practice, 129

Wagner, Ben, 132
Walt Disney Co., Google partnership, 121–22
wealth holders, concentrated (1%), 27
web pages included, Google Search
    index, 13–14
Weinstock, Netanel Neil, 178n94
Wilson, Ben McOwen, 202n68
Wojcicki, Susan, 59–60, 75
World Intellectual Property
    Organization (WIPO)
    Copyright Treaty, 4, 7, 165n6
    Performances and Phonograms
        Treaty, 7
Wu, Timothy, 17, 144, 172n2, 213n41

YouTube, xiv, 83. See also *specific topics*
    *and lawsuits*
  Content ID (*see* Content ID, YouTube)
  Content Verification Program, 118

YouTube Red, 128–29
YouTube Remix, 128–29

Zimmerman, Diane, 126, 129, 209n78